FOOLS CROW

FOOLS CROW

Thomas E. Mails

Assisted by Dallas Chief Eagle

WITH ILLUSTRATIONS BY THE AUTHOR

University of Nebraska Press • Lincoln

Copyright © 1979 by Thomas E. Mails
All rights reserved
Manufactured in the United States of America

First Bison Book printing: 1990
Most recent printing indicated by the last digit below:
10   9   8   7   6   5   4   3   2

Library of Congress Cataloging-in-Publication Data
Fools Crow, 1890 or 91–
Fools Crow / [recorded by] Thomas E. Mails; assisted by Dallas Chief Eagle;
with illustrations by the author.—1st Bison book print.
p.   cm.
Reprint. Originally published: Garden City, N.Y.: Doubleday, 1979.
Includes bibliographical references.
ISBN 0-8032-8174-9
1. Fools Crow, 1890 or 91–   2. Oglala Indians—Biography.   3. Oglala Indi-
ans.   4. Teton Indians.   I. Mails, Thomas E.   II. Chief Eagle, D., 1925–
.   III. Title.
E99.03F664   1990
973′.004975—dc20
90-33803 CIP

Published by arrangement with the author
⊗

To the six directions and the 405 Stone White Men

CONTENTS

CHAPTER 1   THE MEETING
AT LOWER BRULE

In July of 1974, I went to the Rosebud Sioux Reservation, located in southern South Dakota, and to the town of Rosebud to see a Sun Dance. While I was there I contributed some of the food for the meals, and as a result, one night, at a powwow at the town of Mission, I was given an honor dance and the Sioux name *"Waokiye,"* which means "One Who Helps." After the dance, Charles Ross, the superintendent of schools at the Lower Brule Reservation in eastern South Dakota, told me that his people were having their first trade fair in eighty years. He added that they were building a ceremonial dance ground and were badly in need of sod to cover it. "Might you," he asked, "be able to purchase the sod for them?"

As it turned out I could and did, which led to another request from Charles, this time that I come to the trade fair for the dedication of the ceremonial ground. And so it was that in early August I drove from California to my home in Santa Fe, New Mexico, and then on August 8, left there and headed for the lower Brule Reservation.

August 8, 1974, was not by any means an ordinary day, for it was the announcement date of the resignation from office of President Richard M. Nixon. Before I reached Las Vegas, New Mexico, every radio program was preoccupied with the news, and with endless speculations as to what it portended.

As I passed the little town of Raton, left New Mexico, and began the sharp ascent into Colorado's impressive mountains, slate gray clouds closed in overhead. Within moments it started to rain so heavily that individual drops burst like water-filled plastic bags against the windshield. The evergreen boughs were sodden and/drooping, the highway glistened with reflections, and the streams that paralleled the highway were soon rising and overrunning their banks. I stopped for gas at Trinidad, Colorado, and then left the freeway and headed straight east into rural Nebraska, where I would have the pleasure of a quiet back road to drive on.

It rained steadily and hard, and I was forced to make an early stop at a motel. Television was all Richard M. Nixon. The weather forecast, sneaked in between ponderous political comments by everyone from the man on the street to high government officials, was for continual and heavy rain. The prediction turned out to be painfully accurate. All across Nebraska and into South Dakota the water came pouring down. When at last I reached the Rosebud Sioux Reservation and Dallas Chief Eagle's home in the town of Rosebud, I had to run from the car to the house to avoid drowning. Dallas was a good friend, and had offered to go to Lower Brule with me. The two of us resumed the journey the following morning, and the entire countryside was laden with gray-green moisture. The sky itself was so black we drove with the car lights on.

We reached Lower Brule at noon on Saturday, and went directly to the Trade Fair grounds. As we swung into the parking area we saw that only a handful of people were out and about, the fair booths were empty of craftspeople and goods, and the sod of the ceremonial ground showed no evidence of use.

We sat in the car and waited until a break in the rainfall allowed us to step out. When we did, it was into a quagmire of gumbo mud, the like of which I'd not seen since my stay in the Aleutian Islands during the winter of 1945–46 following World War II. The rain began to beat down again, so we jumped back in the car and went looking for Charles Ross, finally locating him at the school gymnasium, where arrangements were being made to hold the powwow indoors that night. It was the only dry place in town large enough to house the more than one thousand Indians who would attend.

Charles told us that over a third of those who had come to the fair had already given up and gone home. He was miserable, and with good reason. The hopes of the tiny Lower Brule band had been high as could be for the fair. Actually, they had advertised it as their Trade Fair Renewal, and it was really a symbol of hope for band renewal. It was what they needed to become something again. So everyone had worked doubly hard to make it as success. Now, however, the rain had almost washed their chances away.

One ray of hope remained. Earlier on Saturday, Charles had taken a filled pipe to the holy man and Ceremonial Chief of the Sioux, Frank Fools Crow, and asked him to split the clouds. It was known by many that he could perform the feat, as could other Sioux holy men who had dreamed of Thunder Beings and thus received the power to divide the rain clouds and keep an area of land dry between them.

For more than an hour Fools Crow stood on the hill above the fairground and prayed in the rain with his double-tailed eagle-feather bonnet on his head. When he came down, he told Charles not to worry, that on Sunday the sky would be clear, the sun would be out, and people should believe this and stay at the fair.

The rain did stop for a time when we entered the gymnasium about eight o'clock on Saturday night, although the clouds were still there and threatening. Inside the huge gymnasium the drums began to beat and soon took on a tripled intensity. The booming sound and the singers' voices reverberated off the walls and ceilings. The miseries of the people were soon forgotten as they were absorbed in dancing and fellowship. I enjoyed it tremendously.

Early in the evening, a Sioux elder and his wife made their way toward the side of the gymnasium where Dallas and I were seated. They were warmly greeted by many people as they came our way. They were a striking couple. She was attired in a full-length blue dress, with an over-all pattern of red and yellow flowers. He wore a western-style fringed buckskin jacket, long black braids—which I later learned was a wig covering the close-cropped gray hair befitting his eighty-some years—and a high-crowned black reservation hat with a broad brim.

They sat down directly in front of me, and in a little while Dallas introduced us. They were Frank and Kate Fools Crow, and he was that very Ceremonial Chief of the Teton Sioux I had heard about earlier. Their faces were marvelous, with the grandeur only an aged fullblooded Sioux can have. Despite the superb dancing by the Indians and an honor dance and star blanket given me in thanksgiving for the sod by the Lower Brule Sioux that night, I found myself staring at Fools Crow constantly. He was chosen to carry the Oglala flag for the grand entry parade, and during the evening I watched several young men get down in front of him on one or both knees when they came to talk to him. No elder passed by him without a nod. I was greatly impressed, and absolutely delighted when Fools Crow asked Dallas and me to come to his tipi for a visit the next morning.

We arose early, and I went immediately to the window and drew the curtain. Off in the distance was a bank of black clouds, but directly above us the sun was shining, the sky was a pure blue, and only a few small clouds could be seen. By nine o'clock the ground at the fairground was firming up, and people were busily setting up their displays. The clouds were split!

Dallas and I went to visit Fools Crow, arriving at his tipi about ten o'clock. The Ceremonial Chief was sitting outside on a folding camp chair, and Kate was cooking. She fed us delicious fry bread, coffee, and I had my first wild turnip soup, which was excellent.

Then, with Dallas translating for both of us, Frank and I began to talk about many things: the weather, the prospects for the last day of the fair, and what was happening among the Sioux. I noted then that his eagle feather bonnet was hanging out to dry on the front of his tipi. It was the only evidence now of a rain-soaked yesterday. "Got wet," he said in one of his few statements in English.

Fools Crow knew my name by now, that I was from California, that Dallas and I were close friends, and that I had a more than deep interest where Indians were concerned. He had seen the sod I had given, and also my honor dance. But he did not yet know that I was a writer and an artist who had done several books about Indians.

Therefore, Dallas and I were both astonished when he suddenly changed the conversation and said that during his last vision quest at Bear Butte in 1965, his god, *Wakan-Tanka,* had told him that "although he was a humble man with little to offer, the time had come for him to tell certain things about himself and his Teton people to a person who would be made known to him." This way the record would be kept and the world would know about it. He knew now that Grandfather had brought me here to Lower Brule for this very purpose; it was for us to make arrangments for a book. Many others had come to him and asked if they could do this but always he had known they were not the one Grandfather meant. Equally fascinating to me was that as we had talked the same thoughts had begun to run through my mind. As it appeared now my long trip to Lower Brule was more than coincidence.

Agreement was immediate, we would do the book. Once the pact was established, I went to my car to get him a copy of my book *The Mystic Warriors of the Plains.* He accepted it with the customary four gestures used by the Sioux to seal an agreement, and without the slightest hint of surprise. He had known intuitively that I was a writer!

Since Fools Crow speaks only a little English, it was agreed that Dallas, whom Fools Crow considers to be his spiritual son, would sit with us to interpret and assist as we talked. There was no way of knowing that day exactly where the discussions would take us. I realized that everything would depend upon how much license Fools Crow felt he had to reveal the secret and most important things of his life. Indians are, by custom, very close-mouthed about such things, but in the end, I learned even more than I hoped for.

This is not to suggest that the information came easily. *Wakan-Tanka* had commanded Fools Crow to tell his story—including the medicine aspects. And there was nothing I waited for more anxiously than for him to lead me onto his secret life of visions, medicine, and prophecy.

Nevertheless, I hesitated to broach the subject, and for a long time he did not bring it up. I understood why, for I knew that discussion of these things would be a trying—even agonizing—experience for him; moreover, I was not certain he knew how far *Wakan-Tanka* wanted him to go in exposing himself to the world.

So I skirted the subject of medicine until we were more than a year along and well into our series of meetings, dealing at first with the ordinary events of his daily life during the reservation years. Finally, when I felt the time and atmosphere were right, I turned the conversation to his shrouded world of mystery.

My fears proved to be well grounded, for as we began, Fools Crow revealed by his reactions that although he knew the questions were inevitable, he would rather part with an arm or a leg than give me the answers. He grimaced, he squirmed, he frowned, he sat like a child in a stubborn posture with his knees together, his fists clenched, and his arms tightly folded across his chest.

After a long silence, he reminded me he had told me of Black Elk's warning that he should not reveal his secret things. But plainly he was caught, as in a vise, between *Wakan-Tanka* and Black Elk, and there was no question as to who would win the contest. The problem was to get him open and started. Somewhat amazingly, it would be Black Elk himself who provided the key.

After we had sparred for a while I put to Fools Crow a question that proved to be more than he could handle. "I appreciate how deeply you feel about holy things, Frank, but why is it that Black Elk was not also bound by his own rules? For in his last years he told John Neihardt everything about his secret life for publication in the book *Black Elk Speaks*."

Fools Crow was stunned. He knew little if nothing about the content of the famous book. He blinked his eyes a few times and then stared at me quizzically, his head cocked to one side and his arms still folded. Then he pursed his lips, looked down at his lap as one does when he thinks back or anew, and began to tell me about his secret life.

To holy men and medicine persons, divinely given power is an awesome and profoundly personal possession, to be handled with the utmost care and concern. A single small mistake or bit of carelessness and it can slip away like sand in an hourglass. One error and the owner of the power might pay for it by a personal disaster, or even the loss of his life.

Every traditional Sioux knows what happens to medicine men who abuse the power that *Wakan-Tanka* has chosen to dispense through them, for the medicine man is but a channel. It is *Wakan-Tanka* who is the source of and does the actual healing or predicting.

As recently as October 1976, I was told about a certain medicine man who had been careless in the handling of his medicine power. Late one night in January, while friends and he were driving in his automobile across a remote part of the Pine Ridge Reservation, a wheel dropped off the edge of the highway, and the vehicle rolled over several times, leaving the medicine man with severe internal injuries and both legs paralyzed. He was released from the hospital for a time, but returned shortly thereafter. The Sioux medicine men prophesied, "No one will see him alive outside the hospital again."

How they would know such things with certainty is a mystery, but they were correct. The medicine man died on December 16, 1976, without having left the hospital.

While in preparation for meetings with Fools Crow I carefully structured my questions, but our discussions often wandered, and what I received was not a chronological record of thoughts and events. In the end, it took some months to rearrange the story and put it in sequential form.

Fools Crow's greatest difficulties were with remembering some details, dates, and spelling of names of white men. My greatest difficulty lay in eliciting ceremonial data, vision information, and personal incidents. Except for a rare extrovert, Indians are not given to the freewheeling recitation of exploits and involvements as is common in the white society. Indians discuss the old days, but in a different manner. On the chance that certain incidents might prove embarrassing to others, a true traditional will skirt many things, will avoid embellishments, and will keep most of his shared memories to himself.

Considering his lack of formal schooling, it might be thought that Fools Crow is a simple man. On the contrary, he is profound and eloquent, although not so complex as was the famous holy man Black Elk.

Fools Crow does speak plainly. His statements are not couched in mysterious language, and he gets directly to the point; for this reason he is able to deal effectively with the ordinary problems faced by the Lakota living on the reservations today.

At home he is besieged by a steady stream of visitors from various places and walks of life. He has no telephone, so local people come to him for social visits, advice, and to solicit his help in proposed ventures. Some come to keep him apprised of what is going on in local and national developments. Other Indian tribes ask Fools Crow to join them in ventures concerning the welfare of all Indians. Non-Indians make pilgrimages to Fools Crow's house seeking information about the old ways and help in carrying out such personal ventures as vision quests. Some of these come from foreign countries, including England,

France, Germany, and Italy. When I went to visit Fools Crow on one occasion in 1976, two visitors from Sweden had just left.

The U. S. Government has for some time solicited Fools Crow's advice on Indian matters. As recently as 1975, he went to Washington, D.C., at government expense, and until Gerald Ford lost his bid for election to the presidency in 1976, Fools Crow had been scheduled to spend additional time with the President in New York City. The Ceremonial Chief, even at age eighty-eight, still makes an astonishing number of business and healing trips to distant places. Whenever I want to talk at length with Fools Crow, I am forced to take him away from home for a few days. It is the only way we can have privacy and get anything accomplished.

At his present age he has lost a few inches in height, but still is about five feet, nine inches tall. His shoulders are broad, and he has a barrel chest. His arms are still solid and muscular. His legs are sturdy but bowed, and he walks in his cowboy boots with a stiff, rocking motion. Stairways are something of an effort for him to climb, but on level ground he hunches his shoulders forward, bends slightly, and easily keeps up with people less than half his age. No one waits for Fools Crow, and his vigor and determination are impressive in all that he does. He chops wood all winter long, carries water, nails on new boards to patch the holes in the walls, and does whatever task is necessary to keep things going around home. All this despite his having had several heart attacks over the past two years.

He is a ruggedly handsome man, and the set of his face conveys wisdom and kindness. His skin is like an eroded granite cliff, in tone a warm-reddish brown with touches of dark purple on the forehead and cheeks. He has the high cheekbones so common to the full-blood, but no arched nose. It is straight, and rounded on the end. His mouth can be a thin, bladelike line when he is being firm, yet it breaks easily into a broad, open smile. His eyes are dark and piercing, the strong and probing kind that appear to penetrate and read your mind. Whenever he laughs they sparkle like gemstones, and are windows of mirth.

With the aid of glasses, his eyesight appears to remain quite good, although he has said on several occasions that he has cataract trouble and is going blind. He has false teeth, and a black wig that is long enough to be worn at times in braids. The glasses, teeth, and wig are always put on when he is taking part in public functions, so that he can make an appearance befitting the event.

His voice is robust and resonant, and his statements are distinct. His vocal range is considerable. When he sings, he can croon as softly as a gentle wind, or roar as powerfully as a booming ocean surf. As he talks, his arms and hands move constantly and swiftly, describing in a remarkably graceful semi-sign language whatever he is saying. He shapes an object, rubs a foot or knee, curls his fingers, turns his palms up to the sky. He stands, he swoons, he holds his head. Once you are acquainted with the subject under discussion, you can, without understanding Lakota, know what he is talking about at any given time simply by watching his face and gestures.

For all he has seen and endured in his span of years on the Pine Ridge Reservation, he has a surprisingly delightful, almost impish, sense of humor. It rises frequently and infectiously. Like a swelling fountain it mounts up to full and bubbling height within seconds. When he is feeling good, he loves to put people on, and as he begins to do so his glinting black eyes will engage theirs to see whether they are catching the spirit of the moment. If they are, they are soon treated to some happy and memorable thoughts.

People magazine, in its October 1976 issue, left its readers with the impression that Fools Crow has become a somewhat feisty man. Yet I have been with him a great deal, and I know him only as generous, kindly, and thoughtful. Even in matters having to do with the mistreatment of the Sioux, he exhibits no bitterness or rage. Little as he has, whenever he is blessed with a gift he shares it. A buffalo would feed him and Kate for an entire winter. Yet when one was given to him in the fall of 1974, he put on a feast for his friends, and the meat was gone in a day.

He is more than considerate where his wife, Kate, is concerned, and is especially so with children. When I visited them one day in 1976, their tiny house was literally crawling with five small children and one woman, the mother, and three men. The children were everywhere at once, wallowing in a litter of cans, boxes, and broken toys. The entire place was a mess, so unlike the way it was when just Kate and Frank were there alone. The woman just sat on the edge of an unkempt bed and the men played cards. Yet winter was coming. The doors and windows needed repair. There was a pile of wood to cut. The whole house needed cleaning. Fools Crow's bedroom had to be locked to protect his personal things. It was he who took the children out in the cold mornings to catch the school bus, while the parents slept. He knew they were receiving some amount of tribal aid, but they never brought food home to share, not even a loaf of bread. They did bring liquor home now and then, either within themselves or in a bottle.

"Why don't you throw the adults out?" I asked. "Because of the little ones," he answered. "There is no place else for them to go, and the little ones would suffer." Besides, they were Kate's relatives, and "Kate would just cry." Fools Crow could not stand that. "Will they eat the food I plan to buy to get you through the winter?" "No, I will keep it at Sharp's Store so they won't know how much I have."

In the spring of 1974, someone ransacked Fools Crow's small frame house and then burned it to the ground. When first I visited them that summer, Kate and he lived temporarily in an aged one-room, split-log, former storehouse on her family property near Kyle. It had a broken-down wood stove, kerosene lanterns for light, and rolls of pink wrapping paper nailed to the ceiling to keep the dust out. When it rained, so much water came pouring through the roof they hadn't enough cans and buckets to catch it all. Yet he was the Ceremonial Chief of the once mighty Teton Sioux, being both a holy man and the highest ranking traditional civil chief of all the Sioux living on reservations in North and South Dakota today. I have not yet adjusted to the situation, even though I understand why it exists. In ancient days, chiefs were always, because generosity was expected of them, poor men. Fools Crow was a continuing part of that tradition, yet it seemed to me that by 1974 there ought to be some limitation as to how far the tradition went.

The robbery and arson took place while Fools Crow and Kate were away at the Cheyenne River Reservation, where he was blessing the first ceremony to celebrate the arrival of spring. When word of the disaster came, a collection was taken for them and they returned home to find that all they had left was what they had taken along: one street outfit, their ceremonial garments, and by good fortune, Fools Crow's sacred pipe. Their few material possessions were gone, along with personal items painstakingly gathered over a period of eighty years; these included photographs, memorabilia, Fools Crow's medicine bundle, all of Kate's beadwork and sewing materials, and their cat.

It seems certain that the fire was set by an unknown arsonist. A policeman who happened to be cruising the area saw smoke coming from the house. He drove up and looked in the window in time to see everything overturned and disorder, as if gone over by a burglar. But the fire was spreading quickly, and it was too late to do anything. Within minutes the entire house and its contents were reduced to ashes.

Fools Crow could find nothing made of metal in the debris, which was further proof of theft before arson. My personal regret was greatly increased when I learned that among the missing items were several things Fools Crow had intended to give me: a fifty-year collection of photographs; a give-away bundle, containing a flag presented to him by a government official in 1915; a tobacco pouch made by Fools Crow himself; and several other priceless items. He told me that since he was giving me his life to put on paper, the bundle and other items were to serve as symbols of the gift.

After the fire, Frank and Kate moved into the sad little one-room log storehouse, and until neighbors came to their assistance, they had no bed, no table, no chairs; only the wood stove previously mentioned. They would live in this poor hut until summer was over.

At the end of June the local Roman Catholic mission gave them an old and very small three-room frame house. I provided the moving costs, and it was placed on the site on June 23. I shall not forget that grand moment when Fools Crow and Kate, Dallas, and I arrived from Martin, drove onto the property about two o'clock, and saw the little house perched there on concrete block piers. It looked like a palace to them, since it was half again as large as the log storehouse, and it even had a built-in kitchen. But it was in miserable repair, and some of the windows and doors were covered with nothing but pieces of plastic drop cloth. It would take weeks of hard work to make it livable, and especially to get it into shape for winter. But it was at least a house for the Ceremonial Chief of the Teton Sioux and his eighty-year-old wife; a house for a gentle man who has devoted his entire life to decency, love, and to helping others by sharing, healing, and leading.

There is much to remember about the hours spent with Fools Crow as his story was put together. Despite his age and heart problems he exhibited energy and enthusiasm that were amazing. We sometimes talked from early morning until 11 P.M., yet his response and interest never lagged. Most of the time he was hunched forward in his chair with a smile on his face, his eyes gleaming, and his arms and hands gracefully acting out every word.

Many times, as he reminisced about the sacred dances of former days, he sang spontaneously in a clear and melodious voice. I tried to catch every one of his songs on tape, since they are simply priceless. How I wished I could see the marvelous pictures that were passing through his mind as he sang. Whenever he spoke the word "Lakota," it was couched in an atmosphere of reverence the like of which I've not experienced in talking with anyone else. In it is summed up all the love he has for the Lakota people, and whenever he says it, one knows instantly that a Lakota is exactly what he is.

His faith was always evident. Whenever we sat down to eat in his home, he said grace; not a rote or a repetitious prayer, but a traditional Indian petition, in which he expressed his gratitude to *Wakan-Tanka* for the food, for bringing us safely to see him, and for the privilege of sharing our company. On our way into Martin one day, we drove through the Porcupine area to the place where Fools Crow was born. As we climbed over Porcupine Butte, he twice asked me to stop the car, once on each side, and to roll down the car windows so he could toss cigarettes onto the roadside. These were gifts for the spirits of friends and relatives who had been killed in automobile accidents at those locations. Six of his relatives had died there in one accident alone, and he tossed out several cigarettes at that spot. He explained that he always left something there when he passed by, and that the spirits of the dead would come for the gifts.

Fools Crow has what we refer to as extrasensory perception. To give but one example, one day as we prepared to say our good-byes, I asked him about his predictions concerning the bad times that were coming upon the world, whether the messages he was presently receiving led him to believe things were getting better or worse. He replied that the signs were "very bad," and in fact that "something terrible is happening at this very moment."

He was right. Less than a half hour later, Matthew King drove up to tell him about the battle in the nearby Porcupine community, where two FBI men and an Indian youth had been shot and killed. It was the most critical situation for the Oglala since the siege at Wounded Knee, and Fools Crow was instantly heartsick. Dallas and I left a half hour later, and by the time we reached the reservation boundary, the entire area was in an uproar. Roadblocks had even been set up to close Pine Ridge off as the grim search for the alleged killers got under way. We weren't stopped, though, and I went on to Rosebud to attend a Sun Dance, which was held from July 3 to July 6.

Fools Crow knew I hoped to see him again. So he promised that he would come to Rosebud on the fourth day of the Sun Dance. When the FBI incident grew even more tense over the days that followed, I wondered whether he really would come. One thing was certain: With the roadblocks still active, he would not be able to bring his hunting rifle along for protection.

True to his word, he arrived with Everett and Ruth Lone Hill about 11 A.M. on the last day—in time to see the piercing. Once again, it was interesting to see how everyone noticed him, and how even the Sun Dance Intercessor, Chief Eagle Feather, paused in the middle of his dancing to nod and acknowledge his presence.

When the Sun Dance ended, we all went to Dallas' house for lunch. Fools Crow was uneasy, and clearly anxious to leave Rosebud in time to get back to his home at Pine Ridge in daylight. But before he left, he took the time to bless the diabetes medicine he had asked Dallas to obtain for me from another medicine man.

We went outside where he could stand in his moccasined feet on the bare earth, and it was there that he did the blessing ceremony. He cut off a short piece of the root, and then prayed with it to the powers of the four winds, the four seasons, to Grandmother earth, to Grandfather, and to *Wakan-Tanka*. He told Grandfather that I was a good man who deserved to be healed, and he asked each of the four winds to individually give me their personal help. When this was done, he took his pocket knife, made a cross in the ground, dug a small hole at the point where the lines intersected, and placed the small piece of root in the hole. Then he covered it over with the excavated earth, and he handed me the rest of the root.

This done, he climbed in his worn-out station wagon, bald tires and all, and with a wave was on his way. These are but some of the things I remember and cherish about my friend Fools Crow, the Ceremonial Chief of the Teton Sioux, an Oglala whose remarkable life has proceeded forth from the first giving of his important family name. The rest he will tell you himself.

CHAPTER 2   THE SIOUX FROM
1700 TO 1890

Fools Crow is an Oglala Sioux, a member of the largest and once the most powerful and best known of the seven subtribes of the Teton Sioux, and before we consider what he has to say about life on the reservation it may be of value to review the history of his people. Unless one is already a student of Plains Indian history, there would be no frame of reference against which to lay his remarks.

The Teton dialect employed by his people is Lakota, in which, although it is not a fixed rule, the "l" is used instead of the "d." And so he calls himself a Lakota, being distinct in language from the other peoples of his Sioux nation who speak the Dakota or Nakota dialects.

The origin of the Sioux nation is shrouded in mystery. They had no written tradition, and it seems as though the dramatic change in their life-style as they migrated from the East and settled upon the Great Plains erased in a moment from memory the ways of the people before that time. Quite probably, the Plains culture the world came to know included extensions of ancient customs, but at this point in time, no one is able to discern and separate that which is very old from that which is relatively new. To all intents and purposes the Sioux are a people who came into being in the late 1600s, when first they moved as a nation into the Midwest and buffalo country.

As far back as 1900, a few anthropologists and historians were speculating on linguistic grounds that the Sioux once resided in the southeastern part of North America. Writing for *Hampton*'s *Broadway* magazine in January 1909, Emerson Hough stated in colorful fashion, "The Sioux did not always live in Dakota, but once dwelt in South Carolina, where their remnants were cleaned up by the savage Iroquois even after the establishment of the English settlements on the Atlantic coast. Long before the white man came a vast body of the Siouans crossed the

Alleghenies, came down the valley of the New River, where the Chesapeake and Ohio Railway now runs, and down the Big Sandy, and the Ohio, and thence passed north into the forest country of Minnesota, following the Mississippi River from the mouth of the Ohio.

"And, so far from being a meat-eating folk who gladly met all comers in any kind of ring with the hard gloves, the truth about the Sioux is that they originally were planters and not hunters; and that when they got into the forest country of Minnesota they were very thoroughly whipped by the incompetent Chippewas, and so forced westward into Dakota."

"There was considerable change and not a little evolution on this continent; and the great Sioux migration is only one of many—one marking an entire change in the customs and character of a tribe."

Unfortunately, Mr. Hough does not reveal the sources used in drawing his conclusions, yet current authorities are inclined for the most part to go along with what he says. In summary, they place the Sioux in North Carolina in A.D. 1500, agree that they made their living mostly by farming, guess that they moved sometime after 1500 to get away from the fierce Iroquois Indians, then settled at the headwaters of the Mississippi River by 1600, and have the Teton and Yankton tribal divisions situated in South Dakota and Minnesota by 1680.

Early explorers were able to determine that the Sioux, much like the Cherokees, who had seven clans whose leaders met around a sacred fire, were known to themselves as the "Seven Council Fires," a title that designated the seven divisions of the nation—Mdewakanton, Sisseton, Teton, Wahpekute, Wahpeton, Yankton, and Yanktonais. Each of these names were derived from a certain characteristic they had or a region they lived in.

The Mdewakanton, Wahpekute, Wahpeton, and Sisseton lived close together by a lake known as Spirit or Knife, and were collectively called "knife." The French changed this to "Santee." They speak the Dakota dialect in which no "l" is used, and call themselves Dakotas.

The Yankton and Yanktonais lived between the Santee and Teton, and were called the "middle people." They speak the Nakota dialect in which the "d" is used in place of the "l."

The Teton, whose name, *tinta,* means "dwellers on the plains," were so numerous that it divided itself into seven subtribes. They are:

The Oglala, meaning "to scatter or pour among themselves." It was and is the largest of these subtribes.

The Brule, meaning "burned thighs," who were and are the next-largest group.

The Hunkpapa, whose name means "to camp at the entrance of the circle."

The Minneconjou, meaning "plants near the water."

The Oohenumpa or Two Kettle, meaning "to boil two kettles."

The Sihasapa or Blackfeet, meaning "black moccasins or feet."

And the Itazipo or Sans Arc, whose name means "without bows."

While the Santee established themselves in what would later be known as eastern Minnesota, the Yankton and the Yanktonai settled on the western border country of what is now Minnesota and South Dakota. The stronger Tetons ranged, beginning about 1775, across South Dakota as far west as the Black Hills into North Dakota, and into northern Nebraska, becoming, once they obtained horses and guns, the strongest and fiercest of the Plains people.

Their invasion led inevitably to friction and warfare with tribes already located in the vast area. They fought with success the Crows, Kiowas, Poncas, Omahas, Arikaras, and Cheyennes, displacing them all by 1800.

From 1800 to 1830 the Tetons reigned supreme. Life was good for them. They relaxed, hunted, socialized, and consolidated their hold over the splendid country they now considered to be permanently their own. In the 1830s they extended their hunting grounds into southern Wyoming, and it was there that the renowned chief Red Cloud would lead them to their greatest triumphs over the United States military forces.

The Tetons had, by then, become willingly and totally dependent upon the buffalo, present estimates of whose number on the Plains in those days range from thirty million to sixty million. It became to them a sacred animal, a unique gift from *Wakan-Tanka,* for it was a walking commissary from which they obtained their basic food and also fashioned most of the items they needed to exist.

The buffalo foraged for grass, and were constantly on the move. So the Tetons moved with them. They broke this pattern every summer in July or August, when each subtribe would assemble in a selected location for a great encampment lasting two weeks or more. During this meeting the Sun Dance would be held, the warrior societies would reorganize, the people would socialize, and the civil, or camp, chiefs would meet to discuss common problems and to plan for the future.

Included in the planning would be the assignment of general areas in which each of the villages making up the subtribe would travel, as conditions permitted, for the next year as they hunted the buffalo. The chiefs might also decide where each of the villages would bed down for the winter, so that individual areas would not be overcrowded and exhaust the wood supply.

The great encampment would end with a communal buffalo hunt; then the mass of people would subdivide into villages and go their various ways. They would cross paths now and then as they moved, but would otherwise maintain contact only through messengers. The pattern of life from early spring to late fall was for each village to make camp for a few days while the men hunted, the meat was brought in and cured, hides were tanned, and then the village moved on to a new location. Consequently, each village became its own social and military entity.

The women did all of the backbreaking work around the camps, and were considered the owners of the home. As might be expected, they made the final decisions regarding it and family affairs. The men were hunters and warriors, killing the buffalo and other game, and doing whatever they felt was necessary to protect the village and Sioux country. Young children had the free run of the camp, and older children were diligently trained to become responsible adults. The people were profoundly religious, and all life centered in this. Few things were done without reference to *Wakan-Tanka,* the highest and most holy One, and to the spirit powers he had created for all creation's benefit.

Life was very hard, and the Great Plains environment was itself a constant challenge. Looking back, the Teton and other Indians described it as "a happy time." Yet this description, for the most part, was based upon a comparison with life as it had evolved on the reservation. For a time at least, they were free people who decided their own destinies, and in those days they managed to fashion a life-way that still excites and enthralls nearly everyone who comes to know of it.

In that memorable period, there were several kinds of leaders for each of the nomadic villages, all of whom held office only so long as the people agreed with their conduct and views. White men called them "chiefs," and the title stuck from common usage, yet few of them commanded among the Indians the absolute authority the title implies. There were civil chiefs who were elected for indefinite terms to manage the movements of the village from one site to another, and who controlled the encampments with the aid of the warrior societies, each of which had its own leaders, or "chiefs." There were also "war chiefs," whose reputations, acquired in defense, horse raids, and war parties, qualified them to lead the other warriors.

Besides the above there were a number of individuals called medicine men (or medicine women) and holy men, whose exceptional spiritual powers gave them special status among the people. A medicine person was one who received from *Wakan-Tanka* the power to heal—usually by the use of herbs. A holy man was a medicine man who possessed in addition unusual wisdom and abilities, and who could often prophesy events of the near and distant future. Included among these holy men would be the famous Crazy Horse and Sitting Bull.

Considering the success of these spiritual leaders in leading the Teton warriors against the armies of the United States, one can easily understand why the government and civilians alike would make them prime targets in the subjugation of the Sioux. Once they were confined within the reservations, every possible pressure was brought to bear upon the healers and their followers in an effort to root out and destroy their influence. And it is not surprising that they withdrew to the remotest areas to carry on until now their traditional ways. This retreat would prove to be a factor of great moment, for while few in number, as the reservation period evolved, the holy and medicine men would play a greater role than expected in shaping the lives and attitudes of the Teton people.

In 1830, the Tetons began to war against the Pawnees, and for the next two decades would do battle with them at every opportunity. In 1840, some of the Oglala subtribe shifted their hunting grounds westward into the country of the Snake Indians, and added them to their expanding list of foes. The Crow also foraged in this area, and while friction with them had lagged for a decade, it quickly became as vicious as it was before.

It was at this point in time that the Sioux had their first serious conflicts with whites. Trappers working the far western mountain ranges assisted the Crows and Snakes against the Sioux, and angered them to where they were soon warring with every white except the traders who bought their hides and furs.

Looking back, one would wonder whether they would not have done well to run out the traders too, since competition among the fur companies caused them to bring cheap liquor to the more than willing Indians in an effort to deceive them and best the opposition. The result of this would be a continuing disaster for whites and Indians alike.

The problems began for the Indians as drunken Sioux started to brawl among themselves. Families were soon alienated, and in a particularly significant act, an aspiring young warrior named Red Cloud became involved in the killing of a chief named Bull Bear. Until now such acts were unthinkable and virtually unheard of, and the leadership of Red Cloud and his friends would be sorely affected by it as time passed.

Further problems arose when, around 1848, an eighteen-month-long epidemic of cholera and smallpox struck the Tetons. Hundreds died, and as these were new diseases to the Indians, the white migrants received the blame for bringing them. The anger of the Sioux mounted. Since 1841, they had watched with apprehension groups of settlers passing through their country on the way to California. At first there was only a trickle, but then the trickle became a river, and by 1850 it

had swelled to fifty thousand settlers per year, all eating buffalo and
other game while their own stock consumed huge amounts of buffalo
grass as they traveled. Even worse, the whites were beginning to estab-
lish forts, and soldiers were in Sioux country for the first time.

The Sioux believed something had to be done, and when their pleas
to Washington went unheard they turned with some reluctance to Red
Cloud, whose reputation as an exceptional Oglala warrior had by now
more than qualified him to lead them to war.

At Fort Laramie in 1851, government representatives at a great
meeting with all of the northern Plains tribes, save the Pawnees, asked
the Indians to agree to impossible conditions. Each tribe was to cease
warring with the others and to stay in its own territory. In addition, the
tribes were not to bother the migrants coming through. Yet to accept
this would change in a moment the life-way pattern of more than a century, and the tribes would not accept it. The tribal representatives went
home angry and with nothing resolved.

In 1854, a cow strayed away from its Morman owners and wandered
into a Brule camp. Considering it a fine gift from *Wakan-Tanka,* the
delighted Indians promptly ate it. When the Mormons found this out,
they went to the commanding officer at Fort Laramie and demanded
satisfaction. In compliance, Lieutenant J. L. Grattan, with a force of 29
men, rode out to discipline the Brule. The discussion did not go well,
and the angry lieutenant withdrew from the camp a short distance.
There he quickly turned his men and without warning had them fire on
the camp. Chief Conquering Bear was killed in the first volley, and the
aroused Brule returned the fire and wiped out Grattan's entire force, except one man. Word of this spread like wildfire, and soon there were attacks and counterattacks by Indians and whites taking place all over the
territory. Finally, Colonel William S. Harney at the head of a superior
force engaged a group of Brule warriors, killed 136 of them, and
dragged the rest in chains to Fort Laramie.

The alarmed Brules and Oglalas scattered immediately to the north
and south, leaving the migrant trail along the Platte River undisturbed
for several years. The whites took advantage of this to add new trails
and thus compounded the situation and pressure. To the trail along the
Platte of the 1830s was added the trail from Fort Laramie to Fort
Pierre in 1855, and in 1862, with the discovery of gold in Montana,
came the Bozeman Trail, cutting through the very heart of Teton country.

The Teton people smoldered within, and needed only an open spark
to set them off again. It came in 1862, when in Minnesota such
awesome violence broke out between the whites and the starving Santee
Sioux as to send shock waves racing across the nation. Hundreds were

killed on both sides. When the eastern Sioux were finally defeated, thirty-eight of their leaders were hanged, those who could escape fled to the Dakotas, and the rest were scattered about on reservations stretching from Nebraska to Canada. Red Cloud considered this well, and saw that the western Sioux had little recourse but to fight for their very lives, which is exactly what they did for the next twenty-six years. Not until 1890, at a place called Wounded Knee, would the struggle come to its ugly end.

The period from 1866 to 1868 is usually described by historians as the time of Red Cloud's war. During these years he led the Tetons to numerous victories over better-armed government forces, forcing them at last to close down forts, abandon trails, and finally to call for a peace conference at Fort Laramie in 1868. At this meeting the government agreed to abandon three forts. They also specified that all of the state of South Dakota west of the Missouri River would be Indian land, and that the Powder River and Big Horn countries would be Indian territory into which no non-Indian could go without permission. Red Cloud, after delaying for a time, signed the treaty on November 6, 1868.

While the Oglalas fought their war, the medicine man Sitting Bull and his Hunkpapas hunted the buffalo and skirmished with other tribes in northern Wyoming and North Dakota. They did not come south to aid the Oglalas. The Hunkpapas had a few sporadic engagements with government military forces in 1863 and 1864, but none of these were of the magnitude of those taking place in the south. When asked to sign the 1868 Fort Laramie Treaty, Sitting Bull refused until he was persuaded to do so by Father DeSmet. In July, Sitting Bull sent Chief Gall to sign the treaty for him, yet he continued to remain skeptical about its results.

Only four years later, in 1872, the government sent out a survey party for the Northern Pacific Railroad to plot a course through the heart of Hunkpapa country. Immediately, Sitting Bull engaged the forces of Major E. M. Baker in the valley of the Yellowstone. In this instance losses were light on both sides, but the message was clear: Stay out of Sitting Bull's country! And, while they did not in the least like it, the government did exactly that throughout 1873 and 1874.

In 1874, Sitting Bull and his people made their winter camp where they had for years, at the mouth of the Powder River. But treaty modifications had changed the boundary lines, and without their knowing it, the Hunkpapas were outside the boundaries and considered "hostile." The government was already annoyed by tribes who wandered to hunt and winter, and was waiting for an opportunity to teach them a lesson. Sitting Bull would make a prime example and target, and immediately word went out to all the Indians to get back within boundaries

by January 31, 1876. The alternative would be to face the military
forces that would be sent to bring them in.

The timing was abysmal. No one could move safely in such deep
snow and bitter cold as blanketed the northern Plains that winter—
neither the Indians nor the Army. Sitting Bull sat fast, yet he guessed
that as soon as the weather cleared, the Army would come. He was
right. In March 1876 Colonel J. J. Reynolds struck without warning, a
village of "hostile" Cheyennes and Oglalas who were camping together
in Powder River country. The camp was destroyed, but Reynolds took
such a beating that he was later court-martialed for it.

The die was now cast, and while the government set to work planning
a massive three-pronged attack, the Indians by the thousands began to
gather in Powder River country, forming a gigantic encampment along
the Little Big Horn River. Eventually it contained as many as fifteen
thousand Sioux, a number of Cheyenne, and a few Arapaho. At least
five thousand of the men there were seasoned Sioux warriors. The
Tetons were encamped in force, with the Oglalas being led by Crazy
Horse, the Hunkpapas by Sitting Bull, and with them were the Minneconjou, the Sans Arcs, and the Blackfeet.

On the evening of June 24, 1876, a confident General George
Armstrong Custer made the fateful decision to press on with his men
through the night in order to surprise the Indians the next day. Most
everyone knows, at least in a general way, the results of that brief but
stunning encounter, which took place on June 25. When it was over,
Custer and 225 soldiers were dead, while the columns under Major
Reno and Captain Benteen continued to be thoroughly mauled throughout that day and the next. Informants put the number of Indian dead at
a surprisingly low 36.

When, on June 26, Indian scouts brought word that another large
force under General Gibbon was approaching, the Indians broke off the
confrontation, struck their camps, and headed off in every direction to
make pursuit as difficult as possible. Many of these, when they were
confronted by government forces later on, would give up quickly and
return to designated reservation areas. Sitting Bull and some of his
followers fled north to Canada, and remained there four years before
returning. Crazy Horse and his people ran until they were starved into
submission because of the absence of the buffalo and other game. When
he surrendered, all effective resistance ceased, and the reservation
period was under way.

Now began the agonizing and frustrating attempt of both Indians and
non-Indians to settle down and adjust to a new way of life together. Details are scarce about those early years on the reservation, but we do
know that for the anxious and bewildered Indians it was a time of

starkest despair, heightened by the death of the revered Crazy Horse, who was imprisoned at Fort Robinson and stabbed to death on September 5, 1877.

From 1877 to 1879, the Sioux were sent to the damp and barren Missouri River bottom to live, while negotiations for the sale of the sacred Black Hills went on between Red Cloud and the whites.

In 1879, Red Cloud and his followers went to the site of the present Pine Ridge Reservation and attempted to make a new beginning. In this same year he, without the general approval of his people, signed over the Black Hills to the government. Back in 1876, the government had reduced the size of Sioux territory by half. Now, in 1879, the various subtribes were pushed onto scattered and even smaller reservations in remote areas of South Dakota, North Dakota, Nebraska, and Montana. Some Sioux stayed in Canada, and their descendants live there today.

In South Dakota, the Oglala were established at Pine Ridge, and at present number close to 13,000. Most of the Brule went to Rosebud, and today number around 8,000. Some Brule went to Lower Brule, where there are now about 650. At the Cheyenne River Reservation there are approximately 4,500 Minneconjou. Lake Traversie Reservation houses 2,300 or so Sisseton-Wahpeton Sioux. Crow Creek Reservation contains perhaps 1,300 Crow Creek Sioux. Yankton Reservation has more than 900 Yankton Sioux. Standing Rock Reservation is home today for 5,000 Hunkpapas. Flandreau Reservation has 275 Santee residents.

Two thousand Sioux are at Devils Lake, North Dakota. Three hundred Santee live in Nebraska. Some Sioux reside on the Fort Peck Reservation in Montana. Approximately 20,000 more Sioux live off the reservations and in the major urban centers of the United States.

For a brief time after 1879 the reservationbound Sioux maintained their own form of government, subject to the approval of a U. S. Government agent who presided over each reservation. Then in 1889, Congress enacted legislation designed to change this. Over a period of several years, land was allotted and deeded in trust to each person. The head of a family was given a certain number of acres of reservation land, which on his death would pass on to his survivors. Each family was issued a few cows and horses, a wagon, pick-axes, shovels, sets of harness, and fifty dollars in cash, with which to build and farm a permanent living place.

The trusteeship was intended to be only temporary, to last until the Sioux could govern themselves under a new form with elected officials. It was, in fact, designed to expire in twenty-five years. But the Sioux were not schooled to handle such things. At the end of its term it was extended for ten years, and then again for ten more—until finally the Howard-Wheeler Act was passed in 1934.

In the midst of these significant changes, the first census of the Sioux was taken in 1886. Thereafter they were required to have a family name. One of the father's names was usually taken by the other members of the family, and everyone was given a distinguishing white first name, such as John or Nancy. Some family names, in translation, were thought unsuitable, so the census takers renamed them with complete English names.

The Sioux chafed at the bit under government programs they seldom cared for or understood. Compounding this, 1889 and 1890 were years of severe drought, and unlike the white farmers, Indians could not move away to better ground. The buffalo were being systematically wiped out by white hunters, and indeed were virtually gone before 1890. In February 1890, the Dakota Reservation was opened to homesteading by non-Indians, and now the Sioux were ready to turn to anything that would offer them the slightest hope of returning to their old way of life. They prayed desperately, and sought visions from *Wakan-Tanka* for guidance and deliverance.

It was at this point that a Paiute Indian named Wovoka entered the scene. In Nevada, in 1889, the Paiutes saw an eclipse of the sun. Wovoka, who was ill when it happened, had a portentous vision in which, he claimed, God told him how the Indians could be united in peace and prosperity, and how they must learn to do a certain sacred dance, called the Ghost Dance.

When Wovoka told of this the people began to regard him as a Messiah, or deliverer. Word of it spread rapidly, and it led to what is known as the Messiah craze. Within months, tribes all over the plains were doing the Ghost Dance. When the news reached the Sioux, they accepted it eagerly, and the Oglalas sent a delegation to Wovoka to learn of his vision and teachings firsthand.

To what they learned, the warlike Sioux added two new dimensions: a painted ghost-shirt that was able to stop bullets and to insure the wearers against attacks, and the belief that dancing would cause the whites to move away while the buffalo returned.

Actually, what they did was a prayer or religious dance, but the already anxious whites living nearby were not, as they watched, in the least comforted. Some still bore the scars of earlier days, and everyone remembered vividly the famous battles. The agent at Pine Ridge was actually terrified, and sent for soldiers. General John R. Brooke came on November 20, 1890, with a huge contingent of troops. Thus the scene was set for the ultimate tragedy, which began when, in an abortive attempt to arrest him, Sitting Bull was shot and killed on December

15. This so frightened a peaceful old chief named Big Foot that he and his followers left their Cheyenne River camp and headed for what they believed would be the safety of the Pine Ridge Agency.

Mistakenly thinking that Big Foot was hostile, General Brooks sent Major Whitside and a company of soldiers out to intercept him and turn him back. They met the Indians on a hill named Porcupine Butte, and upon observing that some of the warriors were ready to fight, Whitside directed Big Foot to camp at Wounded Knee Creek for the night. Big Foot was ill and had intended to do that anyway, so he complied with the order.

The soldiers surrounded the camp, then early the next morning Colonel James W. Forsyth arrived with additional men and took command. It was December 29, 1890, when Colonel Forsyth sent his soldiers among the Indians to disarm them. Precisely what happened then has been hotly debated ever since. But someone did something to set it off,

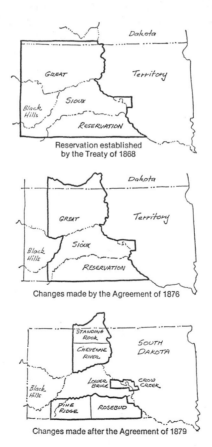

Reservation established
by the Treaty of 1868

Changes made by the Agreement of 1876

Changes made after the Agreement of 1879

The evolution of the Sioux Reservation.

and in moments a savage engagement ensued. An incredible onslaught of fire was loosed upon the Sioux. The fighting lasted only an hour, and when it was over, 146 Minneconjou were dead: 84 men and boys, 44 women and girls, and 18 children. Fifty-one wounded Indians were taken to the Pine Ridge hospital, and of these, 7 died, bringing the total dead to 153. Those who were killed at the battlefield were buried on a hill in a common grave, and a large concrete monument marks the site today. Among the non-Indians, there were 25 dead and 39 wounded.

By noon the next day, close to 5,000 alarmed and angry Sioux had left Pine Ridge and gathered at a place 15 miles away. For an instant they were ready to fight once more and die in an effort to drive out the detested white man. Thanks though to one white man they trusted, a Jesuit priest named Father Jutz, they were talked into returning to Pine Ridge, and on January 1, 1891, the threat of Sioux armed resistance came to an end.

Nevertheless, resistance could continue in another form. The consequences of the broken treaty of 1868 and Wounded Knee would remain to plague forever the deepest consciousness of the Sioux, and as the one-hundredth anniversary of the famous Custer battle was reached, there would still be no real meeting of white and Indian minds.

CHAPTER 3   A CLASH
OF CULTURES

We have considered now what historians have recorded about the Sioux
from A.D. 1700 to 1890. Books and narratives covering this exciting period abound, yet is is astonishing to discover that, although an entire
century has passed since the great Custer battle, little has been written
about what has happened to the Sioux since then, and most importantly
about the Oglala, who fought the hardest to preserve their land and life-
way. Most books about the Sioux either end their story in 1890 at
Wounded Knee, or else they pick up the account within the last decade,
when it has suddenly been recognized that there is a grievous "Indian
problem."

Clearly, the difference between white and Indian views has gone on
compounding for a century. While "out of sight" has been "out of
mind" for most non-Indians, the Indians have themselves been forced
to live in circumstances that have brought, in the long run, neither
progress nor happiness. Not, however, until the fall of 1972, when the
resolute militants of seven national Indian organizations marched on
Washington, D.C., and occupied the Bureau of Indian Affairs headquarters, did the Indians begin to make this absolutely clear and to receive national attention. Then in February of 1973, desperate members
of AIM, the American Indian Movement, began what would become a
dramatic and dangerous seventy-two-day occupation of the historic
Wounded Knee village. When that was over, the entire country was
looking on.

What has happened since 1890 to cause the Indians of the 1970s to
risk their very lives? Obviously, the clashes that began in 1854 went
deeper than the contest for land. There was also a profound clash of
cultures. The whites concluded that the immediate civilization of savage

and heathen Indians was essential. The primary imperative became that of transforming Indians into whites as quickly as possible. No one thought to ask whether the Indians wished to comply, or whether the whites by their own manner of conduct had sufficiently motivated the Indians to do so. There was no moratorium period to quench the bitterness that existed on both sides. The government simply bore in and began the compulsory education of children, while programming the adults to death. The government did this so effectively that most writers about Indians concluded that the heathen would quickly merge with contemporary life and become white men. Only a handful of authors went to the reservations to find out what was going on. Data from 1890 to 1930 for the Teton in particular have been scarce, veiled and unclear. Even among the Sioux, few people have wished, apparently, to give an accounting of what happened during these early years. Today, though, we have learned enough to draw at least a summary picture. It was considered a must in the earliest part of the reservation period to make the Indians self-supporting through farming and education. The allotments of lands has already been mentioned, and that in itself led to incredible abuses. When corrupt government agents saw that the Indians were not able to make efficient use of their land, they permitted the leasing of the land to whites by local agents. By 1916, most Oglala-owned cattle had been sold to whites, and 80 per cent of the Pine Ridge land had been leased at ridiculous prices to white people for grazing their cattle.

The government decided to do its first educating of children through the Christian churches, believing they would be the most effective in civilizing the Indian, but a number of educators got immediately into the act. In writing an article entitled "The Indian Country," (publisher unknown), an author named Harry King stated that the first thing that must be done was to allot the lands to the Indians in severalty.

> This policy [he went on] would be incomplete however unless supplemented by a rigid and vigorous system of education. The instuction of all Indian children in good schools, during a given period of each year, should be made compulsory. In that direction lies the one great hope of modifying and ameliorating the Indian character.

Then Mr. King reveals the nagging doubt that plagued his and anyone else's hope.

> It is uncertain, to say the most, whether the adult members of the wild tribes can ever be induced or constrained to raise

themselves from their abject savagery to the level of any fixed idea of education. . . . But the rising generation is plastic, and can be molded effectually, and to higher uses. The education of children goes to the core of the problem. We must begin at the cradle if we would conquer barbarism and lift a race to a height beyond itself.

Note the words "Indian character," "wild tribes," "abject savagery," and "barbarism." They convey an attitude that could hardly promise much for the future.

In further illustration of the contemporary mood, the November 4, 1876, Omaha *Herald* carried an article the type of which would be common to the media for the next thirty years or more:

The long-expected detachment of Sioux, on their way to the Oklahoma Indian Territory, arrived in Omaha yesterday afternoon. They were accompanied by Maj. Howard, Dr. Daniels and these interpreters: Fred Randall, Henry Clifford, E. W. Raymond, Jeffrey Lott and Louis Robideau.

The Principal men were Spotted Tail, chief of the Brule band; Young-Man-Afraid-of-His-Horse and Red Dog, chiefs of the Oglala band; Fast Bear, chief of the Wahzjahzhah band; American Horse, Whistling Elk, Sitting Bull and many others. Spotted Tail is the elected, and Young-Man-Afraid-of-His-Horse the hereditary ruler of the whole nation.

American Horse had his squaw and papoose with him and there were 11 other squaws in the party. One or two were quite pleasing in the face, but the majority looked as though they were natural-born mothers-in-law. Perhaps this is too severe—they all had the appearance of being amiable at times, and the *Herald* does not wish to say anything really bad about them.

Several ladies passed through the cars, two of whom were evidently officers' wives and somewhat acquainted with the Indian language and customs. The Indians seemed delighted to see these white ladies and took pains to shake hands with them. American Horse's papoose was a chubby, sturdy little beggar, and when one of the ladies spoke to him, he set up a tremendous wail, just as natural and lifelike as if he were human.

How does one measure ". . . just as natural and lifelike as if he were human!" in terms of hope for the Indian future?

Agnes Dean Cameron, in *Pacific Monthly* magazine, August 1909, wrote an article entitled "Citizen Lo! Red Tape and Red Indian," which stated clearly her feelings about the needs of, and aim for, Indian education. She cared not in the least what they wanted. She would give them a practical education in how to run a good farm.[1]

About 1895, F. W. Blackmar, of the University of Kansas wrote an article about Indian education in a publication entitled *Annals of the American Academy*. In it he stated that the recent law for the compulsory education of Indians was a step in the right direction. This law, passed by Congress and approved in March 1881, provided the enforced attendance of Indian children at schools established and maintained for their benefit. Blackmar went on to say that it was not to be supposed that parents of Indian children were capable of determining whether education was good for their children or not. The Indians were too savage for that. Another change Blackmar recommended was to train and discipline the Indian youth by service in the federal Army. Such things as the foregoing were "the only hope of salvation for the Indian race."[2]

Unfortunately, Blackmar's opinions were to become the rule for early Indian schooling. Government-controlled schools became military in character, without tolerance and patience, whose primary goal was to humble the heathen and destroy every vestige of the Indian life-way. As might be expected, they met with resistance at every turn from resentful students and parents, and the educational system on reservations has only recently begun to emerge from this and to function well.

The churches did somewhat better than the government in this regard, providing the only source of acceptable education on many reservations until the government established their schools. Churches did join in the attempt to stamp out tribal customs and culture, but many of their Indian students would become community leaders during these critical formative years when it was essential to comprehend and work with the government officials.

The Roman Catholic and Episcopalian churches were the first to send missionaries to the Oglalas at Pine Ridge Reservation. The Episcopalians had a church building near the Pine Ridge Agency by 1878. The Roman Catholics arrived in 1879, and the Jesuit Holy Rosary Mission was built near the town of Pine Ridge in 1888. Today it is a large boarding school that enrolls over five hundred pupils. In later years other mission schools were built. The Presbyterians and Congregationalists arrived next, and then, from 1930 to 1950, came the Methodists, Church of God, and the Mennonites.

As the years went by, most of the Sioux would be baptized into one denomination or another. Some felt it was the expedient thing to do, the best way to please the whites and to receive rations; others felt that the Christian God presented to them was much like the *Wakan-Tanka* they believed in already, so there was no problem.

Nevertheless, people at Pine Ridge say that one of the loneliest, saddest days of the entire year for Indian families was the day when their children left on the Indian Service school bus for the huge church boarding schools, which were located at the Pine Ridge Agency. Some parents were so unhappy they refused to go along with the compulsory-education law, and hid their children away from the whites. These were the most devotedly traditional people, who continued to believe fervently that the old Sioux life-way was the best. One can easily imagine the friction this caused for all concerned.

A few whites cried out for understanding and justice, but their pleas went unheeded.

General Nelson A. Miles, U.S.A., in an article entitled, "The Future of the Indian Question," *North American Review,* January 1891, made this plaintive statement:

> The Indians are practically a doomed race, and none realize it better than themselves. They have contended inch by inch for every foot of territory from the Atlantic to the Pacific. The strength, superior intelligence and ingenuity of the white race in the construction of weapons of war, and their vast superiority in numbers, have not deterred the Indians from resisting the power of the whites and begging hostilities, sometimes even with apparently little justification, cause, or hope of success; and there would be nothing remarkable in the history of such a warlike people if they made one desperate effort in the death-struggle of the race.
>
> The subjugation of a race by their enemies cannot but create feelings of most intense hatred and animosity. Possibly if we should put ourselves in their place, we might comprehend their feelings. Suppose, for instance, that instead of being a nation of vast wealth, population, prosperity, and happiness, our numbers were narrowed down to two hundred and fifty thousand souls, scattered in bands, villages, or settlements of from five hundred to twenty thousand people, and confined within the limits of comparatively small districts. Suppose this vast continent had been overrun by sixty millions of people from Africa, India, or China, claiming that their civilization, customs, and beliefs were older and better than ours, compelling us to adopt their habits, language, and religion, obliging us to wear the same style of raiment, cut our hair accord-

ing to their fashion, live upon the same food, sing the same songs, worship the same Allahs, Vishnus, and Brahmas; and we realized that such a conquest and the presence of such a horde of enemies had become a withering blight and a destroying scourge to our race: what then would be our feelings towards such a people? In considering this question we may be able to realize something of the feelings of the Indians of today. They remember the romance of the freedom and independence they once enjoyed; the time when they could move from one pleasant valley to another: when they had all that an Indian desires, namely, plenty of food, comfortable lodges made of skins of the buffalo or elk, plenty of their kind of clothing; and when they were allowed to enjoy their customs, rites, and amusements, savage and brutal as they were.

In another sphere, opportunities for corruption were so numerous that the Indian Service became from the very beginning a hotbed of graft and wrongdoing. With few exceptions it attracted men more interested in making money than they were in serving the Indians. Conditions were so bad that an editor's note, introducing an article by Francis E. Leupp, Indian commissioner, entitled "The Red Man's Burden," read as follows:

> What do you know about our real Indian problem? Are you concerned about extending the "square deal" to include the modern representatives of the first Americans? You have read, times without number, of Indians defrauded, homeless, hungry, and have doubtless ascribed it to the dishonesty of the agent. Wrong. His was only the finger that pulled the trigger. The cause goes back to the nation's statute-books, where confusion is spread broadcast, opening the door wide to legalized robbery and tying the hands of those who would do justice. Mr. Leupp, as Indian commissioner, labored whole-heartedly to overcome the handicaps of his office; but the fault he found to be inherent in the system—in our misfit trusteeship. With an intimate knowledge of our many chapters of Indian scandals he tells how they are made possible and suggests such changes in our immemorial policy as will enable us in future to give the Indian even-handed justice.

But the efforts toward help were weak and the pattern was set.[3] Most agents did their best to undermine and ignore the authority of chiefs and leaders who resisted their ways and demands, while they catered to lesser men who would do whatever they were told. In addition, these agents struck hard at the most critical point, uniting with church authorities in a massive effort to extinguish the vital ceremonial life of the Sioux.

As early as 1881, calling the Sun Dance such things as "savage rites," "barbarity," "this cruel spectacle," and "horrible," the whites moved to stamp it out by forbidding its practice on any of the Sioux reservations. Shortly thereafter, they condemned nearly all of the traditional rituals and practices, and those who violated the rule were subject to instant discipline and arrest.

Not for many years would anyone come to the reservations to ask why the Sioux did these things in the first place, and whether what they did might not have important religious substance. By 1885, it was accepted that Sioux ceremonials were rapidly becoming things of the past. On the contrary, though events had fixed, as in cement, the very attitudes that would guarantee the continuance of many of the traditional ways. The Indians were not about to accept in totality the religion of a people such as those who took their land and held them captive.

The holy men and medicine men living in the back country, along with those united with them in heart and mind, became the very perpetuators of the ancient ways. Thanks to them, the Sioux are today even undergoing a minor cultural renaissance. Many customs that were all but lost are being researched and reinstituted, and the religious rites that have been kept are being performed with greater intensity with every passing year.

It is a matter of some consequence to recognize that more traditions have been kept than the outside world has suspected. Much of what was believed to have been terminated by government decrees in the 1890s was in fact practiced in secret over the years and is now done openly. The Sun Dance was one such ceremony, and today it is celebrated publicly each year with piercing. There are frequent Yuwipi ceremonies, constant healings, vision quests, and there are Spirit-Keeping rites.[4] After a long absence, puberty ceremonies are being held for pubescent girls, and Heyoka ceremonies are being held to make sacred clowns. Attempts are even being made to revive the sacred horse dance, last held near Pine Ridge in 1931.

Beyond these things, Sinte Gleska College at Rosebud has become a bustling center for continuing and renewing the traditional Sioux culture, and in co-operation with an association of medicine and holy men, is engaged in a number of events and literary efforts aimed at fostering the Sioux's productive understanding of themselves in ancient and modern history.

In sum, while the Sioux have endured a most difficult hundred years, they are emerging now into an interesting new day. What, exactly, they have come through, how they have lived, and what we can look forward to in the future are what *Wakan-Tanka* wishes Fools Crow to tell us now by revealing the important things about his life at Pine Ridge as a boy, a youth, a husband, a holy man, and a civil chief.

CHAPTER 4   CRAZY CROW

FOOLS CROW BEGINS

You ask me how old I am. It is said at Pine Ridge and Rosebud that every time my age is given, it's different. One time a person will say I am eighty-four and another time someone else will say I am eighty-six. There is a reason for this. Records of Indian birth dates were not being kept on all of our reservations when I was born, and such things can only be decided today by an association of remembrances with known historical events. So all I know for certain is that I was born sometime between 1890 and 1892, and it is thought, either on June 24 or 27. I have a little fun with this, celebrating my birthday one year on June 24, and the next year on June 27. Perhaps the most important thing to remember is that I was born about the time of the tragic battle at Wounded Knee, which took place on December 29, 1890, and my lifespan covers the reservation period extending from that event until now.

I was born in a little log house in the Pine Ridge Reservation district known as the Porcupine community. The house was located on the west side of a flat, grassy meadow. Porcupine Creek passed through the center of the meadow, and the meadow was rimmed on the east by steep hills that were topped by scattered rock formations. There is a different and more modern house on that property now, and at present one of the owner's junked cars, a bright blue one, is close to the spot where the log house once stood.

Whenever I mention my birthplace and birth date I remember that famous battle at nearby Wounded Knee. My people and I can only think of that terrible encounter between the U. S. Army and the Sioux as a massacre. The soldiers slaughtered our people without reason, and

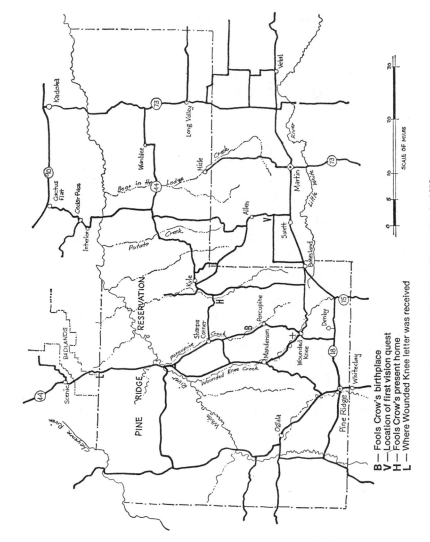

B — Fools Crow's birthplace
V — Location of first vision quest
H — Fools Crow's present home
L — Where Wounded Knee letter was received

Map of the Pine Ridge Reservation in 1979.

we will never forget it. When I was still a boy some of the Porcupine residents told me about a pitiful woman with one arm shot off who came staggering into their camp that cold winter night of December 29. After that rumors spread quickly, and it was soon believed that the soldiers were coming to the Porcupine community to kill as many other Indians as they could. The battlefield was only nine miles away, and although they did not come, the fear that they might at any time continued to haunt us for years to come.

My mother's father was Porcupine Tail, and the Porcupine community was named after him. My mother's name was Spoon Hunter, and she died just four days after I was born. My father's sister, Runs For Hill, cared for me until I was four or five years old. In 1896, my father married Emily Big Road. She was a good woman, who cherished and loved me. She watched over me just as my real mother would have if she had had the opportunity.

My father was given two names, which he later bestowed upon me; Eagle Bear and Fools Crow. He was a big man, about six inches taller than I am today, which would make him at least six feet, four inches. He was very handsome, and had extremely long hair, which he always wore in braids. He was a quiet person who usually kept to himself. He lived his old Indian ways, and did not participate in many tribal activities, even though he was the Porcupine District leader. I compare him in some ways to the great war-leader Crazy Horse, who also spent much of his time alone. But unlike Crazy Horse, Eagle Bear never believed in hurting his fellow man, even if the person was of a different nationality. So he never fought in any battles against Indians or whites.

My father had a lot to do with my early training. He taught me to ride well, to work hard, and he made me run often for long distances to build up my endurance. He also encouraged me to keep the traditional Sioux ways, adding that I should at the same time be industrious, so that I would always have horses, cattle, and food to eat. By doing all of these things, he said, I would have as happy a life as was possible for us Indians in those days.

I never did go to the white man's school. My father did not approve of them, and chose to raise me in the traditional Indian way. He did everything he could to assure this. My relatives also protected me in this regard, and it was not until I was more than eighteen years old that the agent was finally able to catch me and take me to the school. Then, when the teachers started to register me, they discovered that I was too old to compel my attendance. As a result I cannot speak, read, or write more than a little English. Yet I am glad that my father chose to do what he did. Otherwise I would not have learned what I have about our Sioux culture and about spiritual power.

My full name is Frank Fools Crow. I was called "Frank" to distinguish me from my father. Fools Crow is my traditional family name.

As my father told the story to me, our family name was first bestowed by my grandfather, Knife Chief, who received his own adult name in the traditional way of the Lakota warrior living upon the Great Plains in the early 1800s. His father, Holds the Eagle, was a well-known holy man, being called that because he was both a medicine man and a prophet. He was also an independent man who preferred to do for himself. As he grew old, his children and grandchildren tried in every way to care for him and keep him out of trouble, but now and then he would do foolish things.

One blustery winter day, when the prairie was coated with scattered snow and the gusts of wind cut sharply across it like galloping spirits of death, Holds the Eagle went out alone to gather a load of wood. When he had been gone a long time and it grew late in the day, his already worried children became very anxious and decided to look for him. They searched everywhere, and finally found him, just as the sun went down, wrapped in his buffalo robe and sitting on the ground. The bundle of wood was still on his back, and he was dead.

So they carried him back to their camp, dressed him in his finest garments, and wrapped his body in his buffalo robe. Then they gave him a tree burial by placing him on a wooden platform and lashing it with rawhide thongs to the uppermost branches of a tall tree.

While the family was in mourning, Walks Bear, an uncle, brought a red clothbound bundle to Holds the Eagle's son. He told the youth that death was a natural part of life, that he should not mourn overly much, and that the bundle contained something his father wanted him to have. It was an unusually large steel knife, which Holds the Eagle had kept sharpened and ready for this important day when it was to be passed on as a remembrance of himself.

Saying, "Thank you," the young man took the bundle and walked away to a place where he could be alone. He unwrapped it and looked at the knife for some time, thinking about his beloved father and their wonderful years together as he was taught to live the adventurous life of a hunter and warrior. Finally he held it out and up to the sacred directions, prayed with it, and with a firm resolute motion slid it under his beaded belt. Mourning, for him, was over, and his life as a warrior was begun.

Not long after that, as the family followed the buffalo herds and was in the process of moving their camp to a new location, they saw on top of a distant hill an Indian sitting on a black-and-white horse and watching them. He appeared to be a Crow, the Lakota's most bitter enemy.

So the young warrior told his family that he was "going to go up there and get that Crow." No one said a word in reply, for it was not the custom to interfere.

He unbraided his hair, letting it fall loose at the sides, and brushed it straight up like a crown in the front, as the Crows often did. Then he painted his face red, took the huge knife, mounted his horse, and left.

As he rode along he quietly sang a few war songs, and comforted and girded himself with thoughts regarding his knife. His father had been a good and an unusual man, so there must be something holy and powerful about the knife. He was sure he would have success with it.

He made certain that the Crow warrior did not see him leave the camp, and the enemy remained where he was, watching intently to see how many Lakota there were and in what direction they were going. When he first saw the youth close by and coming, he was glad and welcomed him, because he thought he was another Crow.

Much too late he realized his terrible error and sought to retreat to a better position. But the youth rode at full gallop up to him, pulled the Crow off his horse, and while with one arm he held him struggling in midair, killed the man with a single stroke of the giant knife.

He lowered the victim's body to the ground, and then, to give full vent to his hostility, he did as was sometimes done in those days. He cut the man's head off and stuffed it into a large rawhide case, which had been tied to the man's saddle. Then he prayed to the six directions with the knife, and left it on a flat rock there on the hill as an offering to *Wakan-Tanka,* the highest and most holy One. It was a thank offering for his success.

He took the Crow's head, his clothing, weapons, and horse, and brought all of these prizes of war back to his people. Later in the day a victory dance and a naming ceremony were held in his honor, after which he removed the victim's scalp and then buried the head. Finally, everyone prayed about what had happened, and acknowledged that such brutal things must be done, since the Crow was plainly a scout for a war party who would gladly have done the same to all of them.

From that time on, the young Lakota warrior was called "Knife Chief," and he would prove, for his entire lifetime, to be as brave and fortunate as he was on that important day.

In June of 1876, Knife Chief was with the Sioux, Cheyenne, and Arapaho who defeated Custer's forces on the Little Big Horn River in Montana. And, while my Sioux people would not speak of it so, he experienced what whites call "a healing miracle" that historic day.

Early in the day, he went hunting and was shot. By whom, no one was sure, but some thought later it was by Major Reno's advance scouts. In any event, the bullet passed completely through his right arm, through his chest, and came out his left side.

He lay there alone on the ground until a little boy found him and dragged him into a dense patch of bushes to hide him. By now he was so still that when some warriors arrived they thought he was dead. But they sent for help anyway, and shortly thereafter a renowned bear medicine man from Canada who was assisting my people with their wounded came to Knife Chief's side. His name sounded something like "Crutch," and some of the Lakota thought he might have been a Cree. At any rate, he couldn't speak the Lakota language.

Using sign language, Knife Chief's friends asked whether he thought he could help. So he examined the wound, looked at Knife Chief, and smiled, even though the big battle with Custer and his men was fully under way at this time, and all that Crutch did thereafter took place while it was going on.

Crutch built a little fire; then he cut off a small but barren plum branch and stuck it in the ground close beside it. Next he put some medicine in a container, and suspended the container over the fire on a wood rack. After this, Crutch sang a sacred song, and prayed. Then he sang more sacred songs, and while he did so he seized the barren branch with both hands and shook it hard. That is all he did to it, and immediately a small plum appeared on the branch.

He took the plum, rubbed some of the medicine from the container on it, and placed the plum against the hole in Knife Chief's right arm, Then as Crutch blew softly on the plum, it popped into the hole, made a whooshing sound like a sharp gust of wind, and promptly came out the other side of his chest. It had passed entirely through Knife Chief's body by a special power.

Perhaps the plum was a cleansing agent, the Lakota who watched did not know, but Knife Chief sighed deeply, as though he were coming out of pain. In moments, his struggle with death was over.

Using sage, the medicine man wiped the patient's face and sponged the blood from his wounds. By now the medicine was boiling, so he cooled a little of it and had Knife Chief drink it. As soon as he did so he was noticeably better. When the Lakota people left the Little Big Horn area he went with them. In four days he was completely healed and going about his daily tasks. To show his gratitude he gave Crutch twenty-six horses.

In the days that followed, Knife Chief talked often with friends about the Custer battle. Among other things, they told him an interesting thing not known to many people. They did not kill everyone, as is generally thought. An Indian scout was captured but set free because they

1. Fools Crow, the Ceremonial Chief of the Teton Sioux.

2. Fools Crow and Kate at the Lower Brule powwow, August 1974.

3. First meeting with Fools Crow at Lower Brule.

4. "My wife, Kate, and I lived temporarily in an aged one-room, split-log former storehouse."

5. "On May 3 their little house was ransacked and burned to the ground."

6. "A house for the eighty-three-year-old Ceremonial Chief of the Teton Sioux," and Kate taking her first look at it through the doorway.

7. "I stayed in that dark and damp pit for four days and nights without food and water."

wanted him to carry the true story of the disaster back to General Crook and the news media. However, once he had climbed to the top of a ridge he for some reason shot and killed himself. Therefore, many different tales have been told over the years about what happened to Custer and his troops. Knife Chief heard many of these accounts but never corrected anyone. He was certain that the whites would believe what they wanted to anyway.

Although my grandfather was quite old when he died, his mind remained surprisingly sharp, and he remembered well most of the things that took place during his life. He could recall the different areas he had visited and many things about the Sioux wars with their Indian and white enemies. He knew a great deal about Indian tribes. He was acquainted with all of the major landmarks of the vast Plains area, and as a young man could make his way across it with little difficulty. I heard him tell of all these things as the elders visited on long winter evenings. At that time I was very excited by them and remembered well what he said. But as the years have passed the details have gone away from me. It would be hard for me to tell you much about them now. I do recall that he told both his children and me that the Sioux people and life-way are integral parts of the country in which we live. Therefore, we have no choice but to protect it against other nations. I have tried my best to do this.

But let me go on with the story. Knife Chief had two sons. When the older one was only eighteen, he was killed by Crow Indians. When the news of this came to him, Knife Chief cut his braids off and went to a lonely place to pray and mourn for his son. While he was there he cried out against the Crows, saying that they were crazy for killing his boy, since now they would have Knife Chief himself to contend with.

A Lakota woman friend happened by as he mourned, and when he arose to return to his village she walked with him and consoled him by agreeing that the Crows were senseless people.

Back at the village a feast had been prepared for a group of warriors just returned from a raid, so when Knife Chief and the woman arrived they were invited to share in it. After they had eaten, the woman gave Knife Chief a good horse and said, "It was a terrible thing to lose your older son. So that it will never be forgotten, why don't you give your younger son, whose 'calf name' is Eagle Bear, the additional name, Crazy Crow?"

What she meant was that Knife Chief should give his son a name that would encourage him to fight the Crows and avenge his brother's death. Knife Chief thought it an excellent idea, and promptly named his son Crazy Crow. Later on, people translated the name from Lakota into English as "Fools Crow."

There was, however, no revenge. When Custer was defeated, the fullest might of the United States military forces was loosed against my people, and against the Cheyenne and the Arapaho. Soon the Indians were beaten, captured, and confined to reservations for good.

My father, Fools Crow, became a quiet man and he was not inclined toward violence. He preferred for himself the name Eagle Bear. He settled in the Porcupine District of the Pine Ridge Reservation of South Dakota, and for the rest of his life applied his efforts toward reconciling himself and our people to the new way of life as a captive people. As was the case with all Indian families, the names of that period became family names to be handed down from generation to generation. I was the only son by his first wife, Spoon Hunter, who as I said died only four days after I was born. Shortly after that a naming ceremony was held, and I was named Frank Fools Crow.

Two other men besides my father played important roles in the shaping of my early life: Iron Cloud and Stirrup.

My uncle, Iron Cloud, was one of the greatest of the Sioux leaders during the early reservation period. He and his devoted wife, Runs For Hill, lived in a log cabin on the grassy hillside above and to the northwest of our family home. When my first wife, Fannie, and I were married in 1916, we built a log house close to theirs. Both cabins are gone, but the spot can still be identified by a nearby strangely shaped sandstone formation, which has an evil reputation. People sometimes heard the eerie voices of unknown spirits coming from the sandstone, and so stayed away from there. Some are afraid even today to go near it.

Iron Cloud was not a medicine man and could not teach me to be a holy man, but he did teach me the most about how to lead a spiritual, moral, and productive life. And I have followed his guidance faithfully until now.

I am certain that *Wakan-Tanka,* the one called God by the white people, intended this to be so, since Iron Cloud became like a second father to me. On August 14, 1917, just three days before he bled to death as a result of a farm machine accident, Iron Cloud sent for me and gave me his ceremonial pipe, which he had used most of his life. It has been my most cherished possession. I have prayed with it in every ceremony I have done, and even took it with me on my European show tour in 1921.

Iron Cloud taught me much of what I know about *Wakan-Tanka,* and how to have a good and close relationship with him. He also taught me many things about how I should live; how to take care of my body; and how to get along with people. In the evenings we would sit by a fire, either inside or outside his log house, and talk for hours about many things. Sometimes others joined us, but usually just the two of us exchanged ideas.

Iron Cloud was a sharp judge of people. He would talk about a certain person and tell me why the person had no friends, or what was wrong with his outlook and why he was having problems. All of these discussions were helpful lessons. He told me to buy as many horses as I could, and to try to have other useful possessions of my own. He said that if I didn't develop this habit I would never have anything worthwhile. My only choice would be to take someone else's things in order to survive. He would name Indians who were forced to steal, and he would describe in detail the trouble it brought them.

Stirrup did not become an influence in my life until I was thirteen years old. At that time I began to have strong inner feelings that I was supposed to become a medicine man. Following the way of my people, I told my father about this, and he responded immediately by taking me to a well-known holy man named Stirrup. This man talked to me about my feelings for some time, and then performed a special and secret ceremony for me. A few weeks later, he took me on my first vision quest, and after that became my teacher in the secret things necessary to begin my career. This included some instruction in how to lead a Sun Dance, but I learned the rest by watching many dances and finally leading them myself.

As I have said, my father, Iron Cloud, my grandparents, and Stirrup were my main teachers when I was a boy, but my education took many forms.

When I was still very young, perhaps only five years old, I was taken to the agency headquarters at Pine Ridge, where I saw my first white man. His appearance was really something, and at first I doubted that he was a human being. I was frightened, and clung as tightly as I could to my father's leg. The white man's face had hair all over it and his skin was like white clay. His huge green eyes scared me even more because I had never seen eyes that color. My father saw my fear and told me that the man was our field agent, the one who came out to help the Indians start their new homes and farms.

Later on, I found out that one of the reasons we boys were taken to see the bearded white man at the agency was to frighten us, and hopefully to improve our behavior. Boys are always doing something they shouldn't, and each time I misbehaved, for a long time after that my father or stepmother would say, "If you don't behave yourself we are going to tell that white man with all that hair to come and get you." Some of the people at Pine Ridge still use this method to discipline their children. When my granddaughter's little boy acts up, she tells him she is going to leave him at the local filling station and let the white man have him. It works pretty well. And whenever I hear her do it, it reminds me of that memorable time when I made my first trip to the agency. Then I smile as I see again in my imagination that hairy face and those huge green eyes!

Reservation life and white ways brought us many new experiences, some of which caused us to do foolish things we laugh about now. For example, the first time clothing was issued to us we didn't know what to do with stockings. So we put the shoes on first, and then pulled the socks on over them. How would you have done it if you had not known? A lot of pictures were taken by whites and Indians to record our awkwardness during that period, and I have often wondered what happened to them.

The first time I tasted sugar was at a grocery store in Porcupine in 1902. The owner gave me a few sticks of what was known as barber-pole candy. I really liked it. But it was only later that I tasted the granulated sugar that we buy in boxes today.

Most of my boyhood days were spent doing chores, such as taking care of my father's horses and the other livestock. As time permitted, I relaxed by riding and by going swimming with friends. Even when we were very small we swam in the White River, which in those days had lots of water in it. We boys would compete against each other in speed races and in underwater swimming, seeing who could stay underneath the longest and go the farthest.

I also went fishing quite a bit. My stepmother taught me how to do this, and I caught them for her sake and because it was fun to do. There were lots of bass in the creeks. They like to hang around rocks, and this is where I positioned myself. The water was only a foot or so deep in some places, and for a line I used a loop made from the white braided hair of a horse's tail. I would lay down on the bank and watch the schools of fish. The bass have a habit of going through things, so I maneuvered the loop in front of them, and then as one went through it I would just pull it tight to catch him.

I really enjoyed fishing in this ancient manner, and at times I brought plenty of fish home to my stepmother. She always fried them, and then my father and relatives would gather for a grand feast. I have never in my life eaten fish, because I just don't feel right about it. Still, when I buy groceries today, if I am able to I include some mustard-sauce fish or sardines for my wife, Kate, because she truly likes them. When I was nine or ten years old, my grandfather, Knife Chief, made me a bow and some arrows, and taught me how to use them. I began to hunt rabbits, prairie dogs, and prairie chickens, and in time I became an excellent marksman, bringing a considerable amount of game home to add to our food supply.

I know you are anxious to learn whether the Sun Dance played a part in our life then. It certainly did! It is commonly believed that when in 1881, the government agents told my people to stop doing the Sun Dance, we obeyed and held no further dances until the two large public dances were held with government permission in 1928 at Rosebud and in 1929 at Pine Ridge. But this is not so. The Sun Dance was celebrated at Pine Ridge almost every year, and with piercing. It was always held in a remote area, where the crowd would be small, and where precautions could be taken to avoid discovery. It had to be so. The Sun Dance is our religion, our highest way of paying honor to God; therefore we celebrated it in secret nearly every year, and the favored time was the last part of July. I attended most of these dances. White spectators, friends of the Sioux, were also present at some of the Sun Dances where there was piercing. But they knew what was being done was against the law, and did not report it. Sometimes white men even joined in the dances with us, although they did not pierce at any I attended.

Other Sun Dances were held now and then without piercing, because these were not flatly outlawed so long as we Sioux did them quietly. For private purposes we could go ahead with everything but the torture aspects: There could be no flesh piercing or flesh offerings.

As I said, the Sun Dances with piercing were done in secret and with the threat of arrest always hanging over us. We were even afraid that our Indian police would turn us in, so the men who pledged to do the dance started dancing each day when the sun came up, and quit when the sun went down. They did this every day for four days, going to their homes at night and coming back the next morning. Individual men might be pierced on any of the first three days. The group piercing always took place on the fourth day, about 10:00 A.M.

Most of the piercing was the commonly known type, where the man was attached to the sun pole by long buffalo-hide thongs tied to two small sticks that pierced his chest. Occasionally a man would be pierced in the back and drag around a single buffalo skull, with the skull turned upside down and the horns digging into the ground. I saw several men do this, but I never in those days saw anyone pull more than one skull at a time. They are very heavy, weighing as much as twenty-five pounds, and with the horns digging in one is plenty to handle.

There are other methods of piercing. When I was only five or six years old, I was taken to a secret Sun Dance at a place south of Whiteclay. There were quite a few Indians there, and one young man was pierced with wooden sticks and tied with buffalo-hide thongs to four poles, two in the front and two in the back so as to make a square. He was held upright by medicine men, pierced and tied, and when they let him go, only his toes touched the ground. He hung there between the poles for two days, with the skin of his chest and back continuing to stretch and stretch. He was in terrible pain, and struggling all the time. Even at my age I could see what an ordeal it was for him. Finally, he tore loose from all four of the ropes. Nevertheless, he continued to dance between the poles for another two days and nights without food and water. I don't know his name, but he was about the bravest man I ever saw.

You asked why, at the Sun Dances you have attended at Rosebud, the announcers say repeatedly, "This is our religion, this is our religion, this is our religion," and you want to know what kind of spiritual power the dance really has for my people.

The Sioux are raised with the Sun Dance, and it is the highest expression of our religion. All share in the fasting, in the prayer, and in the benefits. Some in the audience pray along silently with the dancers. Near relatives will often fast for the full four days, and these will come to the sun pole and stand close to the pledgers as they are pierced on the fourth day. Their presence in the mystery circle at that time reveals that they have been praying and fasting. They do not just come to stand with the dancers as a token show of sympathy and comfort. Everyone is profoundly involved, and because of this the Sioux nation and all of the peoples of the world are blessed by *Wakan-Tanka*.

It is sad that the white people did not try to understand the purpose of our Sun Dance or any of our religious ways. Instead, they believed we worshiped false gods and needed to become Christians. So missionaries came by the dozens to our reservations. Some built small church buildings and then wanted to build larger ones with schools.

About the time I was seven or eight, I went on a trip to the town of Pine Ridge with my grandfather, Knife Chief. While we were there a discussion arose among Knife Chief and some other leaders as to which if any of the missionaries were going to be allowed to remain and build larger churches and schools on the reservations. American Horse and Little Wound solved part of the problem by saying they would become Episcopalians and accept that denomination. Red Cloud and Knife Chief said they would go along with the Roman Catholic Church. In fact, there was a black robe, a priest, present at the time. When he came over to where they were sitting and shook hands with them they told him they were going to be Catholics, and that he was welcome there.[5] The missionaries were told they could go ahead with their plans.

Later on, there was a big meeting in St. Louis, Missouri, at which an agreement between the Sioux and the churches was drawn up and formalized. Knife Chief was supposed to go to that meeting as our tribal representative, but was ill at the time. So Red Cloud went instead. The development of the Holy Rosary Mission, which is also called the

Red Cloud Mission, was one of the results of that meeting. Actually, the schooling of children rather than the Christian religion was always the main concern of our Indian leaders when they permitted the missions to be built and expanded, but they did not know that even in the schools an attempt would be made to turn us away from our culture and into white men.

I've mentioned the Roman Catholic and Episcopalian missions. Actually, there were four denominations who established missions on our Pine Ridge Reservation in the early days. The Congregationalists and the Presbyterians were also there. My stepmother, Emily Big Road, became a Roman Catholic, and my father, Eagle Bear, became an Episcopalian. It was not, however, until June of 1917, when I was twenty-five or more years old, that I gave in to the persuasion of the priests and decided to become a Roman Catholic. They baptized me and then gave me a few instructions about who the Pope was, some of the important things Catholics believe in, how to receive Holy Communion, and how to confess my sins. About three months later I was confirmed, and I am still a practicing Roman Catholic. I go to Mass once or twice a month, and I receive Holy Communion whenever I can. My first wife did not attend church. My second wife, Kate, whom I married in 1958, is also a Roman Catholic, and we attend worship services together.

At the same time, we live according to the traditional religious beliefs and customs of our people, and we find few problems with the differences between the two. Many things we believe about God are the same. Today, most other Sioux feel as we do, but it was not always this way. Some of the things the new faiths said were hard to take, especially their belief that we did not know the true God and that Sioux medicine and ceremonies were things of the Devil. So we rejected these views until their positions began to change.

I want to point out, however, that my uncle, Black Elk, became a Roman Catholic in 1904, and I am certain his first name, which was Nicholas, was given to him at that time. Black Elk was very interested in the teachings of the Roman Catholic Church, and spent many hours talking to the priests about it. When he and I were discussing it one day, Black Elk told me he had decided that the Sioux religious way of life was pretty much the same as that of the Christian churches, and there was no reason to change what the Sioux were doing. We could pick up some of the Christian ways and teachings, and just work them in with our own, so in the end both would be better. Like myself, Black Elk prayed constantly that all peoples would live as one and would cooperate with one another. We have both loved the non-Indian races, and we do not turn our backs on them to please even those of our own people who do not agree.

While I am on the subject of churches, I remember something that puzzled me no end about them in those early days. We Sioux prayed to *Wakan-Tanka* personally and constantly. We even thanked him for the lessons that hardships taught us. We could see that through each experience he had given us light with which to see into our future. So both the good times and the bad times taught us valuable lessons about life and about daily prayer. What confused me most was the fact that the churches had books with prayers already written in them by white people who lived a long time ago, that these were the only ones we Indians were to say as members, and even then only inside of the building called the church. I couldn't figure out how prayers like that could fit our daily needs. They were not personal enough.

Nevertheless, we Sioux did the best we could to follow the rules when we joined the churches. It was, after all, like any other change we made. As always, we adapted to whatever presented itself because we trusted people, and felt that if supposedly responsible white leaders recommended something, it was probably the best thing to do. In time, though, we finally learned our lesson and knew better than to go blindly along with everything the whites said was best for us.

You ask me whether, during the early reservation period, parents and grandparents followed the ancient custom of teaching children by telling us legends and stories. Yes they did. But I am told that many of our tribal legends and stories are already in other books, so I will only tell you a few things I learned to help you understand how it was for me. Remember too that *Wakan-Tanka* did not say he wanted me to tell much about these things.

While I was still a boy, my grandparents passed on to me many of the ancient legends of the Sioux, and also stories about important things that happened to the Lakota in the early days.

On one occasion, my grandfather, Knife Chief, told me a story about the time the great Chief Crazy Horse went on a vision quest to Bear Butte in the Black Hills. When Crazy Horse returned, he said he had learned that one day there would be terrible wars all over the world. Crazy Horse accurately described the physical shape of the world by talking about where the sun comes up, and goes down, and then comes up again. So he must have known that the world was round. And he said there will one day be fighting and big fires all over the world. People will be suffering, and our women will cry. Men will be brutal to women everywhere. But in the end, God will come to the earth to judge it.

I was also taught that our Indian people have more knowledge than white people think they do about the earth and about creation. For example, we know that some of the Indians who live on this North American continent came from Alaska, and some came from South America. But we real Indians go way back to ancient times, when Great Grandfather, the Great Spirit, molded us from the ground and gave this land to us. He placed us here, and told us that it is our land. So we are part of it and one in spirit with it. That is why we seek harmony with all creation. We share the same Creator and heritage.[6]

As for what I was taught and believe about God's judgment and life after death, I will tell you what I have seen in my visions and discussed with old-timers who are gone now. There are three spirits that are involved when a person dies, and each person will enter one or the other. If he enters the first, his spirit will travel around and all over. If he enters the second, his spirit will remain in the immediate area of his home. If he enters the third, his spirit will be buried in the ground. Then there will be a judgment day, when Grandfather will hold court. Two pathways lead out from there. The spiritual people will go on one path and be happy forever. The others will go on a path where they will be eternally confronted by problems and live in bad circumstances. They will suffer all of the time. I have seen all this in my vision quests, and it has always been believed among my people.[7]

Another story having to do with the shape of the earth that both my father, and my grandfather, Knife Chief, told me, was about three men named Eagle Elk, American Bear, and Brown Dog, who disappeared from the reservation back in 1890. They were gone so long the people at home began to think they might be dead. Then, one day four years later, a group of Sioux who had traveled to the West Coast to put on a show noticed a big crowd and heard Sioux Indians singing and performing. Jim Brave Heart and Jim Grass were among those who went on the trip, and who later told what happened.

Jim Brave Heart thought he recognized the voices, and shouted the name of one of them, adding, "Is that you?"

In reply they shouted his name. "Jim, is that you?"

"Ho, yes!"

Then the performers and the group started crying, and they all hugged each other. They took the three men back to where they were staying. Their appearance was terrible. Their clothes were worn and ragged, they were skinny, and their braided hair was so long and unkempt they looked like wild men. It was obvious they had had a rough time.

First they were given water, and then food. Then everyone chipped in to provide them with street clothing, and also donated parts of their costumes so they could dress up and join their show. Then when they finished the tour, Jim and the others brought them home.

As the days passed, their entire story became known. They had decided to settle for themselves the argument as to whether the earth was round, and had been around the world, making their way as performers. Two became wire walkers, and the third served as the singer and helper. Sometimes they would even do Indian dances on the high wires, taking collections wherever there were enough people in order to earn their way. When they first went away they had fine costumes and pretty good clothing. But whenever hard times came, they would sell something so they could eat, until finally they had little left. It was in this condition that their friends found them on the West Coast.

What their trip did do that was important was to confirm that the world was round. This idea had been known to us long before the white man came to our country, and now we had proof from our people that it was really so. Another thing the three men learned was that the numbers of white people were endless. They found so many in their travels they could hardly believe it.

After they returned to Pine Ridge the three performers did their act for the people during one of our annual celebrations, and then it was seen that they really were good. As one sang and played the drum, the other two, dressed in their costumes, even danced the Grass Dance on top of that wire. Those who watched could see why it was that the famous Buffalo Bill had watched them do it in some country, and was so impressed that he brought them back to the West Coast of the United States.

My father once said that when he was only a child, he was told that his great grandfather was one of those who believed that the earth was round and turned. According to him our pipe was designed to be like the world we live on. The bowl we put the tobacco in is round, like the world. And outside this bowl is the endless universe where the stars are. That is why the pipe is so sacred, why it is used for every ceremony, and for prayer to *Wakan-Tanka*.

My father also told me that in the early days our people often had long debates about the stars. Some believed the stars were worlds too, and that the larger worlds were much like ours. They insisted that the stars were round, and that they turned just like the earth. Some felt there were people on them, and my father said that someday, if what these three men who went around the world had said was true, their expanding populations might force them to come to our world.

This is why, each time I hear of someone who claims to have seen a flying saucer, I wonder whether some of those other worlds are overflowing now, and if their leaders are sending people here to see whether there is room for them.

CHAPTER 5   THE STONE
             WHITE MEN

When Stirrup took me on my first vision quest in 1905, he was assisted by Daniel Dull Knife and Gray Dull Knife. The place where I vision-quested is a grassy, wooded location that can still be plainly seen from the paved road that runs from Martin, South Dakota, to the town of Allen, and it is about nine miles southwest of Kyle. Whole villages of Sioux used to camp in this area in the old days, and it was called "Yellow Bear Camp" after the name of the Yellow Bear band leader. The creek running through it is known as "No Flesh Creek."

We went to the Yellow Bear area early in the morning. When we arrived, Daniel climbed up the vision hill, which was located about a quarter of a mile north of the camp site, to dig a pit for me to lie in. The rest of us put up a tipi and built a sweatlodge, which was covered by blankets and a buffalo robe. The three men would stay at this camp and pray for me while I was in the pit.

Late in the afternoon a purification ceremony was held in the sweatlodge. We sang songs, we chanted prayers, and we prayed individually. Then, as the sun was going down, Stirrup put a black cloth hood over my head so I could not see where they were taking me. Stirrup led the way, and Daniel and Gray helped me walk as we climbed the steep hill. All I had on then was a breechclout, and they brought along a blanket, which I would use to keep warm at night. When we arrived at the questing pit the hood was removed and I saw that it was all ready for me. It was about two feet wide, four feet deep, and six feet long. Sage had been spread on the bottom to purify the pit and to make a bed. I jumped into the pit, and following Stirrup's instructions I laid down with my head toward the west. Then the men stretched a buffalo hide over the pit, pegged it down tight, and left me there alone.

I stayed in that dark and damp pit for four days and four nights without food and water. On the fourth day I had my first vision, and in the middle of the fourth night I woke up and discovered that the buffalo robe had mysteriously and silently disappeared. Early the morning of the fifth day, Stirrup and the two men came for me, and took me back to the camp. When we arrived there, I was amazed to see that the buffalo robe that had disappeared from the pit was draped over the east side of the sweatlodge. Some might say that Stirrup took it to make me believe in the power of the spirits. But if that is so, what actually would he be accomplishing? Who would really be fooled, me or Stirrup and his companions?

I told Stirrup about my vision and he helped me understand it, but *Wakan-Tanka* would not want me to reveal here everything I saw. It remains a very personal experience. I did see and learn many things. I was transported by the power of the spirits all over the world, and I saw a lot of good things and a lot of bad things. It was a furthering of my education in telling the difference between the good and the bad, and in how to avoid the bad. I also was given 405 Stone White Men helpers.

These helpers are the entire 405 good spirits who serve *Wakan-Tanka* and Grandfather. These helper spirits belong to him, and if *Wakan-Tanka,* God, should take them from me, I will be just an ordinary man again. The good spirits are the ones who perform the great things through my mind and body. So while it is hard to serve God, it is at the same time an honor and rewarding to be his instrument in healing sick people and in helping others to solve their problems.

I want to tell you more about this. There are 405 good spirits or powers, called Stone White Men, which are known to the Sioux, and which operate in the created world as they serve Grandfather. Perhaps the good spirits are a gift to the whole of mankind, but it seems that Grandfather has chosen the Sioux medicine men to be the intercessors through which they dispense their blessings.

The 405 powers are divided into four groups, each of which renders service in a given area. One group is involved with nature's medicines. These are the herb and root medicines that are used to cure people. Another group has to do with nature's power to understand what is important about a given matter. These spirits work through plant herbs that are taken into the body as medicines to help one think and perceive. A third group helps with dreams. These spirits use medicines to make a person dream, and then help the dreamer understand what the dream means. The last works in the area of the inner person. They help the holy man and the medicine man look within himself and other creatures to see there the things that cannot otherwise be seen with the naked eye.

The 405 spirits are not subdivided into four equally sized groups. I do not know how many spirits there are working in each division. The first three work through medicines, while the fourth does not. This one is very interesting. . . . When you want to look deep within yourself, to probe into a realm of consciousness that goes beyond the ordinary, you paint the stem of your pipe black, and then you take it with you to a lonely place where you meditate intensely. When you do this, you must be brave, because you are asking for a response that the human mind cannot at first absorb or comprehend. When the answer begins to come, it does so in a startling way. Bright red lights that gleam like red fires often appear close by and around you at the four cardinal points. Then you will be given the message. You will either see it or hear it, and you are often given a great deal of knowledge in a brief period of time. It is a powerful experience that almost overwhelms you. Your mind expands and contracts rapidly, as though you had been holding your breath for a long time. When it is over you are exhausted.

This fourth division of spirits is also employed when, for example, a person comes to me and wants to know something about his innermost self. He wants to understand himself so that he can find peace and live in a more secure way.

I take this person out to a certain remote place, and leave him there to pray while I go to another location and meditate with the pipe. Then after a while I get him and we go into the sweatlodge together. While we are there I pray with him, and with the spirits' help the answers come to me in the powerful way I have said. As they come, they are passed through me to the man at the same time. Without our speaking, he will learn exactly what I have learned.

This is not a thing only I can do. Anyone who is sincere with the pipe can do it, and gain the insight he wishes. If this person takes his pipe and goes out by himself, if he takes plenty of time, as long as is needed to get the message, he will learn what he wants to know. And these ceremonies do not belong to Indians alone. They can be done by all who have the right attitude, and who are honest and sincere about their belief in Grandfather and in following his rules. This is why *Wakan-Tanka* has taught me to make proper use of the spiritual colors.

Whenever it is possible, when I am doing my ceremonies I put my black flag here (west), and that is a man; I put my red flag here (north), and that is a man; I put my yellow flag over here (east), and that is a man; and I put my white flag over here (south), and that is a man. These are the spiritual representatives of all races, and they remind me that Grandfather's spirits serve others as well as the Indian. We are the keepers of certain areas of knowledge, which we are to share for the good of mankind. And the blacks and the Orientals and the whites are each keepers of knowledge that can and should be used to benefit us.

Sometimes, all 405 Stone White Men are used by *Wakan-Tanka* for a single ceremony, which means that all four groups are called upon at once. At the beginning of World War II, a young part-Sioux by the name of Ed Magaw came to my house to tell me that he was going to join the Air Force. And he wanted me to give him a good medicine, one that would bring him home safe and sound. I did a ceremony for him in which I set up the four flags in the ground to make a square and then laid out a small bed of sage in its center and spread a black cloth over it. Then I placed on the cloth a string of 405 small bags of medicine to call forth the 405 good spirits.

I asked them to give him a medicine that would protect him and bring him safely home. Within moments, an almost perfectly round black rock appeared in the center of the black cloth. The 405 powers had placed it there. So Ed took it and wrapped it in a piece of deerskin. Then he tied it with a thong and hung it around his neck. He was sent to Europe, and made 110 flying missions, returning from all of them without a scratch. On his last flight he saw a huge American flag wrapped around his airplane. He said the Yuwipi (spirit) people did that for him, to let him know he would return home unharmed. So we know the 405 spirits were indeed present in that ceremony. When he landed at his home airfield after that last flight, he was so happy he jumped up and down, shouting with joy. Then when he got back to Pine Ridge he vowed he would give thanks by participating in four Sun Dances over a period of four successive years. He did, and I think they were the dances of 1968, '69, '70, and '71. Later on, I asked for the return of his sacred stone to see what he would say, but he said, "No, uncle, it has brought me great luck. I want that to continue the rest of my life, and if I can, I'd like to keep it." So I let him. The last I heard he was an attorney, and if I remember correctly, the head of the Indian Studies Department at the University of Minnesota.

Once, when a group of white people heard about my 405 Stone White Men helpers, they wanted to know how I could, not knowing much English, count into the hundreds. So I counted for them in Lakota. They must have thought we were really dumb. One last thing, whenever I do a ceremony, all 405 helpers come to it as the ceremony begins. The reason they do this is to decide which of them will stay to cure the disease and return the patient to health and active life.

You can see by what happened to me at my vision quest in 1905 and during the rest of the early reservation years, that although the government officials and the missionaries did their best to destroy it, our traditional religious practices remained a vital part of our Teton life-way. In fact, there were many holy men and medicine men, all of whom are gone now, who made what I believe were the most important contributions to our people during the first thirty years of the twentieth century. They kept our traditions alive and helped us to preserve our roots. Those who became ceremonial chiefs in the years just before my time were Chokecherry Seed, Red Shield, Running Shield, High Wolf, Drum Carrier, and Spotted Horse. Chokecherry Seed holds first place in my life, not because I knew him personally, but because he taught Stirrup, who was my teacher. Chokecherry Seed died before I was born. As you know now, Stirrup was the one *Wakan-Tanka* used to give me my holy powers and my basic instruction.

Actually, while I learned many individual things from Stirrup over a long period of time, it was not until after my second vision quest, in 1914, that we spent a full and concentrated training week together, working day and night while he revealed some of the profound secrets I would need to know to begin my career as a holy man. Stirrup taught me some of my ceremonial songs, and the two of us became in our mutual experience closer to one another than blood relatives; a spiritual father and son. It was Stirrup who gave me instructions in the basic preparations for the Yuwipi ceremony, showing me how to arrange the altar items, and how to make the other special preparations. He also taught me some of the secret things a holy man must know about the Sun Dance and the sweatlodge ceremonies. My father, Eagle Bear, gave Stirrup three horses in payment for this. I use in my ceremonies all that he taught me, and so in a way I carry the ceremonies on from him. Whatever was not clear or not explained by Stirrup I learned later on in my visions, and added this to his basic information.

You ask me how Stirrup compares in stature to other medicine men. My uncle, the renowned Black Elk, has earned a place above all of the other Teton holy men. We all hold him the highest. I have never heard a bad word about him, and he never said a bad word about anyone. All he wanted to do was love and serve his fellow man. Black Elk was my father's first cousin, and so he is my blood uncle. But in the Indian custom, he was also a father to me. I stayed with him quite often, and sometimes for long periods of time. We also made a few trips together, and over the years talked about many things. I learned a great deal about *Wakan-Tanka,* prophecy and medicine from him.

Other Sioux holy men of importance I have known well over the years are Small Eagle of Kyle; Four Thunder, a holy man from Newton, North Dakota; George Poor Thunder from Kyle, who was a very holy man;[8] and Joe Ashley, who used to live about two miles from Wanblee, South Dakota. Joe told me what God looks like, and I have lived happily with this picture. Two men from Wanblee who should be included among the great holy men were Horn Chips and Moose Camp. I mention all of these because I feel everyone should know who the true Sioux holy men of this century have been. They not only did amazing things in their ceremonies, but also their manner of life measured up to the high standards of what a holy man's life should be.[9]

By the end of 1905 I was experienced enough and mature enough to be interested in and understand some of the things the older people talked about when they gathered for various purposes. Many of their conversations included references to the legend of the Sacred Calf Pipe of the Teton Sioux. This really fascinated me, and in time I learned the legend by heart. Although the legend accounts are numerous, and vary a little in their details, the story is known by all our traditional people. And, from the moment of my first hearing it, I had a burning desire to see the great pipe, which was and still is in the possession of a keeper on the Cheyenne River Reservation. I also became a keen student of the proper use of the pipe. Any reference to it caught my attention, and like the squirrels do their food, I stored what I learned about it away for future use.

One day I heard my father tell his friends that, when my mother had died and I was only four days old, he prayed with his pipe, and he was sure this was why his sister offered to care for me. He went on to say that although she already had an eight-month-old son at the time, she put her son on solid food, breast-fed me, and continued to care for me for four years. So my father believed from this, and many other proofs, that prayers made with the pipe will always bring what you ask for, or as *Wakan-Tanka* and the spirit powers in their wisdom see the need, something better. I often saw the pipe employed with reverence and effectiveness by the holy men and medicine men. This too had its effect on me, and I resolved to make correct and constant use of the pipe throughout my life.

No ceremonial item is more important and vital to my people than the sacred pipe. It is not enough to call it a peace pipe. It is much more. No traditional Sioux man is a whole person without one, some women use them, and no holy man or medicine person could do his ceremonies without his pipe.

Some of our pipes are quite plain in design, while others are carefully carved and decorated. Yet the pipe's actual value has always been determined by its use rather than its appearance. Except for some of the ancient tribal pipes prepared for important rituals such as the Hunka, or making of spiritual brothers, a plain-looking pipe will often contain far more power and worth than the most beautiful one ever made.

Every Sioux pipe has its origin in the first pipe brought to my people by the holy Calf Pipe Woman, who is also called White Buffalo Calf

Maiden. Since that time the pipe has been the central item in all our Sioux ceremonies and in our life-way. I was taught that this great event took place as much as eight hundred years ago (sometime between A.D. 1200 and 1500).

I know that most non-Indian authorities will not agree with this dating for Calf Pipe Woman, since they say that the Sioux and the pipe came to the plains sometime after the year A.D. 1700. But I was taught as a boy, and have had it confirmed in visions, that small hunting parties made journeys as far west as the Rocky Mountains long before our entire nation migrated to buffalo country, and that it was during one of these trips that the original Sacred Calf Pipe and instruction for its use in prayer was given.

The seven sacred tribal ceremonies that feature the pipe were given to us and practiced after our Sioux nation was settled on the Plains, and many, many years after Calf Pipe Woman first appeared. I am not bothered by the fact that more recent winter count robes tell of a mysterious woman in white coming among the Sioux. She has returned many times since her first appearance. At this very moment [June 1974] she is walking about the United States in the company of another young woman. This is a bad omen, which tells us that the end times are upon us.

Ever since it was first given, our Sacred Calf Pipe, which is wrapped in a cloth bundle, has been kept by a succession of custodians. Indians who have seen it know they are not supposed to talk about it, so complete descriptions of the pipe have not been given. It is presently kept in a small wooden building at Green Grass, on the Cheyenne River Reservation in South Dakota. The Keeper is Orval Looking Horse. He is a handsome young Lakota man who lives according to our traditional ways and speaks little English.

In the old days, some Indians tribes had a special tribal ceremonial pipe that was only smoked when it was necessary to make a truce between enemies. Sometimes a pipe like this was placed on the ground between two enemy groups as a pledge of peace during trade talks. Pipes were sent around villages to gather warriors for a horse raid or war party. The one who led the raid carried the pipe to the tipis of those he wanted to go with him. And war party leaders usually carried a small pipe that was specially blessed by a medicine man. The warriors smoked it along the way, and if circumstances permitted, celebrated a short ritual with it just before the enemy was engaged.

Among the Sioux there have always been three different uses for pipes. The least important kind is one that is used for social purposes. It is filled with regular tobacco and smoked with friends. Anyone can smoke it. A higher kind is the personal pipe that we use to make and continue friendships, and it is the one that is filled and sent as an offering to a medicine man when his services are needed. The third and most important kind of pipe is one that is used by its owner for ceremonial purposes, such as sweatlodge rites, vision quests, and the Sun Dance. The third kind is also the pipe used by the holy men and medicine men for their private rituals, for healing patients, and as they lead the various tribal ceremonies.

When the Sioux smoke the two higher kinds of pipes, the bowls are filled with a tobacco mixture known as *kinnikinnick*. It is made from the dried and crushed inner bark of the red willow tree combined with a certain hard-to-find plant root. I am always looking for some. We call this mixture a fruit from Grandmother Earth, and when we smoke it, it makes a living four-way bond among the people, the rest of creation, *Wakan-Tanka,* and Grandfather above. Each grain of tobacco placed in the pipe bowl becomes something God has created, so that when the pipe bowl is filled, all of creation is held within it and made a part of the pipe ceremony. Its sweet smell when burned is welcomed by *Wakan-Tanka* and by Grandfather, and he gladly receives the prayers that go up to him in and with the smoke.

I have made several pipes and can tell you how it is done. The head is made first, and the stem is designed to balance it, so that it is a good work of art. Heads can be carved from black or gray stone [using steatite, argillite, shale, and limestone], but a red stone that has been called "catlinite" ever since the artist known as Catlin [George Catlin] visited the Minnesota quarry site [in the 1830s] is the material we like best. It has been used by the Sioux since the year A.D. 1700. Catlinite is very soft when the piece of stone is first cut from the cliff, so years ago the pipe maker, who was always a man, was able to take a layer of stone, and using only flint stone tools, to rough out a block the size he wanted. Then he cut and shaped the bowl, after which he finished it by grinding the surface smooth with another stone and rubbing it with tallow. But in my time metal tools have been used for cutting, and a final polish of beeswax is applied to the stone to make it shine.

I know of an ancient pipe bowl that was styled in the shape of a cross, but its use was discontinued when the Sioux learned that Jesus Christ was crucified on a cross.

Our earliest pipes were just a single piece; the bowl and stem were a straight tube. Some were simply an animal leg bone wrapped with sinew to keep it from cracking, and others were made of stone. Later on, we began to make the two-piece pipe everyone is familiar with. Its stone bowls were L-shaped or T-shaped. Some of the mid-Plains tribes used a flat, disk-shaped bowl, and some northern nations made a stubby style (called Micmac), but we Sioux did not make these. Ornately carved

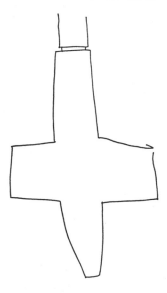

Fools Crow's drawing of the ancient pipe in the shape of
a cross.

bowls, and those inlaid with silver and lead strips, only appeared after
1850. Some of these were created by Indians, and others by non-Indians and used for trade items and awards after 1864. Many pipe bowls
had file cuts [a carving process called "incising," wherein grooves were
cut and ridges were left to form a washboardlike pattern].[10]

Pipe stems are sometimes made of catlinite, but while these are good-
looking, they also break easily, so our stems are usually carved out of
wood. For several reasons, ash is the material we like best. It absorbs
any poisons in the tobacco, it seldom bends more than a little, and even
when it rots, it remains straight. Because of this, the stem stands for
straightness of speech, mind, and body.

The shape of the stem is simply a matter of the designer's preference.
Some stems are round; others are broad, thin, and flat; and some are
carved with a twist or a spiral. A few are covered with a wood-burn
pattern, some are painted, and the best are wrapped at the mouthpiece
end with porcupine quills or beadwork. Animals or other creatures
carved on the stem stand for, and thus pull into a ceremony, all of the
four-legged creatures of the earth. Eagle feathers tied to the stem stand
for the winged creatures above. Colored ribbons stand for the four cardinal directions, and in modern times have become a prayer for the
well-being of all the races of mankind.[11]

We medicine men say that when the ceremonial pipe is used properly it has enormous power. There are fixed rules to be carefully observed in lighting it, in passing it from one person to another, in disposing of the ashes, and in doing the pipe ceremony proper, in which the smoked pipe is pointed to the six sacred directions. When these things are done correctly, they release the powers that reside in the directions, where since the beginning of time they have awaited opportunities to promote the good of all creation. When the pipe is used correctly, what happens is like the opening of the flood gates of a dam that contains the water of life, or it is like throwing a switch that releases the power that energizes the universe.

In these six directions is found everything needed for renewal, physical and intellectual growth, and harmony. There is *Wakan-Tanka* himself, God, the "highest and most holy One"; there is *Tunkashila,* Grandfather, who corresponds to the Son of God; there is Grandmother Earth; and there are the four cardinal directions, moving in order of importance from west to north to east to south. *Wakan-Tanka* is unlimited [infinite], and has given to each of the other directions sacred powers that are their own to impart as they see fit, including such things as purification, joy, good health, growth, endurance, wisdom, inner peace, warmth, and happiness. The directions are holy and mysterious beings. *Wakan-Tanka* remains above them in power, and they are not separated even though they are distinct and identifiable. The powers do the will of God, yet they have a will and intellect of their own. They hear and answer prayers, yet their powers and ways remain mysterious. With them and through them we send our voice to God.

In our pipe ceremony, which is really very simple, the pipe is smoked and pointed stem first and horizontally in a clockwise direction to the west, north, east, and south; then down to Grandmother Earth; up to Grandfather; and finally in an almost imperceptible higher movement to *Wakan-Tanka*. So while we speak of six directions, there are actually *seven* movements of the pipe, and our God is a Trinity, consisting of *Wakan-Tanka, Tunkashila,* and the Spirits. As the Pipe Ceremony is done, the pipe first of all opens the gates to release the powers, and then becomes the very channel through which the powers flow, moving from the six directions to the one who prays, blessing the person, and then through the person and out to bless the rest of creation.

Therefore we say that the pipe itself has the power to transport power, and it is sacred. *Wakan-Tanka* sent the first one with Calf Pipe Woman, but any pipe used in the same way as the original one is just as sacred and effective.

Thus it follows that those who smoke the sacred pipe with understanding and reverence will receive uncommon help. I believe that it is the key to the world's survival today, and when we talk about the future later on, I will explain why this is so. The sacred pipes are indeed beautiful, but more than that are powerful, and should be handled and considered with utmost respect.

CHAPTER 6   RUNS FOR HILL AND THE KETTLE DANCE

I am not able to remember everything about my boyhood years, only the big things that affected the direction in which I was going. In 1908 a dance was held at Porcupine, and my father, stepmother, and I were invited to attend it. Much to my surprise, Iron Cloud's wife, Runs For Hill, the aunt who cared for me as a child, took my hand and led me out to the center of the dance arena, while the large crowd formed a huge circle around us.

While the two of us stood there, a crier announced that Runs For Hill wished everyone to know she was becoming a spiritual mother to me. In the Sioux way, spiritual relatives are closer than blood relatives. So this was a great moment. She was declaring a mother-son relationship between us in which she was promising to do even more for me than my real mother would have been required to do.

To demonstrate her sincerity, Runs For Hill then gave twenty-six horses to the poorest people present, asking them at the same time to always remember me in their prayers. They should pray always that I would continue in the traditional way of life that Iron Cloud; my father, Eagle Bear; and Stirrup had taught me, and they should pray that I would live up to their high expectations.

I treasure that day and honor, and because of it I have done my best to maintain self-respect as well as concern for the elderly, the poor, and the sick. Whatever I have, I share it with people who are in need. And I have not, under any circumstances, violated the bond that was made.

My spiritual mother did fulfill her promise to watch out for and to help me. And I believe the people she asked to pray for me must have done so, because while I have been faced with great temptations in my life, with God's help I have overcome them all. Grandfather heard their prayers and made me strong. I have lived this long, and during my life I have accomplished many of the things they hoped I would.

After that day in 1908, the Lakota people began to show special regard for me, and I began to have a special concern and respect for them. Public honors that continue traditional customs have a special way of shaping and directing our lives. Once Grandfather begins to touch us through these things we can never be the same again.

Five years later, in the spring of 1913, I was riding in the hills near my home when I saw my first vision in a thunderstorm. This gave me the power to learn to lead the Sacred Kettle Dance Ceremony, and my grandparents taught me how to do it. Then in November of 1913, I conducted my first Kettle Dance. Long, long ago, God showed the Sioux how to do this sacred dance as a prayer for rain and plenty of food. It is so old that our ancestors were still roaming about and homeless when they first learned it.

Actually, a Kettle Dance could be done at any time during the year, but one was always included among the first dances held in the spring. Whenever it was done, it was always the last dance of the day to be performed. Only when the other dances were finished could the Kettle Dance be held.

A dog must be eaten as part of the dance. That may seem strange, but in the old days dogs were very precious animals to the Indians. Every family had to have several to use as pack animals. So the dog was held in great respect. It had power and could give power. It was a holy gift from Grandfather, and so was used in the Kettle Dance and the Yuwipi ceremony because of this. The cooking kettle the dog was put in must always be made by the women in the ancient manner. A buffalo stomach was hung on four upright sticks so as to make a bag, and then was filled with water. Nearby, a fire was built and rocks were heated. When the rocks were as hot as they could get, forked sticks were used to place them one by one in the water.

As I indicated when I mentioned having my vision, the leader of a Kettle Dance had to have seen visions in thunderstorms. Only those who had seen these could be taught how to kill the dog, and how to paint special lightning lines on a leader's body. The painting of my body for my first Kettle Dance was done by my uncle Sam Stabbe, who was also a medicine man. Participants in the dance always went to the medicine men and asked them to put the designs on their body. In my case, because I had dreamed of thunder beings, my uncle painted red lightning designs all over my body. The lines ran up the front of my body, over my shoulders, and down my back. Other lines were painted down the sides of my legs and arms to the ankles and wrists. Yet another line ran in a U shape across my forehead and down my cheeks. All of the lines were forked at the ends, as thunder-being lines should be. This tells people that we can split storm clouds to keep rain away from an area. Thereafter, every time I did a Kettle Dance, my body was painted this way. All I wore as a costume was moccasins, a breechclout, a feather bustle, and a headdress.

The dog had to be slain in a certain ritual manner. Since I was the leader this time and had been taught how it was done, I took a wide rawhide thong, put it around the dog's throat, and swiftly choked him to death. The dog, it usually was a puppy or at the most a young animal, hardly realized it was happening before it was over. When he was dead, his body was first washed, and then the hair was singed off. After that, I cut him up and dropped the pieces in the boiling kettle.

At this point, a medicine man assisting me chose and blessed with burning sweetgrass eight male dancers. These men were chosen because they were worthy of the honor. Once this was done, I called the eight men to come forward and to dance four times around the kettle. At this time the men were wearing only breechclouts, moccasins, and armbands. In addition, two men had buffalo robes wrapped around them. After this the men put on their feather-dance bustles and divided themselves into two groups, with four men on the east side of the kettle and four men on the west side of it.

Now the dance proper began. Both the drumbeat and the dance step was very slow, so the spectators could observe its details very carefully. The eight worthy men, four coming from each of the two sides, danced up to the boiling kettle, acting all the while like they were going to plunge their hands into it. Then they formed a line behind me and followed, dancing as we went, while I circled to each of the four sacred cardinal directions and prayed. After this the eight men and I went forward to the kettle and backed up four times. On the last approach and to the great wonder of the spectators I plunged my bare hands and arms deep into the boiling water and pulled out the dog's head. This act could be done with a pointed stick, but a really worthy leader would do it in the ancient way and use his bare hands. He never got burned if he knew how to do it, and, of course knew the medicine man's secret. The reason we leaders didn't get burned was that we had a herb medicine that we rubbed on our hands and forearms before and after we immersed them in the boiling water. I once had quite a bit of it, but lost it all along with the rest of my other medicines when my house burned down in 1974. I know of places where more is growing, though. We passed a location just the other morning when we were on our way to the town of Martin.

Experienced Kettle dancers knew when the dog was cooked from the appearance of the water, and it was always still boiling then. After the

8. "I was a rider in the last horse dance held by the Sioux."

9. "If the spirits do not at first speak to me through the rocks, I sing the song again until they do."

10. "It was, however, my first and my last buffalo stunt, because I had never taken such a wild ride in my life."

11. "So I looked up, and from the west through the clouds came four riders on four horses."

12. "My years with Kate have been good ones."

leader pulled out the dog's head, the other dancers could reach in and grab a portion if they wanted to. But usually most were afraid to do it! Kate's father used to be a leader in the Kettle Dance, and he was never afraid to put his hands in the boiling water and come up with the dog's head. Neither was I.

As for the use of the dog's head itself, it was customary for the leader to dance a couple of times around the kettle with it and to then give it to a young boy. It can be given to either a young girl or a young boy. Doing so was a prayer that they would one day have a family of their own, and that they would remember this ceremony and encourage their sons to do the Kettle Dance.

The Kettle Dance is a prayer for a good spring and summer with plenty of rain, so that the gardens and the wild plants will flourish and the grass will be abundant for the livestock; our Kettle Dance prayers included thoughts of wild chokecherries, plums, currants, buffalo berries, sand cherries, wild potatoes, and turnips. We prayed about our horses and cattle, and about our cellars being full of food for the coming winter. That is why the Kettle Dance was and is so sacred to us. I will try to tell you word for word the prayer that was used when we did the dance in the early days.

After the dog's head was given to the young girl or young boy, the rest of the meat was passed around to the dancers and to the people who were sponsors because they had provided food and money to help the leader put on the dance. Then the leader took a piece of meat, and holding it up high in both hands prayed to the four winds, to the ground, and to the sky. The words he used have never been changed. They have been the same as far back as anyone remembers.

> First the leader looked toward the west, and said:
> O Great Spirit please hear our prayers and hear our request for many things that will come from the earth. Of this meat that we are going to eat we are giving you a piece to show our gratitude.
> Then he faced north, saying:
> O Great Spirit from the north, please give us the most wonderful winter we could ever pray for. Please let us stay healthy through your winter months.
> And then he turned to the east:
> O Great Sun, give us the light and the warmth that the Great Spirit has always put in our hearts. And always make the days as bright as they have been in the past through your help.

Then he turned to the south:

O Great Spirit of the south, please help us by bringing the warm winds and the wonderful birds that come in the summertime, that we might enjoy the summer months with the pleasure of your warm climate.

Then he held the meat toward the ground:

Grandmother of the ground, you know what comes from the ground and what we have put into the ground. O Grandmother of the ground please let what we have put into the ground grow.

Finally, he held the meat up to the sky:

O *Wakan-Tanka,* this prayer is sent to you from every person in our nation. It comes from their hearts. And, it is only a simple prayer, but please hear and grant our requests. And let us always remember that you are continually in our hearts.

When the prayer was done we offered the first piece of dog meat to *Wakan-Tanka* and Grandfather. When I led the dance, I took the piece of meat some distance from the dancing area, dug a little hole, put the meat in it, and covered it up. It was buried in Grandmother Earth, but it was actually a gift to God. It is his. Then we burned the dog bones because the dog was holy.

After the offering to *Wakan-Tanka* was made, everyone joined in a huge feast. Then the singers went to the middle of the dancing circle. The leader was given a stick, and the singers began a song. As they sang, the leader went to everyone present and touched them with the stick. Then they got up and danced a round dance. The exception to those dancing were the people who were there for a giveaway. These remained seated until the round dance was completed. Then they brought their gifts out in the center and held their giveaway. Once this was done, the Kettle Dance was over.

While I sometimes took part in Kettle Dances as one of the eight dancers, the last time I did the dance I was the leader. I am not able to remember for certain what year it was; perhaps it was 1952. I know it was shortly after the Pine Ridge courthouse burned down, and, judging from my relatives who have died since then, I would say it was at least twenty years ago. The way that dance happened, Jake Herman and Ben Chief told me to get my costume and bring it to Pine Ridge, because they were going to have a dance and wanted me to take part in it. But they didn't say what kind of dance and what I would be expected to do.

So I took my costume to Pine Ridge, and when I arrived there, to my surprise they announced to the assembled crowd that they were going to have the Kettle Dance, and that Frank Fools Crow was going to lead the dance and get the dog's head. I guess they had heard that I could do the dance, and were trying to test me to find out whether I would really put my hands in the boiling water. So I asked them to give me just five minutes, and I took off. Only a short distance away and right alongside of the road, I saw the very medicine I needed. I took some and chewed it, rubbing the saliva all over my hands and forearms. Then I came back to where the crowd was.

By this time they had already selected the other eight dancers. So we did the Kettle Dance, and when I was supposed to get the dog's head I reached right in, pulled it out, and handed it to Ben American Horse. It was too hot for him to handle. He tossed it from one hand to another like a hot potato, and hastily threw it in Frank Afraid of Horse's lap. Frank yelled, jumped up, and threw it to another man. They kept tossing it until it was cool. Then they all came to examine my hands, and were amazed to find there was nothing wrong with them; no burns, no blisters, nothing. I dried my hands off with sage, and that's all there was to it.[12]

CHAPTER 7 LONGNECK AND THE NEW LIFE

The early years on the reservation brought constant and significant changes in our life-way. You would need to be one of us and live through them to even begin to understand what it did to us. The government had passed the Dawes Allotment Act in 1887, and two of our oldest leaders, Fast Horse and Ghost Bear, decided that we too should have our own allotments. So they went to Washington, D.C., and got the program approved for us.

At first, we Sioux were really sad and upset about having to change. My ancestors had been relatively happy with the nomadic life, living in small camps and traveling most of the time in search of buffalo. It was all they knew, and settling down in one place was entirely strange to them. Under this new program, they, and those of the first reservation generation, would have to separate and live as families on our own land. We all knew it would not be easy to be tied down and dependent on someone else for the things we needed to live.

It was actually 1906, or 1907, before the allotment program went into effect at Pine Ridge. By now the reservation was divided into eight districts, and each family was assigned to a district. People lived in many kinds of dwellings: log houses, cellar houses, canvas tent, and in tipi fashioned from deer hide and the few buffalo hides that were left. The buffalo were all gone, and all I knew as a boy about buffalo was the stories the old people told about how many there used to be and what sport it was to hunt them.

As a matter of fact, the first time I saw a living buffalo was in 1913, when we were on a train on our way to Salt Lake City. We passed by a place where a white man had eight of them. He was out there feeding them, and they were tame. This was contrary to everything I had been told about them, and I was amazed. My people had said it really took courage to go after a buffalo and bring him down. So it made me wonder what kind of a white man this must be who so fearlessly fed these monstrous animals.

Most people think that our early years on the reservation were our most difficult ones, but that is not actually the case. First there was a period of comparative happiness, and then later on the tragic times came.

As the allotment program got under way, the government provided each family with a wagon, a plow, two horses and harness, an ax and a shovel, and a few other items, such as gardening equipment. This would not have helped us much were it not for the white settlers who provided us with additional teams of horses, more harness, more wagons, plows, milk cows, chickens, hogs, turkeys, and ducks. They also taught us how to use all of these things, and it was a common and amusing sight after that to see an Indian with his long braids chasing chickens or sitting alongside a cow and milking away.

In their kindness our white friends even watched out for us, since they knew that in this new manner of life it would be some time before we could take care of ourselves. They would come around and see what they could do for us, and then teach us whatever we needed to know. So it was a sad moment when the government decided later on to force a lot of the good whites, including some who married Indians, to move off the reservation.

Of course, there were problems, and some very painful ones, that resulted from agency rules. It was especially hard to have the children sent away to school, and that was resisted, as was the order to cut our hair short. People were also unhappy about relatives being moved to reservations some distance away. And we were not pleased about the interference in our religious ceremonies.

But at the same time, the new life proved before long to be challenging and interesting. It even brought a new kind of unity to our people, for we at last had the peace and security we needed to rebuild our lives and nation. We now had new things to talk about and to do, and we made progress quickly. By 1909, we were already well into the farming life.

The men were learning where and how to plant crops, how to raise cattle, and how to take care of poultry. The women were busy and even excited, learning new ways to cook using cookstoves, and how to eat at tables with dishes and tableware while sitting on chairs. They learned how to use soap to wash clothes, and how to iron them and repair them with needles and thread. It was even a happy experience to learn to cut things with scissors. And we all learned not to try to pull the feathers off a chicken without first soaking it in boiling water.

For the first time now, we learned to make butter. And as was the case for everything, we tried to come up with better ways of doing it. One morning, when I was getting ready to go after the horses, my stepmother came out and told me she wanted me to help her make butter. So I said I would as soon as I returned. But she brought out two flour sacks, each containing a lard can, and tied them to my saddle strings. Then she told me to gallop my horse out, to round up the horses, and then to come back. I did this, and when I arrived back home I found that, while the cans had at first been full of cream, I had made about six pounds of butter that morning without even knowing it. After that, it became routine for me to make buttermilk or butter this way.

We kids were actually happy in those days because we knew how to plant and harvest watermelons, squash and onions, potatoes, and we really enjoyed the cow's milk. All of this made for closer relationships within the family, and it increased respect between neighbors because we had so much in common. We had things to exchange and accomplishments to be proud of. We were learning a new kind of interdependence, and we were gaining a new kind of self-respect.

In some ways, conditions were even better than the old buffalo-hunting days. In the fall of each year we helped one another to gather the harvest, and to store it in root cellars. Winters in our country had always been difficult to live through, and being able to store food like this was a proud and comforting achievement.

In this early period there were always ambitious and clever men who showed us the way to improve our circumstances, although we often learned later that some ways were not such a blessing as we first thought, and resulted in jealousy. One ambitious fellow was a man named Four Horn. He had a small garden in which he grew such things as corn, potatoes, squash, watermelons, and onions. He neither spoke nor understood English, but as he traveled off the reservation he saw what white men were doing with their large farms. So he came home one day determined to plant huge acreages of wheat, corn, and beans. And he did. Then when these were ready to harvest he went to the agent and asked him to provide the equipment and operators to harvest them. The agent agreed, obtained the help, and then offered to do the same for any family who wished to follow suit. His support gave Four Horn recognition, and it encouraged others to try harder.

Speaking for myself, I know that my family was so busy and content that it felt good to take a break and go someplace once or twice a month. This was about all the time we had to relax, though, because we were always working. The reservation was a beehive of activity.

Another step that brought control and unity to the reservation was our new system of law and order with courts and policemen. We needed this, because the old way of camp life in which warrior societies served as policemen was gone, and there were no others but white soldiers to control the people. Once we were permitted to have our own Indian policemen and courts it reduced tension, and permitted parents to concentrate upon bringing up their children in the new way, while at the same time doing what they could to continue some of the traditional customs.

In those days there were forty-eight Indian policemen for the eight Pine Ridge districts, and four of our elder statesmen served as judges for our court. These four sat in judgment on Indians, but could not judge white men who broke the law on reservation lands. If a white man killed an Indian, the Indian policemen would capture him and then turn him over to the white authorities. But you can't even do that now. The Sioux have no jurisdiction over a white man, even on a reservation. It did not, however, work the same way in the early days when an Indian killed a white person off the reservation. For example, when a man named Two Sticks killed a white man, the Indian leaders caught him and turned him over to the white people. They hung him immediately without a trial.[13] That's the way it was. We were always willing to keep our word as to what we would do, but most of the time the federal and state governments did little more than make promises.

The settlers were different, and I have mentioned the considerate white people who went out of their way to help us in the early years of reservation life. We truly appreciated this, and we have not forgotten them. In fact, one white man, named Oscar Tolcheck, became my best friend. He is still alive, although he is half paralyzed. He lives right next to the store at Allen. He has leased some of my reservation land for over twenty years, and we have never had an argument. Whenever I have needed something I asked him, and he either gave it to me or got it for me. He has always treated me very well. Mr. Malone, who runs the store at Porcupine, is another fine and generous white man.

John Brennan, our reservation agent in those earliest days of the twentieth century, was one of the nicest men I ever met. Of course, we could not pronounce or write the white man's names, just as they could not pronounce ours, so what we did was give them a name of our own based upon some feature in their appearance—whether they were tall, short, fat, or whatever stood out about them.

Brennan was such a nice man that we had no desire to insult him. But he had a very long neck, so we called him by a name that could best be translated as Longneck. I doubt that anyone ever explained what the word we used for him meant in Sioux, and if he ever found out he never complained. In fact, he seemed quite happy that he had an Indian name, whatever it was. He had a lot of respect for the Sioux, and we admired him. He tried to understand our ways, and in time learned to speak a little Lakota. Every other month he visited all of the districts, asking what the people needed, and what he could do to improve the government services for them. Whenever a storm hit, he came out immediately afterward to see what the damages were.

If Longneck was still here today (1975) we would not have been exposed to that scene we saw this side of Scenic last night. No group of drunken kids would be trying to stop our car, or to leave us wondering when we passed by whether they would shoot at us.

Longneck would not have permitted such a thing, and he fought as hard as he could to keep liquor off the reservation. I can't remember how long he was the agent for us, but he was certainly popular during the years from 1908 to 1910. The women liked him so much they took presents to him every time they went to Pine Ridge. The men weren't jealous, they liked him too.

Longneck did a number of special things that helped us adjust to the new way of life and that hastened its acceptance. One was to make it a rule that every two weeks all of the people were to come to the agency and camp there. Then in the evening a *wacipi* (powwow) would begin at a location near his house, and it would last all night. Longneck enjoyed this tremendously, and so did we. The next day was ration day, when nearly everything we needed to balance what we were growing and producing was handed out to us. We received beef, bacon, flour, coffee, sugar, beans, rice, prunes, and dried fruits such as peaches and apples. Besides clothing, we were given quilts, blankets, and pillows. Then we would take our gifts and go home.

Of course, some Indians argue today that these were not gifts, that they were really nothing more than fair payment for all that was taken from and done to us. But that is a meaningless argument now, and it does not change the fact that we were happy again and no longer struggling against the new way. We had food and clothing and homes to go to, and it was far better than the horrors of Wounded Knee.

I feel it was important that the men had work to do that occupied their minds and bodies. In former days the women did most of the work around the camp, while the men hunted, made their weapons, defended their territory, and went on horse raids and war parties. When this lifeway ended, the men were restless, frustrated, and felt unproductive. Now everyone had something valuable to do.

I should add that the Indian police did a good job of protecting things for us, just as the warrior societies once did for our ancestors in the old days. The Indian police patrolled the reservation boundaries, and among other things would bring home stray horses or cattle belonging to Sioux or white men. If these animals belonged to non-Indians living outside the reservation, they charged one dollar a head for returning them. No one ever asked what happened to that money they collected. Things were so good that we all had everything we needed, we weren't jealous, and we didn't care.

The reservation policemen were actually very good men, and very helpful. People did not fear them at all, except in regard to turning us in for forbidden medicine practices and doing the Sun Dance. Even then we knew they only did so because they would be in bad trouble with the authorities if they didn't. If we wanted to butcher a cow, all we had to do was notify the police, and they would come over. After checking the brand to be certain it was our own cow, they would shoot it for us. Today you can drive anywhere and see the carcass of a dead cow someone has killed, just to steal some of the meat and sell it for booze. This happens here at Pine Ridge, and on the Rosebud Reservation too.

Another thing Longneck did was to make it possible for us to go to other reservations and visit our relatives and friends whenever we wished to. Our families and friends were close-knit in those days, so this was a generous and considerate act on his part, and it helped to keep us peaceful.

Whenever we wanted to go on a trip, we went to the agent, and he would make out a travel permit for us. It stated where we were going, and the length of time we expected to be gone. The agent also provided us with the food we would need for the journey, since such trips might take several days. Upon arriving at our destination, we were required to go to that agent to register and give him our permit. Then he would send us to a storage building where we could obtain most of the food we would need while we were there. We could even get a time extension by having the agent telegraph our agent for it.

Sometimes, if government work projects were under way where we were visiting, such as road building, cutting trees, or building log houses, we were offered temporary jobs and an opportunity to earn some money. We received ten or fifteen dollars a month for this, and our food. Actually, money meant little to us at first. We did not yet know what it was for. But the work was always a challenge to the men, because by now we were into the work habit, and as the men applied themselves they were aware that they were encouraging their children to grow up doing the same.

Of course, liquor was not yet allowed on the reservations, and the penalty for being drunk was a year and a day in jail and a five-hundred-dollar fine, so everyone was alert and physically fit, had lots of energy, and always looked forward with anticipation to the next workday. Later, when the Reorganization Act was put into effect in 1934, this attitude would change drastically.

Wherever people went in those early reservation days there was mutual respect and a desire for healthy competition. In prereservation times, after the fall buffalo hunts were over and things were pretty well ready for winter, the people would have feasts and games before settling down in their wintering places. It was a good way, and we wanted to continue it, so in our new way of life, sometime around October, after the harvest and all the corn, potatoes, vegetables, and hay were stored away, criers would be sent to notify the districts that a festival would be held at a certain location. Thousands of people assembled for four days of games, feasting, dancing, and contests. We competed at these annual gatherings to see who had the strongest team of horses and who could do the most work at certain harvesting tasks. We had foot races, horse races, and squaw-wagon races. In these the women were the drivers, and the men stood behind them and whipped the horses. So in those early years we could practice in one more way at least a semblance of our old life, and on land that belonged to us without dispute.

Besides this, we could invite anyone we wanted to live with us. Friends and strangers alike could camp on our property as long as they wished. Or we could go to someone else's property and do the same. In some ways Pine Ridge was like a big, old-fashioned Indian camp that covered thousands of acres, much like the great summer encampments of yesterday. And I think there were more Sioux at Pine Ridge then than there are on the reservation now.

We also had annual celebrations on the Fourth of July. These were begun in July of 1891, the summer after the Wounded Knee battle. Actually it was at that time a memorial celebration for us, a prayerful event in remembrance of the Indians who had died at Wounded Knee. Following Sioux custom, once the appropriate services and ceremonies were finished, there would be a big feed for everyone and social dances. Many of the songs that came into being at that time were results of Wounded Knee. The decade that followed the massacre was a melancholy period, during which the impact of what was happening to the Sioux really struck home. A beloved life-style was either ending, or at the very least changing drastically, and the people sang spiritual songs that expressed their hope that their fears and losses would be wiped away, and that such tragedies as Wounded Knee would never take place again.

But in time, the memorial part of the Fourth of July celebrations faded, and they became more joyful events. Time heals most wounds for all people, and it did so for us as well. I want to say again that contrary to the opinion that the early years on the reservation were a bitter and frustrating experience for us, we were relatively happy. Things were in no way perfect, but compared to now, and to the desperate period between the end of Red Cloud's War and 1900, the situation was very good.

Besides our farm produce and the agency supplies, fish were plentiful and so was wild meat. The year-round hunting was great, even though we had to do it with bows and arrows. The women could obtain permission from the agent to purchase the knives they needed for housework and tanning. But there was a federal law forbidding Indian men to have firearms, knives, or liquor. Usually, four or five of us young fellows would get together, obtain authorization from the agent, and go hunting anywhere we wanted to on the reservation. Sometimes we would be away from home as long as two weeks. We brought home deer, antelope, prairie dogs, and all of the wild animals you can name that Indians ever ate—except members of the cat family. We Sioux would not eat this. After 1915, we began to go over to Custer, to the buffalo park there. They had a small buffalo herd, and since a lot of townspeople and National Parks Service personnel wanted to see Indians on horseback killing buffalo, they let us shoot a few of them with our bows and arrows.

As far as bears were concerned, very few were considered sacred and not to be killed. Sometimes word would get around about a certain holy bear, so people were afraid of it, wouldn't go near it, and would not shoot it. Outside of that, the Indians killed bears and ate them. We do have many legends and tales about holy bears, but people who hear these should know how it really was. I myself have never eaten bear meat, and in 1927 an incident happened that strengthened my belief that I shouldn't. That year I made a trip to Interior, which is close to the Cedar Passes and the Badlands. And there was a huge bear hung up there, already skinned. They asked me if I wanted to eat some of it, but it looked too much like a human being. This explains why, while a lot of Indians will kill bear and eat it, I won't. When you skin them they look too much like a human being.

As far as I know personally, pheasants came late to the reservation area. It was less than thirty years ago when I saw my first one. Two fellows named something like Manendora and McKeen leased some land and brought them here.

I continued to hunt with my bow and arrows until last fall, and was still a good shot. I used them to pick off cottontails. But a friend of mine from California wanted the bow, so I sent it to him. For over seventy years my stalking method remained the same. I followed along the edges of creeks. And when I saw or heard a prairie chicken or any other bird, I would frighten them and as they flew up in the air would send an arrow right through their throat.

Perhaps people will wonder at my enthusiasm for these early reservation years, at my saying we were learning more, and about my claim that life was more interesting in some ways than it was before the white man came. But from what I have been told, our old life-way was constantly assaulted by white pressures from the middle of the nineteenth century until the Custer affair in 1876. And while the pace did slow some after that, our situation did not really change for the better until at least ten years after the Wounded Knee massacre in 1890. You can easily imagine what that fifty-year period did to the Sioux.

So when you ask me whether, if I had a choice, I would prefer to live during the reservation period or back in the prewhite days, I will answer as follows: I enjoyed most of the early years of my life, and in particular the twenty-year period between 1908 and 1928. All our people lived happily then. Life was different than it had been for us, but at least parents could raise their children close to the way they wanted to. Still, I imagine I would choose the prewhite days for two reasons: There was no liquor then, and it would be pleasant to live without the havoc that has worked among us. Also, in the ancient days our religious life was respected and powerful.

In the period from 1895 to 1910 we Sioux learned a great deal about our new home life, family life, and social life. Some of our young people kept wishing we could return to the old ways, but our elders made it plain that it would not happen. They said the new way was here to stay, and the Sioux had no choice but to learn it.

I continue to look back on those early years as wonderful ones, because I learned so many interesting things in such a short time. The changes brought about by the new government laws and policies were major challenges to all of us. And as always, Longneck came to the rescue by adapting what he could of each program to our Indian manner of doing things. It is too bad that all of the reservations did not have an agent like him.

I want to say more about Longneck. He would come regularly with an interpreter to visit each district. Here he would be met by a respected Sioux leader, whose main job was to serve as spokesman and grievance man for the people in his district. The spokesman was always chosen by his people for his intelligence, fairness, and honesty. He must also have been living a traditional life. Whenever someone had a request to make to the agent, the leader first evaluated it as to its actual need. Then if he agreed with it, he passed the request on.

This system made it possible for the agent to become well acquainted with the leaders of each district. So when he needed someone to send to Washington, D.C., to seek changes in reservation laws and policies, he knew which man would do the best job in each instance. It was a simple form of government, but it worked well, as had our similar system of camp chiefs and society leaders in the old days. Our wishes were being evaluated, and we felt needed and responsible. It was different then from what it is today.

We followed this custom of working through the spokesmen for our personal business trips, too. If, for example, we wanted to go to Omaha, Nebraska, we discussed our reasons with the leader, who then talked to the agent, and he would authorize the trip, giving us whatever help we needed to go. On our return we advised the leader of the results, and discussed with him how they might be put to the best use.

All in all, it encouraged mutual respect and the keeping of the laws. People seldom left the reservation without permission, and if they did and were caught, they received little sympathy. There was a just penalty for doing that. If arrested, they were brought back to the reservation and jailed for anywhere from six to nine months. But it seldom happened because of Agent Longneck's good sense in handling reservation affairs.

The mutual respect that existed spilled over into our relationships with all of the white employees who were on the reservations. The doctors and nurses, the government employees, and the settlers who leased land learned to appreciate our ability to conform to laws and policies that were similar in nature to what our people had known in prereservation times.

I am aware that we made mistakes, and we were deservedly punished for it. That was fair, I feel, since the only way a people can live secure and productive lives is to follow clear-cut laws. There must be control, and there must be understanding as to why each rule is needed.

For instance, I was born and raised in the Porcupine District, which is a large area encompassing many square miles. Since my father, Eagle Bear, was for a long time the leader of that district, the agent sent him on many trips to Washington to effect changes in laws and policies. They also talked together about sensible family planning. My father often passed on to me the things the agent felt we needed to do to have a controlled, family-oriented life. One suggestion had to do with children. Everyone knew it was a wonderful thing to have them, but if the children were to be healthy and cared for, they should be limited in number to what their parents could handle well.

So the fathers would be advised to discuss this with the mothers, and together they were expected to arrive at a sensible decision. They were to bear in mind, as they talked this over, that with a restricted amount of land available they could not support an unlimited population. And furthermore, they were to remember that circumstances on the reservation could change very quickly.

The future of the children was very much on our minds. Ultimately, families decided on an average of six children. This may seem a large number in view of what I have been saying, but it was believed right for our time and needs. Remember that we were farmers and stock raisers. There was much work to be done, and we believed that fairly large families could if industrious, make their own way. I think that most American farmers felt the same.

Another suggestion made to and accepted by our leaders was that we put aside for a time our anger over the loss of our land, and concentrate on getting along with one another and with the non-Indians living around the reservation. If protests were to be raised about this, they should be done through the legal means open to us. We would have to negotiate with the Great White Father in Washington, even if there were little hope in it for us. And I am proud to say that while it could easily have been different, we never sought to avenge the wrongs done to us by attacking the white settlers around us. We did not attempt to take back our land by force.

Nor did we revolt against the authorities who were suppressing and controlling our religious life. Longneck was kind about this, but even he had to follow orders and control or outlaw certain ceremonies. We were under constant pressure to give up our healing ceremonies, as well as our rituals for prophesying and spiritual guidance. Spirit keeping was discouraged, as well as the Sioux marriage custom. Of course, except for the Ghost Dance, we actually gave none of these up that still were useful and essential in our lives. We simply practiced them in a quiet way and out of the government people's sight. How could we give up that which kept us close to *Wakan-Tanka,* to Grandfather, to Grandmother Earth, and to the powers of the four directions? So we controlled our anger, and found ways of going on with both the old and the new.

Of course, things did not always go so smoothly as I may seem to be suggesting. But whenever pressure started to build on the reservation our elders would step in and remind us that our traditional way of life ruled out jealousy, hatred, and, yes, even revenge. It had permitted revenge for the loss of a relative in war, but our people were not, by bullets at least, being killed any more. Every father was encouraged to teach this to his children, and so to build a base for future peace and happiness.

Moreover, there were those things we could do openly to maintain something of the Sioux life-way. I have already explained about many of these things, and about how agent Longneck made it possible for us to have dances at the agency at ration time. Every two weeks we could do certain dances like the Buffalo Dance and the Kettle Dance, which are religious dances, and social dances like the Grass Dance and the Rabbit Dance. Adding these to what we did secretly, we got along. We were, in any event, too busy with our homes, crops, and livestock to do much more.

CHAPTER 8   ALL THE IMPORTANT
DANCES

I have already spoken about the Sun Dance and the Kettle Dance. Now I will tell you about some of the other important dances we did for religious and social purposes in those early days. Dancing has always been very important to the Sioux, and it was a great source of comfort, strength, and pleasure as we made the difficult adjustment to our new way of life. My heart aches now because many of these dances are no longer performed.

One dance we did was the Buffalo Dance. The Buffalo Dance is a sacred ceremony, so its song is religious. It is a prayer that is sung. In it, the Sioux thank God for all he has done for them, and they pray that they will always live as he wishes them to. People do far less of this now, so anyone can see why religious dances like this are not being done today.

Anyone who knew how to do it, and who was considered worthy in the eyes of the people, could join in. The performers wore a buffalo skin headdress made from the buffalo's head, and a piece of the hide with the tail attached hung down their backs. Porcupine quills had to be part of the costume, and for this purpose, arm, wrist, or knee bands, or quilled moccasins, were worn. Each dancer carried a gourd rattle in one hand, and a pipe in the other. The rattle did not have a buffalo tail attached to it.

The last Buffalo Dance I saw was held about forty-four years ago at a place near Whiteclay, Nebraska, which is just south of the town of Pine Ridge. The gathering was a four-day affair, during which time we had the Buffalo Dance, the Horse Dance, and the Eagle Dance.

Some of the performers did an excellent job of preparing their buffalo headdresses. The finished ones looked like real buffalo heads. They used the skin of the full head, shaping and drying it in such a way as to keep its original form. They did not use wooden blocks to make the eye and nose holes as the Mandans did. The performers kept the actual eye and nose holes open until the skin dried, and then looked and breathed through these when they danced.

In doing the dance, the performers entered the dancing arena and formed a circle. Then when the music began they imitated the actions of real buffalo. They would make noises and frighten each other. They would chase each other and fight, pawing the dirt in a fierce way and then bumping heads like fighting bulls.

There were a fixed number of songs for the dance, and the dancers kept track of them as they were sung. About two thirds of the way through the ritual, some of the performers used sticks that were imitation bows and arrows and lances to kill one of the buffalo. He fell to the ground and lay there while the other performers danced around him four times. At the end of their fourth circle he struggled slowly to his feet and joined them. He was alive again, and this meant that the buffalo would continue to be available to the Sioux. Finally, there was joyful shouting and singing from the audience, who were happy because Grandfather would continue to provide for them by sending the buffalo.

Another religious dance whose song was a prayer was the Horse Dance. I was one of the riders in the last true and sacred Horse Dance, which was also held that day at Whiteclay in 1931.[14] It was an amazing event. Poor Thunder, Danny Otheo, and Standing Little Boy were the other riders. Four singers and four wild horses were used for the dance. One horse was black, one was sorrel, one was buckskin, and one was white. The horses were brought in and put in a corral that was set up near the place where they were going to dance. A fire was built next to the corral, and Poor Thunder made a medicine by taking some red-hot ashes and mixing them with the smoke. The horses had never been ridden and at first were frightened and unruly, stomping and rearing. But when Poor Thunder took his medicine over to the corral and let the wind blow it through the rails and across the horses they calmed down in moments and were no longer wild.

All we riders wore for a costume was a breechclout, and a black cloth bandanna, which covered our entire face and was tied in a knot behind. It was thin and we could see through it. A hole was cut at the mouth so we could insert an eagle bone whistle through it and blow on it. A couple of young boys opened the corral gate for us, and we walked in and directly up to the horses. Poor Thunder went to the black horse and petted it. Then without the aid of a bridle, halter, rope, or anything else, he climbed on top of it. I went to the sorrel horse and did the same thing. Danny Otheo mounted the buckskin. Standing Little Boy went to the white horse, petted its face and shoulders, and climbed up on it. Remember that these were wild horses! We prodded our mounts with our bare heels, and each of them walked calmly through the gate. Then the singing began, and the horses started dancing, really dancing. I was so excited I could hardly stand it.

The singers were excited too, and broke into song. I will tell you how it went. "The riders and the horse dancers are coming, they're coming dancing, they're coming dancing." Then we riders came forward side by side. Looking at us from the front, the white horse was on the left, the buckskin was next, then the sorrel, and the black was on the right. It had been a sunny day, but huge black clouds formed in the sky. Thunder began to boom, and about ten yards ahead of us, lightning started to strike. Amazingly, the horses did not bolt and run. Whinnying and snorting, making all of the strange sounds horses can make, they danced straight toward the lightning. As they did so the lightning moved in a semicircle, and we followed it while it kept striking ahead of us in a broad flashing curtain of light. Not once did the wild horses run away or even turn their backs.

Poor Thunder and I started to sing and pray, and the storm and the lightning split in two, as though the curtain of light were torn in half from top to bottom. The power of our prayer did this. Now we rode to the east, then we turned and faced the south. The drums were booming, the song was started again, and we blew sharp blasts on our eagle-bone whistles. Once more the horses began to prance and dance. Then we faced the west, and as the intensity of the drumbeat rose and the singing gained momentum, the horses really had fun. They were spirited as could be, with their necks arched and their tails sticking almost straight up. They really enjoyed the sacred dance.

Whenever we halted our horses at one of the four cardinal directions, Poor Thunder and I took a position in front and sang and prayed, while Danny and Standing Little Boy were directly behind us and blew on their eagle-bone whistles. This was the only sound there was besides the cries of the crowd, the thunder, the lightning, and the horses.

After our final stop at the north, we rode our dancing horses back into the corral. We dismounted, took sage grass and wiped them down, and then we threw the gate open and let them go. Responding like wild horses once again, they took off running as fast as they could go. Years later I saw one of them out on the prairie, but that was all. It was some experience, that dance. There was a great amount of thunder and lightning, and it was a terrifying time. The performance of the horses was truly amazing. A big crowd of Indians attended it—so many, in fact, that they were pushing against one another, and every one of them cried out in fear and wonder many times. Sacred dances like this are not being held anymore because so many of the people are drinking and misbehaving, and in truth some act like they are out of their minds. You have to be a good person and in the right spirit before the spirit powers can and will help you. People simply do not realize how far the Indian has fallen because of liquor. Most only see the surface damage.

The Eagle Dance was also done at Whiteclay in 1931, and that too was the last time I saw the Eagle Dance performed in the traditional way. The eagle's power is almost equal to that of the 405 good spirits, so we use his feathers in our ceremonies. In the dance we ask God to help us through the eagle. The Eagle Dance is not the same as the Eagle Ceremony. In the Eagle Dance we usually had four men dancing. Their costume consisted of huge wings made with eagle feathers, a white clothlike hood that was pulled over the head and tied around the neck, an eagle-tail shaped like a fan at the back, large bells on straps below the knees, and moccasins. Each performer held an eagle wing-bone whistle in his mouth.

The eagle dancers entered the dancing arena in single file, crying out again and again, "The eagles are flying, the eagles are flying." They continued on, dancing in single file, and made four complete circles around the arena. After this, the tempo of the drum and singing increased, and while they shouted, "The eagles are here, the eagles are here," they imitated the motions of flying eagles. Four more circles were made while they cried out in this way and blew their whistles. When they had done this and finished their dancing, the white hoods were removed and a holy man blessed them with the smoke from burning sweetgrass. Then they left the arena and the dance was over.

In my boyhood days the Sioux did an important but infrequently performed dance called the Stick Dance. Large numbers of people would assemble for the event and group themselves according to districts. It was actually a ceremony designed to encourage selected young men to prepare themselves for tribal leadership. The leaders of the eight districts would sponsor the Stick Dance.

To begin the dance, each leader would bring a special stick and place it in the center of the dancing arena. Then he would stand by his stick. The singers would go to where the sticks and leaders were and sing an honor song for the leaders. When that was done they started another song. While they did so, the eight leaders picked up their sticks, and each leader walked toward the people of his own district. He had already decided upon a young man who, in his opinion, could one day be an outstanding leader. He went to the youth and touched him with the stick. This was a high honor for the young man, and when he responded to the touch by taking hold of the stick, as he always did, it meant that from that day forward he would strive to live the traditional life and prepare himself for leadership. Then the eight young men went together to the center of the arena, and the singers sang a special song for them. It was a proud moment for the young men and for their parents.

Sometimes, when the Stick Dance ended, a Night Dance was held. It would be sponsored by from two to four families, and at their special request. If the parents of one of the young men chosen in the Stick Dance had arranged in former years a marriage agreement with the parents of a girl, the Night Dance was used to bind the agreement. The parents of the young people would bring the couple out to the center of the dancing arena and then have a giveaway. In other words, it was an engagement dance, and a social one.

I was always extremely happy for the young couple when that happened, because their future had been decided and the chances for success were much better. Time has changed everything, and people would question such customs today. Yet marriages made on these occasions usually proved to be among the most prosperous and progressive on the reservation. The couple worked diligently to live up to their memorable beginning, and to what was expected of them. The girls were usually wonderful mothers, and the boys became outstanding fathers and leaders. Their children were frequently the best behaved on the reservation. When our ancient dances are properly performed, they can bring to pass wonderful things.

The purely social dances we did for enjoyment in the early days were the Owl Dance, the Rabbit Dance, and the Grass Dance.

The owl song was, "An owl, you will think of me once in a while." People danced it with different partners so that no one ever danced alone. As we danced we thought of the owl, so that we could become wise and unafraid like he is in our relationships with other people.

The Rabbit Dance was always a lot of fun. Couples danced in a line with everyone facing in the same direction. The line moved clockwise, except for the tail-end couples, who danced counterclockwise. Whenever the drummers hit loud beats each couple would spin around. It was hard to keep together and to keep up. The reservation agents tried to stop this dance because of its song and the things it suggested, namely an affair between two people who were not married to one another. But nothing was meant by it, and it and the Owl Dance are still being done today.

The Grass Dance got its name from our custom of wearing grass in our belts while dancing. The grass represented the scalps our warriors took from their enemies in the old days. It has also been called the Omaha Dance, because the Sioux got it from the Omaha nation many, many years ago. It stressed bravery and generosity among my people.

The giveaway was always part of it. Because all of these things were emphasized, everyone sang loudly and danced wildly. We were very happy. This dance too is still being done wherever Sioux people are, but often without the grass.

Sometimes, when people talk today about the old dances, the Bear Dance and the Prairie Dog Dance are mentioned. But these were really healing ceremonies, and not dances as people usually think of them.

These are all of the important dances we did besides the Sun Dance and the Kettle Dance. They were a central part of life then, and we who shared in them miss the ones that are gone. I wish that people behaved better and believed in *Wakan-Tanka* more so that all of them could be done today.

Of course, while we danced and enjoyed ourselves, I hope I have made it clear that not everything was the way we preferred it during those earliest days at Pine Ridge. We learned, as time passed, to listen to the authorities when we were supposed to listen, and to talk only when we were asked to talk—both of which often required great patience. During those years of changing over to the new way of life I saw several white men hit Indians, but I never saw an Indian attack a white man. I guess our tolerance was better than theirs. So while conditions were quite good, some things were hard for us. Still, I feel we had in those days the strength and wisdom to make the right decisions. Our morale did not give way, and we did not become confused, as we so often are now.

I hope that you will not think I am overdoing this when I say again that I give much of the credit for this to Longneck, since his wise administration and material help made allowances for our ancient faith and aided our progress with our homes, livestock, and poultry. With these things we were almost content, well fed, and occupied. Hungry people cannot be patient. Without proper clothing people are ashamed. When people are freezing, and have the feeling no one cares what they think or do, they lose all hope and sometimes do rash things.

Through the first fifteen years of this century we were sometimes very troubled, but never over vital things. John Brennan, Longneck, was a great Indian agent, and I for one will never forget him. He knew that the Sioux are a proud people and a strong people, and that we deeply appreciate those who give us an opportunity to be what we are with dignity and respect. Few of us living today are old enough to recall those stirring days, and how in such a short time we were able to alter so drastically our former way of life. Many an Indian song was made during that period, and countless memories were engraved upon our minds. To me, it seemed like we were standing on the top of a hill on a beautiful day without too much to worry about.

CHAPTER 9   STIRRUP AND FANNIE

In 1911 I saw my first automobile. I was visiting the agency at Pine Ridge when a man named Hegel, from Rushville, Nebraska, drove up. He was hauling mail for the government.

I remember the occasion well, because the thing he was riding in was so strange-looking. It wasn't very big, and it had solid rubber tires. Yet Mr. Hegel claimed it could go as fast as a horse, even thirty miles per hour.

At that time we Indians didn't know what miles per hour meant, but we weren't in the least ready to find out either. He offered to give all of us there a ride, but no Indian would even touch that thing. Everyone was afraid. I know that I for one wouldn't get off my horse because I couldn't tell what exactly it was, or whether it might suddenly lunge toward me if I did.

It was 1913 before I went on my first long trip off of the reservation. John Apple and Emil Afraid of Hawk made the arrangements, and fifteen of us went to Salt Lake City for a dancing contest. There were ten men and five women. We went on a train, and I enjoyed it so much that I still prefer to travel that way. The meals were very good. There was plenty of meat. And that was fortunate for us, because all we had with us were gingersnaps and cheese. Since our funds were limited, we rode in coaches, and sat up all the time. Usually the cars were cool, and the windows could be opened for air. The only time we were bothered by soot and smoke was when the train was coming to a tunnel or making a turn. So whenever we were coming to a tunnel, the conductor always warned us to close the windows.

While we were at Salt Lake City, Emil took all of us out to the famous Salt Lake. I urged him to ask a white man there if I could go out in the lake to swim. The man said, "Sure, go on out there and swim if you want to." So I took all of my clothes off except my underwear and walked out into the water. But the deeper I got the more it felt like some bad spirit beneath the water was pulling at me and trying to drag me under. Finally, I was really scared. The people on the shore could see this and were laughing at me. So I knew that something was haywire. But I was not going to take a chance, and I just got out of there as fast as I could. Only then was I told that you can't swim in such salty water in the usual way, but that you can float easily. So later on I went back in the water and found this out for myself.

I won first prize at that dancing contest in Salt Lake City. I did a traditional dance, and my prize was fifty dollars.

During the years from 1910 to 1920, I competed in many dance contests like this, and also in many horse races. A certain trader friend bought a one-year-old bay horse for one hundred dollars, and I rode that horse more times than I can count. He was a big horse, and no one knew whether he was a thoroughbred or not, but he outran every horse in the area. My riding partner was Robert Iron Cloud, and between us we won several races at Martin, South Dakota. Then we went down to the Rosebud Reservation and were victorious in all our races there. We took the horse to different places in Nebraska and won there, and after that to Rapid City, where we did the same. That horse could win races ranging anywhere from 300 yards to 2½ miles in length. I always tied a special Indian medicine on his mane and tail to give him added stamina and speed. As soon as I did so he would flare his nostrils and stamp his hooves. He was ready to go.

In 1913, a lot of Sioux men went to a meeting at the agency that was chaired by Charles Red Cloud, Flying Hawk, and several other district leaders. A white man named Miles was there from the Defense Department in Washington, D.C. Speaking through an interpreter, he explained that the government had decided that our leaders should approve a request from the Great White Father concerning our participation in the armed services. If there was a war between the United States and another country, our men would agree to either volunteer or to be drafted into the Army, so as to defend our country. Miles said that we should sign it, because it was our country, and in any event we had no way of turning the request down.

As everyone there recognized, all of the elderly Sioux men had proven themselves to be great fighters in the wars against the United States Army. So we knew well what war was like, and we had always defended our land in a powerful way. Ignoring for the moment the political and moral questions that were plain to us all, Charles Red Cloud and Flying Hawk put their thumbprints on the paper that Miles had brought. But then we began to ask aloud why the white men, who had defeated and humiliated us, felt we should join them in a war against their own kind. They had done their best to put an end to our ability to make war, and had put us on reservations without weapons. Now they wanted us to agree to fight by their side against the very countries where they came from originally! Their answers did little to satisfy us. But what could we do? We were helpless and dependent upon them. All of the district leaders made their thumbmark on the paper. Yet it brought chills to everyone, for we sensed that things were about to change again, and just when everything seemed to be going so well.

In 1914, Stirrup came to visit my father. Stirrup's purpose was to obtain Eagle Bear's approval of Stirrup's choice of me to carry on his work as a holy man, and especially a Yuwipi man. He knew it was Eagle Bear's wish that I become a holy man. Nevertheless, Eagle Bear still wanted to know why he had chosen me for this great honor. Stirrup answered that he had considered several young men in the different districts, but had always been led by *Wakan-Tanka* back to me. So my father wanted to know how I felt about it, and whether I would accept the challenge and holy calling. I told him I wanted to do it, although I knew that the first step demanded of me would be another vision quest, and that not everyone was successful at this—my earlier experience with Stirrup near Allen notwithstanding. Sometimes men quest and don't see or experience a thing. In fact, not many people do manage it successfully, let alone going on to become a Yuwipi man and a holy man. But I was pleased with Stirrup's offer and not afraid. I knew that Stirrup had helped and healed many people. His life had proven to be a happy one, which he clearly accepted and loved. Indeed, it was the highest possible calling for any Sioux, and I knew that I would strive to live just as Stirrup had lived.

Shortly thereafter I traveled on horseback the long hundred-mile trip to Bear Butte, the most awesome vision-questing place in the Black Hills of South Dakota. The greatest Indian leaders had made their vision quests on this mountain for several centuries, and it was the questing place to which Grandfather called me. Sonny Larvie went with me, and waited at a base camp while I fasted and prayed on top of the butte for four days and nights. On the third night I had a vision in which I learned many secret things about being a medicine man, and was given a special herb to use in a special sweatlodge ceremony, but I remained on Bear Butte until the traditional four days and nights were finished.

I left some tobacco for an offering to the spirits, and took about an hour to descend to where Sonny was waiting for me. We returned to Porcupine, where Stirrup spent a full week showing me the medicines he used for different kinds of sicknesses, and explained how he performed his Sun Dance, Yuwipi, and sweatlodge ceremonies. He also described the ways in which other medicine men had helped him.

Stirrup included several warnings about the kind of life I would be expected to lead. He said that while Indian people usually had to pay when they went to a white doctor, there would be many instances when I would be called upon to cure people without pay. It was a sacrifice I should expect to make many times. He also said I could never argue openly with any Indian about political issues or laws—either from the government's side or from the people's side. Even if I was strongly against something, I could not stand up and debate with my own people. I could never engage in war or in a personal fight, and I could never hate anyone or indulge in jealousy or revenge. It was a challenging life I was confronted with, but I accepted it, and I have kept faith with the sacred life-way entrusted to me. For the first time, I felt well settled. The pattern of my life was beginning to be established, and the shape of my future could be seen in at least a hazy way. But my life as a healer would not begin for some years. I was still a young man, and I cherished my freedom as young men do.

In 1916, there was a well-publicized foot race in Gordon, Nebraska. It was advertised as a fifty-yard contest, and all of the best white and Indian runners in the area were invited to compete. The prize was fifty dollars, and that was a lot of money for just running. All of the best sprinters came, and I laugh now as I remember that Dallas Fire Place and I ran barefooted, outran the rest, and tied for first place. We had to split the first and second prize money, which totaled ninety dollars, and came home with the huge sum of forty-five dollars apiece. We were rich men for a while! Dallas is still alive and lives in the town of Batesland. I am sure he could tell people a lot of exciting stories about those early days.

This same year I went to Cheyenne, Wyoming, and while I was there I was selected by the Indian dancers to lead them in the Frontier Days grand parade. That was a great honor, because large groups had come to Cheyenne from many Indian reservations. We had a large group there too. Fifty-two Oglala from Pine Ridge had made the journey. There were thirty-two men, fifteen women, and five children. We went by train, and the group was really a special one. Besides my uncle, Black Elk, it included such men as Flying Hawk, Little Horn, Looks Twice, White Bull, Holy Bear, Little Soldier, Long Soldier, Jim Grass, Jim Braveheart, Tommy Grass, Tommy Little Elk, Brown Eyes, Little Committee, Hand Soldier, Black Horn, Charley Whistle, and others. Charley Whistle had a huge herd of beautiful horses at that time, easily the greatest number owned by anyone on the reservation.

While we were riding the train toward Cheyenne, Black Elk took me aside and talked with me. After we had talked for a while, he told me that as a medicine man I would learn many sacred secrets and perform countless ceremonies for people. He said that over the years, Grandfather would show me wondrous things, that I would receive valuable messages and signs, and that solutions to reservation and healing problems would come to me during my vision quests and rituals.

Black Elk went on to say that, as I traveled to competitions and toured with Wild West shows, word of my healing and prophetic power would spread. Then people who were doubters would ask me to prove what I could do by telling my visions and performing my ceremonies for them. Black Elk also said, "Even then they won't believe you unless you perform your most powerful ceremony. One of these days doubters will come to the reservation and ask you to do it. They will do their best to discover why and how you heal. And they will want to know who helps you perform your healing and prophetic work. In fact, they will attempt to learn everything about you, but you must not tell them about your 405 Stone White Men helpers, which the Great Spirit had made available to you." Black Elk was right. This very thing has happened to me many times, but I have not until now revealed any of the most important things.

During that same conversation we had on the train, Black Elk predicted that annual trade fairs would soon come to our people. And he was happy about this, because he knew it would bring about a spirit of co-operation in a time when it was badly needed.

I have always thanked Grandfather for this wise and holy man. In a way, his prediction about people wanting to know my secrets began to come true while we were still in Cheyenne. I used my prize earnings to purchase my first automobile, a much-used and battered Model T Ford touring car. A fine young white man taught me how to drive it. I had a terrible time learning, and while the many lessons required were under way the young man told me he had a deep interest in what I did and in the Sioux culture. As a result, while I did not say too much about myself, I did teach him more about life on the reservation than he taught me about driving. I had an exciting trip home, and from then on I always owned a car; but never a new one.

That same year, 1916, Black Elk gave me my first eagle feather headdress. It was a beautiful head bonnet, and it had thirty or more tail feathers in it. The headdress was made especially for me as a reward for my success in relay horse races at the Cheyenne Frontier Days, at Colorado Springs, at Salt Lake City, at Chicago, and at Cedar Rapids, Iowa. I came in first in all of these, and so was given the bonnet.

During the depression, and sometime after 1930, I sold it for one hundred and fifty dollars, which was a lot of money in those days. I have many times regretted its sale, and whenever I do I remember a story. Knife Chief told me to emphasize the importance of the eagle feather headdress. He said that in his time the warrior's trail bonnet, one with an eagle-feather tail hanging clear to the ground, was highly respected. In fact, the people were in great awe of anyone who was able, because of his successful war deeds, to wear an eagle-feather bonnet with such a tail. Then he told me a story about Eagle Shield, a leader who, while mounted on horseback and wearing his trail bonnet, performed heroically to save his people. Once, while his camp was under attack by Indian enemies, Eagle Shield rode everywhere in a desperate attempt to keep his people together and fighting. If anyone panicked and ran, he went after them on his horse and brought them back, including women and children.

Eagle Shield also carried a long lance, and when all else had failed, he drove it through the tail of his headdress and pinned it like a soldier sash to the ground. The tail was so long that he was still mounted on his horse when he did this. Then he drew his bow and arrows and remained there fighting until he was shot from his horse and killed. But the camp was saved. This shows, Knife Chief said, how brave and worthy the trail-bonnet wearers were, and why they were held in such great respect.

In those happy days I was in excellent physical condition and I could do well at anything I put my mind to. I was a jockey, ran foot races, and I danced. I suppose I did most of the things any ambitious young man does to build his confidence and make his place in his own world.

The year 1916 turned out to be an eventful one for me. On July 4, a big four-day celebration got under way at Kyle. I was there with a few racehorses and a relay team. The evening of the first day, just as I was sitting down to dinner with my family, a friend of ours named Fannie, the youngest daughter of Emil Afraid of Hawk, came to our camp and told me her parents wanted to see me. So I went along with her without eating my supper, and all the way there I was wondering what it could be about.

When we arrived at her camp, her parents fed me supper, and when I was finished, Emil came over and shook my hand. Then he told me that Fannie had fallen in love with me. He and his wife approved, and wanted very much to have me for a son-in-law. I was really shocked by this, and was speechless for a moment, because I really hadn't thought much about marriage; I thoroughly enjoyed my freedom to travel and enter contests. Finally, I said I would need to return to my camp and ask my father what he thought about it. When I did so, my father smiled and said they had already discussed it with him, and that he whole-heartedly approved. In fact, he was the one who had suggested they ask me that day.

So I thought about it for a while, and said I would marry her. Right then I went to her camp and we collected what few belongings she had and moved them to my camp. As simply as that we were wed. I feel it was one of the best decisions of my life, for we had a wonderful marriage, even though we lost most of our children while they were very young. Our firstborn was Mattie, in 1923. She died at the age of three —from pneumonia, I think. She was terribly sick, and just died. In 1925, we had twin girls, named Grace and Marie. Grace passed away from pneumonia at the age of three. Marie is still living and has a family of her own. In 1930, Fannie and I had twin sons, named James and Andrew. Both of them cried continually, and they lived only six months. It was common for reservation people to lose their children like this in those days. The weather was a factor, and the kind of medical care we now have at hospitals was not available. The medicine men also did their best, but had no success whatsoever in treating pneumonia.

I knew that, as a married man, things would be better for us if we had either a regular food source or an income, so in 1916 I took my first job. The telephone had come to Pine Ridge in 1914 or 1915, and in the winter of 1916 the agency people offered me a job as a lineman. I was to service the line from Porcupine to Kyle, a distance of about twenty miles. This line ran from the main agency office to the farm agent's branch offices. The farm agents were the white men who now served as middlemen between the head agent and the Indian district leaders. So I traveled each day in a wagon between Porcupine and Kyle to check the condition of the wires and the poles. If a wire was down, I put it back up. If a pole needed replacing, I would get one and replace it. The poles were not as big as they are now. I received no money for the job, just rations, and worked at it for about eighteen months.

Until now, neither the telegraph nor the telephone had been popular with the Sioux, since in the last part of the nineteenth century there was a big battle that the Sioux almost had won. Then the Army used the telegraph to summon help, and the Sioux were driven away. For a long time we thought of it as bad medicine.

Time was passing swiftly, and world-shaking events were taking place. Without my realizing it, since few of us Sioux could read English and thus understand much of what that paper really meant that Miles had brought from Washington, my marriage was to save me from going to war. As soon as the United States entered World War I in 1917, we were told that all of the men must go to the agency to fulfill the commitment to fight that the leaders had made. So I went, and together with the others put my thumbprint on a government paper that said they could take us as they needed us. I was very unhappy, because Stirrup had told me I should not fight. But as it turned out, only single men were taken, and I never had to go.

I hardly regret this, because so many who went to war came home wounded and crippled. Others were physically well, yet never mentally the same again. A person cannot return easily to normal life once he has been in that kind of a war. The elderly people of those days understood this. They knew very well what it was like to return home after fighting other Indian tribes and the whites. So as the veterans arrived back at Pine Ridge the elders and the older religious leaders did what they could to restore and renew them. They gave the veterans sweatbaths, which cleansed and purified their bodies and souls; they gave them the best food available; and they talked with them for days on end.

Then when the time was right, the parents and relatives of the veterans put on huge feasts to thank *Wakan-Tanka* for bringing their young men home, and these feasts were always followed by the traditional giveaway. From that time on it became the custom for many traditional parents to select only those who had served their country honorably in war to be the ones to bestow upon their children, in a naming ceremony, an Indian name.

CHAPTER 10   IRON CLOUD'S PIPE

In 1917, Fannie and I were invited to go with a group of Indians to Cheyenne, Wyoming, to participate in their Cheyenne Frontier Days celebration. When we arrived there, a man named Charlie Airring came to see me and told me he had heard about my abilities as a relay jockey and rider of racehorses. He wanted me to ride for him. I explained that I was married now and couldn't travel like I used to. But Fannie was really understanding, and in fact really happy about my opportunity to ride again. She spoke up quickly, and said I should not give up everything I was doing before we were married.

Since I could get away from my lineman job, I rode in relay races at Cheyenne; at Salt Lake City; at Gordon, Nebraska; and also at Cedar Rapids, Iowa. I did very well in these, and for several years after that, I often made as much as six hundred dollars a year just by riding in relay races. I used three horses in each race, and each horse would run a half mile. Even if I started last I would win.

One day, just as Fannie and I arrived home from a race in Iowa, we received urgent word that my uncle, Iron Cloud, wanted us to come quickly to his house. When we arrived there we were surprised to find him in bed and not looking well. He explained why he had sent for us. It was to pass on to me his ceremonial pipe. I knew, of course, how highly he valued it, and what a surpassing gift it was. His prayers sent up to Grandfather through it had all been answered, and it had enabled him to help many people. Most of the Sioux knew about its power, and hundreds had come to ask him to smoke it with them in prayer on their behalf. They knew that his traditional way of using it assured success.

But when he prayed now to the six directions with the pipe and then handed it to me I was very sad. I knew that when a Sioux elder spoke this way and gave you his pipe, which was his most treasured possession, it meant he was certain he would soon die. Only then did Iron Cloud explain that he had been badly injured in an accident on one of his farm machines, that he was bleeding internally, and that he knew he would die.

Fannie and I returned home with the pipe, and were overcome with grief. We understood that such things were part of life, but this loss would be an especially difficult one to accept. Iron Cloud had meant so much to me throughout my life, and I could not conceive of his not being there to talk with and share thoughts. Three days later, on August 17, 1917, Iron Cloud died, and my life would never be the same again.

I have explained that I was thirteen years old when Stirrup took me on my first vision guest. During it I received my first vision, my 405 Stone White Men helpers, and I was told what principal medicine I should use to heal. As of that moment I had the power, but I didn't realize how important that was or what I was supposed to do with it. I knew of course what my role in life was, but it was only after years went by and certain things took place that I began to apply my power.

It was with me like it is with any youth. He may know about certain things and what they are for, he may even know what is expected of him, but he does not know the importance of actually doing it. Something has to happen to change things. It was 1918 and I was close to thirty years of age before I really started to use my medicine power to heal. The gift of Iron Cloud's pipe changed things for me. I had to use it, and I did. Once I started, I never stopped. Whenever possible I have used either the Yuwipi or the sweatlodge ceremonies for healing, but these are not the only ways I can gain information and cure. Often there is no time or place for these long and complicated rites, so I commune in prayer with *Wakan-Tanka,* Grandfather, and the spirits, and I am told how to heal a certain illness. Then I do exactly as I am told. Because of this, and unlike many medicine men who can treat only one kind of illness, God can cure anything through me.

The Yuwipi ceremony that Stirrup taught me is an ancient Sioux ritual used to cure, to learn which herbs to use for curing, to prophesy about the future, and to find things that are lost. In each instance of need, God helps us decide whether to use it, the sweatlodge, or some other ceremony. Many times, when I have been called upon to cure someone, and if time and circumstance permitted, I have held a Yuwipi ceremony first. During the Yuwipi I ask Grandfather to help me, and to show me in the Yuwipi or in the sweatlodge what medicine to use for the person he will heal through me. Everything there is is here on earth for a purpose, even the people who are ill. So when a person is ill,

Grandfather shows me in my vision what medicine he has placed on earth to cure that illness. Grandfather has the power and the knowledge. I am only an old man serving as his instrument, an intercessor for his pity.

The Yuwipi ceremony is held inside a house after dark, and it lasts about two hours. It may be in the patient's house, but it can be in anyone's house. We clear all of the furniture out of one room and build a little square altar on the floor in the center of the room. The four corners of the altar are marked with black, red, yellow, and white cloth flags tied to sticks and set upright in cans filled with dirt. I also make a string of 405 tobacco offerings, because as I said, I have 405 good spirit helpers. There must be one offering for each spirit.

I must have at least four singers to help the spirits. There are about sixteen singers around the Kyle-Porcupine area who know the Yuwipi songs. When I am going to hold a ceremony, I notify four of them, and they always come. I also have four Yuwipi rattles, which are placed on a bed of sage grass near the altar, and they fly all over during the ceremony. Their sound comes from every part of the room.

Besides the four rattles, I have a special rattle that I sometimes use in my Yuwipi ceremonies. During the ritual, it moves about on its own. And if there are people present who do not want the curing to happen, or who doubt the power of the ceremony, this rattle talks to me and tells me who those people are. On occasion this rattle will even go and hit those people. It does not injure them, but it scares them and shakes them up enough to disturb their doubts. If I sense they are still skeptical after being hit, I do not ask them to leave. The spirits take care of that for me, and the doubters just disappear. Maybe they go through a crack in the wall, because nobody sees them leave through the door. The spirits take them out the way they deserve to go.

When everything is ready, another medicine man ties my hands behind me, and even ties all of my fingers tightly together. Then he wraps me from head to foot in a quilt. I cannot see and I am in complete darkness. After this, buffalo-hide thongs are wrapped securely around the quilt and tied with firm knots. When all of this is finished, they lay me face down on a bed of sage, the patient sits in a circle with the others, and the lights are put out. The ceremony takes place in absolute darkness. While the singers sing and I am wrapped up, I pray and meditate until the spirits come and show me a picture of what medicine to use to cure my patient. I see very clearly what it is, and in what stage of growth I will find it. The next morning, when I take my pipe and go out to pray, a good spirit guides me straight to where it is, and I find the medicine very quickly. It is usually standing alone so as to be easily visible, and whatever the season, it is in its proper condition for use—dry, green, or stubble. I pull it out, and I place four medicine bags in the hole it leaves as gifts to the spirits. After this I administer the herb to the patient.

Sometimes, when I am inside the blanket in the Yuwipi, I see several kinds of plants I need to cure people who have various kinds of illnesses. Then in the morning I am guided to them, and I store them away in my medicine bundle for future use.

After I have my vision, the spirits untie me and remove the quilt. The room is still in darkness when this happens. So, since 1965 when God put the holy stones into my body during my great vision quest at Bear Butte, I throw sparks all over the room. The sparks come in showers from the stones in my hands. Sometimes, but not every time, while I am still wrapped up and praying, the person who is to be healed actually comes inside of the quilt with me. Then, to show that he will be healed, the spirits make us both sit up, or stand up, or even walk around. No matter how ill the person is, this can happen.

The spirits tell the singers when I am untied, and the lights are turned on. The Yuwipi ceremony always ends with a meal, and the main meat is dog. When I described the Kettle Dance earlier I told you why dog meat is used for some of our rituals. Some people don't like to eat dog meat, but everyone present at a traditional Yuwipi must eat at least a little bit to fulfill the requirements; otherwise the ceremony will not work.

Yuwipi is a very old and powerful ceremony. My people hold it and the medicine men who can do it in high esteem. Doubters have tried many times to prove that some person and not the spirits free the Yuwipi man from his quilt-and-thong bindings. But no one has ever been able to do this. We don't know exactly how it is done, but we know who does it. We understand the power of *Wakan-Tanka* and the spirits.

I also have been given a sweatlodge ceremony that I use for healing. It is almost always held at night. When in rare instances I must hold one in the daytime, I do it before the sun comes up.

When I set up my sweatlodge for a healing ceremony, the arrangement of the items depends upon whether or not the patient can be present. Sometimes the patient is too ill to come to the sweatlodge, and I make provision for this by the way the lodge is arranged and the ceremony is conducted.

First, though, I will tell you how I arrange the lodge and conduct a ceremony where the patient and his relatives can be present. I build the sweatlodge framework in the traditional way, always using a basic group of twelve willow branches stripped of their bark, bending them over, and tying them together with strips of the bark. No nails, wire, or string are used. The entrance door always faces west, and the dome-

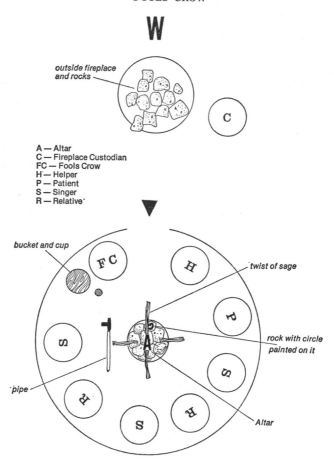

A — Altar
C — Fireplace Custodian
FC — Fools Crow
H — Helper
P — Patient
S — Singer
R — Relative·

The arrangement of the sweatlodge when the patient is present.

shaped lodge is nine or ten feet in diameter and about four feet high. It is large enough to seat from eight to ten people.

I put down a layer of sage around the outside edge of the lodge for the participants to sit on; then in the center of the sweatlodge I dig a shallow, round pit for an altar. It is about eighteen inches in diameter, and perhaps fourteen inches deep. A small incline, like a chute, is made on the west side of the altar to slide the rocks in. In all, twelve rocks that have never been used before are put into the altar pit for my healing ceremony, and individual prayers are said for each of the first six as they are passed into the lodge by the custodian who helps me. The twelve make a pile whose top is higher than the wall of the altar pit, and when they are together they are considered to be one rock. The first rock I put in has a small red circle painted on it. It is placed on the west side of the altar pit.

Usually the rocks are heated in an outside fireplace before the ceremony begins. If, however, I am going to do my most sacred ceremony for a very serious illness or a special occasion, and which I have done only four times during my lifetime, the rocks are just stored in a loose pile near the sweatlodge before they are passed in.

I sit on the south side of the sweatlodge entrance, and a helper sits on the north side. As the rocks are passed in, the helper places them in the altar, using a forked wooden stick or a deer antler to arrange them. I watch him to make certain he places them correctly. If one is out of order I tell him so, or else the ceremony will not work. After the first rock is placed at the west side, the next rock goes on the north side, then the next on the east, and the fourth rock is placed on the south. The movement is always clockwise. The fifth rock is placed close to the center of the altar pit. It is for Grandmother Earth. The sixth rock is also placed at the center, and it is for *Wakan-Tanka* and Grandfather. I stop praying then, and the other six rocks are passed in and piled on top of the others.

Four twisted, not braided, pieces of sage, which I prepare before the ceremony, are then placed at the four directions, so that one end of each piece is leaning on the rock pile and the other end is on the ground. These represent the powers of the four winds, or directions. Next to me is a metal bucket and a wooden water cup. My pipe is laid on the ground on the south side of the Altar, with the bowl toward the lodge entrance, or west.

I usually have three singers, and they sit on the south and east sides of the lodge. The patient and his relatives ordinarily sit on the north side, but they can sit anywhere, except where the helper and I sit.

As soon as the twists of sage are in place, the custodian closes the door flap and makes certain that the walls seal out light and are airtight. Then, while the participants sit in the darkness, I take the sacred medicine that Grandfather showed me in my 1914 vision, I chew it fine, and then I blow it on the rocks four times. After each time, I pour a little water on the rocks and they make a sound. By the fourth time I pour the water the rocks are red hot and glowing. The red glow is so bright everyone present can see it clearly, and the heat of the lodge is hotter than it is when the rocks are cooked in the outside fireplace in the usual way. Those who have seen this happen with their own eyes and have felt the heat have been absolutely amazed. They tell me they have never experienced anything else like it, and find it hard to believe.

After I have finished with the stones, a close relative of the patient, it can be a man or a woman, speaks, explaining what they think is wrong with the person, and adding their wishes that the patient will be healed and live. The wish always includes the statement that [he or she by name] will live through the coming four seasons. When the relative is through, the singers begin to sing. I sometimes use three, but more often four, songs. The singers know the songs, and only those who know them well are permitted to sing. They learn to do this by going to many sweatlodge ceremonies, and when they are ready, they demonstrate their ability by joining in. After these introductory songs, I pray to *Wakan-Tanka* and Grandfather, and ask them to cure the patient through me. Remember now that the prayer request has been made for the patient to live through the four seasons. So when I have completed the four seasons part of my prayer, I take the water cup and I bless it by moving my finger around the inside of the cup four times, praying all the while I do so.

Then I bless the water in the bucket and I fill the cup. I pour a little on the rocks at the four cardinal points, beginning at the west and moving clockwise to the north, east, and south. At the south I pray to Grandfather and Grandmother Earth. I pray aloud while I do this, and the heat and the cloud of steam are terrific!

Now the singers begin to sing the sacred songs again, and as they do so, sparks of light that come from the stones in my body begin to float in the darkness, especially during the second time they sing. When the singers finish, I pray for the spirits' power to come inside the sweatlodge so that the patient will be helped. I also pray for all of the Sioux people. Then there is complete silence for a while, while we all wait for the rocks to speak. It is the rocks who will tell us what is wrong with the patient, and what medicine to use to cure him. They speak to us in the Lakota language, and everyone present hears them.

Usually just the father and mother of the patient are present, but there might be as many as four relatives there. At this time they offer prayers of thanksgiving, gratification, and humility. Then the singers sing again, after which there is another period of silence. If I think they have finished too soon I might ask them whether they are done. They should take this as a hint to sing another song. If they fail to catch my hint, I instruct them to go on, and as they do so, the rocks make further sounds, even though no more water has been poured on them.

By now the heat is really pressing in on us, and it is performing its purification rite. If someone is not able to stand it, he says *"mitakuye oyasin,"* which means "all my relatives." If the custodian does not hear him and fails to open the door flap, I tell the custodian to do so. This cools off the lodge a bit and lessens the ovenlike pressure of the steam heat.

After two or three minutes I tell the custodian to close the flap again.

Then I pour more water on the rocks, and the sacred songs are sung again. Now we can hear the rocks speaking Lakota in joyful sounds and whoops, like "how, how"—that kind of sound. All of us in the lodge join in with this and make happy sounds until the lodge rings with the noise. At this time, I pour into the cup a little of the holy water I have saved. I drink some of it, and I pass it clockwise to the others just as the people do with the pipe when it is used. If there is any water left over when the cup returns to me, I pour it on the rocks.

For the entire healing ceremony, a minimum of four sacred songs are sung. Sometimes it takes a while for the rock spirits to get ready to speak, so I might ask the singers to do five songs, or even seven. But there must be at least four, because there are four stages to the ceremony, and when the door flap is opened the fourth time, the water is completely gone.

I tell the custodian when to open the door flap the last time, and while the rest of the people file out counterclockwise, so as not to pass between the pipe and me, I remain there praying. The pipe is filled with Kinnikinnick before the ceremony begins, and by now it has taken on the power of the spirits. So when I finish praying, I pick up the pipe and bring it outside.

The people who have shared in the healing ceremony form a small circle near the sweatlodge, with each person standing and occupying approximately the same position they did inside, and they wait there for me. When I join them, I give the pipe to the patient. The custodian has built a little fire, and he picks up some hot ashes on a slender piece of wood or bark and puts them in the pipe bowl. The patient puffs on the pipe to start it going, and then offers the pipe to the west, north, east, south, to Grandmother Earth, and then to *Wakan-Tanka* and Grandfather. The pipe is passed clockwise around the circle, with each person smoking it and offering it to the directions, until it returns to the patient. He smokes it and then returns the pipe to me, and the healing ceremony is ended. Afterward, the relatives usually prepare a feast for all who have shared in the ceremony, and we all go to the relatives' home and eat.

When I am asked to do a healing ceremony for a patient who cannot be present in the sweatlodge, the arrangement of the items within the lodge is different. If the patient is not able to come to my home and ask me personally to do the ceremony, someone related to him comes in his place. It can be a parent, grandparent, or a brother or sister. The traditionalists make this request in a customary way. They bring their pipe to me filled with Indian tobacco, light it, and after offering it to the six powers, they give it to me. I seldom refuse it. By accepting the pipe and smoking it I agree to do the ceremony. I can smoke the pipe as long as

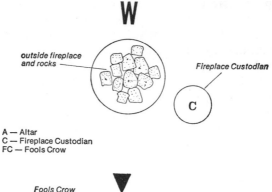

A — Altar
C — Fireplace Custodian
FC — Fools Crow

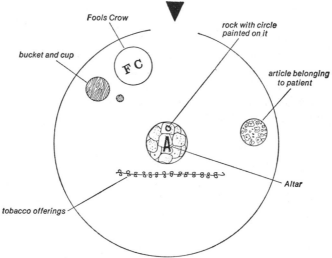

The arrangement of the sweatlodge when the patient is not present.

I want to, even until it is finished. If I do not finish it, though, I hand it back and the other person completes it. One of us must smoke it until it is empty.

The person making the request also brings a string of tiny tobacco offerings in the form of a rosary. Each little bag is tied to a string, and the entire string is wrapped in a piece of cloth. I do not see how many bags there are until after I enter the sweatlodge. The bags can be any color of cloth, as long as one or more of the four sacred colors—black, white, yellow, and red—are used. That same evening I hold the ceremony, and I only need one person to help me, the custodian who heats and passes in the rocks. This man also takes care of the door flap, and gets the water bucket and cup ready.

For this ceremony there is no pipe in the sweatlodge, and no twisted pieces of sage are used. But on the east side of the lodge, on a line running from north to south, I unwrap and place the string of tobacco bags. Usually the number of bags is twelve, but it can vary according to whatever number of bags the person requesting the ceremony brings to me. Each bag represents a sacred spirit, and the number of bags determines the number of spirits who, of all those 405 coming, will remain for the ceremony. I also have a piece of something belonging to the patient in the lodge. It can be apparel or anything else.

The number and placement of rocks are exactly the same as for the ceremony where the patient is present. Before the custodian starts to heat the rocks in the fire, I paint the red circle on one rock, and that is the first one passed in to me. I place the hot rocks gently in the altar pit, and using a short forked branch, I move them into their proper places. I do my own praying and singing for this ceremony, and as before, the door flap is opened four times before the ceremony is finished. Once again, there will be sparks floating in the air. And often, when I am alone like this, there are even more sparks. Perhaps it is because of the sacred atmosphere and holiness I feel. The spirits may feel more free to come when I am alone.

Right after the door flap has been opened and closed the first time, the spirits in the rocks begin to speak to me as I pray. They tell me the things I need to know about the patient and the medicine. During each of the four stages of the sweatlodge ceremony I pray. I talk to the rocks and the tobacco offerings, and I listen intently. I also sing a certain sacred song, and if the spirits do not at first speak to me through the rocks, I sing the song again and again until they do.

When the rocks do speak, they ask me why I am having the ritual, and who it is for. Then they ask me whether I know what the ailment is. During the fourth period they ask me what the patient desires; what he wants. In all, four main questions are put to me, and it is the spirits in the rocks who eventually tell me what medicine plant to use and how to apply it. The rocks are what I call "the workers." Suppose the patient is near death. You recall there is an item belonging to him in the lodge. It can be a piece of a dress or a shirt, a headband, a glove, a shoe, or anything. The rocks ask me where the patient is, and how far away he lives. Then using their sense of smell like a hunting dog does, the rocks take a scent from the article and go immediately over to where the patient is and examine him. They can go anywhere in the world, make an examination, and quickly return. The rocks spirits travel like God does. When they return they tell me they have found the patient and know what is wrong with him. Then they tell me what the right medicine is and how to apply it.

The role of the tobacco bags is to help bring the spirits into the sweatlodge, and they determine how many will come and work. But the tobacco bags do not speak to me; only the rocks do that. Remember too that I do not see the string of tobacco bags before I go into the sweatlodge, where I unwrap them and lay them out. Until then they remain in the wrapping cloth used by the person requesting the ceremony, so it is only when I am in the lodge that I discover how many spirits will actually work on a given case. It could be the entire 405, since there are that many good spirits, and that is how many helpers I have available to me, or it could be only a dozen. Before the door flap is closed the first time I spread the string out on the east side of the lodge, and I count them.

As great and as trusting a friend as my uncle Black Elk was, when word reached him one day about what I was able to do with the unheated rocks in the sweatlodge he came to me and asked if it was true. I told him it was, and since he was a medicine man I would do it for him. After all, it has always been permissible for our holy men and medicine men to share with one another like this. Before I did the ceremony, he asked me several questions, and I answered them all. I described what items I used, what they meant, and where they were placed. He wanted to know why I used new rocks each time. I answered it was because it was one of the things given to me at Bear Butte in 1914.

He saw with his own eyes that the cold rocks were placed in the altar pit by hand. Then I did my ceremony, chewed my medicine, and spewed it on the rocks. The heat came. The singers sang the special songs, and by the time I put the water on, the rocks were red hot. Black Elk held his hands out toward them and said the rocks might even be hotter than they are when heated in the usual way. When we were finished we were both perspiring as in a regular sweatbath. Afterward, he shook my hand, said he believed in me and in the power of my prayers, and went home thoroughly convinced.

You ask me what kinds of ailments I healed first? What people came to me for? In those days, the twenties, one of the most common ailments I treated was kidney problems—kidney stones and gallstones. No one else except the public health doctors knew how to deal with them, but they usually operated, and sometimes with bad results. So the Sioux people who didn't want surgery came to me. Over a hundred people came to me for just kidney problems alone, and in addition to this others came with complete or partial paralysis. That was common in those days too.

I was always successful in curing these diseases. I really have a sacred gift, and every one of my healing ceremonies has been successful. I have cured everyone who has come to me, I have not had a single failure. I am not boasting when I say this. Some of my patients have since died, but of other causes, not of what they came to me for. I cured them of that.

For example, in the early 1920s, we were eating our evening meal when a lady came to our home crying pitifully. She just kept it up and we had a terrible time getting her to stop. Finally, between sobs she told me that her husband was completely paralyzed. He couldn't even move his tongue.

We closed the door of our home and pulled the shades. Then, following my instructions, they wrapped a black cloth around my head till it was completely covered, and the lights were turned out. I prayed to God for help, and speaking through my medicine bundle stones he told me which herb medicine to give the lady.

She took it home, and I finished my meal. The next morning her husband came riding to my house to bring me a white-faced buckskin horse. It was a gift to show his appreciation. No sign of his paralysis remained.

You want to know whether, when the cloth is put on my head, is it made like a bag or hood and tied at the neck with a string, or whether the cloth is simply wrapped on. It's a cloth wrapping, put on so tightly that I am in total darkness and I can't see beyond it. I do this because God told me in a vision to do it this way. I never do anything different than he tells me to, and I never disobey him.

You have pointed out I did not mention that the woman whose husband was paralyzed had brought me a pipe. In most cases a pipe is brought, but you must understand that not everyone has a pipe. In the old days and even now some bring a little tobacco or a few cigarettes— even home-rolled ones. The woman brought me some tobacco. If someone brings a sack of tobacco it is the custom for them to roll the first cigarette I smoke. In any event, it is still the custom for me to smoke the entire pipeful or cigarette before proceeding with the healing ceremony.

You wanted to know the other day whether I had been to the Custer battlefield before? I started to answer you and we got off onto another subject. I'll tell you about it now because it has something to do with one of my early healings. I have gone there, and in fact I have made the trip almost as an annual pilgrimage. I remember an instance as far back as 1921, when I went there with a large group of Sioux. Jim Red Cloud was tribal chairman at the time, and all of the Sioux tribal leaders went along. No sooner had we arrived when a young Cheyenne came looking for me, saying that his family had been trying to contact me, but had no address. His father was very ill, suffering terribly from pain in his lower back, and he was hardly able to move about. He wanted to know whether I would come and heal him.

I told the youth that I would come and do it the next day if Red Cloud didn't mind. With Red Cloud's approval, our entire Sioux group went together to the sick man's home, and I performed my ceremony and healed him. We stayed that night with the Cheyenne family, who fed us well and gave us food for the journey home. We were also given blankets and cloth, valuable things in those days. I am sorry to tell you that later on the man I healed and two of his children were killed in an automobile accident.

Healings like this and for people on all of our Sioux reservations occupied much of my time for the next few years. I do not want to tell you about too many of them, though. People who read what I say will think I am boasting. As we visit, I will tell you about some of the cures God worked through me in later years, and that will be enough. You know that it is not our custom to talk about healings. Instead, our words and hearts are sent up to God in prayerful thanksgiving for them. We tell him this in our private prayers and in our ceremonies. No medicine man or patient makes a big thing of it when a healing takes place. This is why sick people do not come to me or to other medicine men in greater numbers. Most know very little about us outside the reservation.

CHAPTER 11   LEADER OF THE DISTRICT

By 1921, the wounds of war were beginning to heal, and the people of America and Europe were attempting to be friends again. Someone in our government thought it might be a gesture of friendship to send Indian shows to the different European countries, including Germany. So I and fourteen other Oglala men, five Oglala women, and four Oglala children were sent there. We stayed and performed for a long time. Thirteen months passed before we were home again. We went by train to New York City and then on a big ship to Europe. We traveled all over Germany, dancing and singing, and with me doing the pipe ceremony using Iron Cloud's pipe. The terrible consequences of war could be seen everywhere, but the German people were happy to have us there and we were greeted and treated in the most friendly fashion. In fact, we were honored wherever we went. So we even sang our sacred songs for them, which is more than we were willing to do for non-Indians in the United States.

We returned home, and not too much happened for a while. Some of my time was spent in healing people. Our first child, Mattie, was born in 1923, and in 1925 Fannie and I had twin girls, Grace and Marie. Then in the summer of 1925, a truly great thing happened to me. There was a big celebration at the Porcupine District. As you might expect, I was at the place where they were having the horse races when Chief Red Hawk came to get me. He said that my father, Eagle Bear, wanted to see me over where they were having the ceremonial dances. Red Hawk did not say why he wanted me, and although I wondered, I went along anyway. As soon as we arrived, several leaders escorted me directly to the dancing arena, where a huge crowd had assembled. I was led out to the center of the arena, and they brought me an eagle-feather headdress.

Fannie was sent to our camp to get my pipe—the one Iron Cloud had given me—and while everyone waited for her to return, I asked my father what was going on. He did not answer, he just smiled as if to say, wait and see. When Fannie came back, Chiefs Red Hawk, High Wolf, Turning Hawk, Black Fox, and my father, Eagle Bear, brought the pipe to me and put the bonnet on my head. Then my father announced to the people that this was the day he had chosen to turn over his leadership of the Porcupine District to me. He said his son had a home, a family, and livestock, and that I had followed the traditional way of life as he had taught me and hoped that I would. "This," he went on, "is a good boy. I am getting weak with age. So today, my son will take my place and fill my position as leader of the district."

At this point my father gave me an entire buckskin outfit, with beautiful fringes and beading. It included a shirt, leggings, moccasins, and a pipe bag and pipe. Later on, that pipe was stolen from me. Iron Cloud's pipe has never been lost because I keep it with me at all times, at home or wherever I go.

All of this celebration had been arranged without my knowledge, and for once I was speechless. I did not know what to say or do. Then my father announced that he was giving me his honor song, which was then sung to me:

> Young man, young man, strengthen yourself
> From here on you are going to lead the people.
> You will never turn around, and you will always move forward.
> Because old people, old men and women, have also selected you,
> you must move forward.
> You are the leader of this land.

At this moment the full weight of what they were saying struck me. I was not only to be the leader of the Porcupine District, but also the people hoped I would become the Ceremonial Chief, the highest ranking of all the leaders of the Teton Sioux. It was an overwhelming honor. I did not expect it, and I was not at all sure I deserved it. Now Red Hawk came up to me and shook my hand. Then he gave me the first advice I would receive as a leader. He said, "You will never forget this day. Now you are the leader of a district. And this means you must defend these people and look out for their health and welfare. You must continue to practice our traditional way of life, so that the people will respect you. Once you have gained this respect, it will be your assurance that they know you have a true regard for them. Already, while you are still a young man, we have seen evidences of your concern for the people and of your desire to live the traditional life. So we have chosen you, and the agent has agreed with our choice. Therefore, congratulations. May the power of the Spirit remain in your heart, and may *Wakan-Tanka* increase the wisdom we believe you already possess."

When Red Hawk stepped back, Turning Hawk came forward. He shook my hand and said, "You are the leader of this district. You are their spokesman. You are their medicine man. You know what it is to be an energetic young man, and you know what it is like to grow up in a home that is blessed with love and understanding. Now you have both your own family and a district family upon which to bestow your love and understanding."

Then he stepped back a little, and he finished with a statement that really caught my attention. He said, "And remember to always pray to God."

What struck me was his use in this instance of the term, "God." As long as I could remember, for ceremonial purposes we Sioux always referred to the Supreme Being as *Wakan-Tanka,* or as Grandfather, which is *Tunkashila.* It was clear now that the white man's religion was making deep inroads into our traditional life-way, and I knew that my leadership would require me to help the people adjust to it. That would not be impossible for me. I was already attending the Roman Catholic Church. But it would be hard for many who were still fully immersed in our traditional culture.

By the time I returned to my camp that evening, my passionate interest in such things as horse racing and foot racing had already begun to fade. And I knew that my principal concerns from now on, in addition to medicine, would be the civil and the social activities of the Porcupine District. My life changed its course again that day, and I can still close my eyes and hear the voices of Red Hawk, Running Hawk, and my father as they spoke. One thing more: I had already received the family name Fools Crow from my father, but on this day I was given his other name, Eagle Bear, so from then on I was known by both names.

In my estimation, the greatest Sioux civil leaders during the first part of this century were Knife Chief, Red Hawk, Turning Hawk, and Eagle Bear. Other leaders of significance were Good Back, Pretty Hip, Joshua Spotted Owl, Come American Horse, Ben American Horse, Little Wound, Iron Cloud, Weasel Bear, He Crow, and Lone Hill. Most of these are names that are not well known to white historians, but we Sioux know who our real leaders were. I still feel that Eagle Bear ranks above all the rest. He was a truly great father and leader, and bearing both of his names is one of the highest honors of my life.

You have noticed that I did not include in my list the famous Chief Red Cloud. As was the case with the foremost holy men of the early days, the civil leaders who accomplished the most for us were those who lived in such a way as to bring honor to us all. Many of the traditional Sioux do not care for Red Cloud today for two important reasons. The first is that he either murdered or joined with several others in murdering the top leader of his time to gain his leadership. No Sioux is supposed to do this. He did it because he was jealous, and for this reason a lot of Oglala warriors never did follow him. Red Cloud was never able to unite our people in all things, even though he had a superb war record. In his last years, while we were on the reservation, Red Cloud did do some fine things in achieving for us more consideration and material assistance from the government. He did some good things in the field of education too. But his rash act of murder, plus his second mistake when he sold the Black Hills to the U. S. Government, made it impossible for him to gain the position he might otherwise have had.[15] The same thing happened to Chief Crow Dog when he ambushed and killed Chief Spotted Tail on the Rosebud Reservation. Chief Crow Dog never became as great as he otherwise would have. When a leader breaks tradition, is not honest, and behaves badly, he loses the respect of his people, and he can never unite them.

The next day after I was made a chief, the people held a ceremony to honor me as their new leader. I knew they would expect me to wear my new ceremonial outfit, so I put it on and went over to the dancing arena, which was surrounded by the circular shade arbor we always use to shelter the spectators. A tremendous crowd was there awaiting me, and they put me out in the center and sang my honor song again. It was another high point I would never forget. Chills ran up and down my spine, and I felt like I was being lifted up to the clouds.

As I left the arena, Running Hawk caught my hand and took me aside for some last advice. "This is your land," he said, "and it is your people's land. You are the leader among your people and in this country. Don't ever turn your back on them." I told him I would not do so. It was a monumental privilege and responsibility to be chosen as a leader, and especially to have it done according to our ancient custom. Ever thereafter, I thought and dreamed of doing great things for my people, and I took up my duties with great hope. But it was not going to be that easy. The winds at the top of the hill were already changing. Black clouds were forming, and soon a chilling frost was felt in the air. The time soon came when our days were not so beautiful anymore.

My personal awareness of this came forcefully home two years later in 1927, being provoked by a seemingly innocent statement from people at the agency that they would like us to have public Sun Dances again. However, and this was the catch, they asked me to work out a way it could be inoffensively done for the numerous tourists who were coming to the reservation in the hope of seeing our most sacred ceremony. In other words, they wanted a sideshow without its most sacred aspects: the healing, flesh offerings, and piercings.[16] To do this and to omit these things would trouble the agency people little, but the very idea tormented me and the leaders of all the other districts. I told the superintendent I would have to think about it. So when I returned home after a meeting with the leaders, I told my wife I had to go to Bear Butte and pray. She did not ask why I was going. And this is something I always appreciated about her. She never kept at me with questions when I told her I was going to do something. If I chose to explain it, then she might mention something that bothered her, and we would talk it over. Otherwise she just assumed that I knew what I was doing.

I arrived at Bear Butte a very troubled man. In fact, I was truly afraid. It was clear that things were going to change for the worse for us. The seemingly innocent request for the public performance of the Sun Dance was but the first of a series of disasters to come, and somehow I knew it! I prayed as hard as I could to *Wakan-Tanka,* requesting answers that I could take home to the Oglala and to the other bands; something that would serve as a secure shelter for them in the stormy days ahead.

I sat there on top of the magnificent purple butte, mindless now of the sweeping view of green valleys and mountains that stretched out below as far as my eye could see. I held Iron Cloud's pipe tightly in my hands, and I prayed without ceasing. Before long, a flood of remembrances swept over me. Apparently, whatever answers I would receive would emerge from a review of the past, beginning with my earliest recollections. I needed to go over the good things and the bad things, to go back to the happy moments and the sad moments, before I could see ahead.

I recalled that, from 1895 to 1920, we Sioux had learned what unity was; what it was like for a family to work together, and what it was like to co-operate with relatives and neighbors. We had achieved in those days a measure of both independence and interdependence. We gained self-respect, and were able to continue much of our traditional way of life—which was first to show love for one's family, relatives, and friends; second, to learn about and to relate closely to nature; and third, to appreciate the things *Wakan-Tanka* was giving us in such a way that we would never cease to thank him for it in our daily life and in our ceremonies.

I recalled that children had been especially happy when winter ended and it was time to plant their gardens. I remembered what it was like to help the mares have their colts and the cows have their calves. It had been a wonderful experience to watch the eggs crack open and see turkeys, chickens, and ducks come bursting forth. The litters of pigs were a great delight as they squealed and squirmed around like a bunch of large worms. I saw again the potatoes, the corn, the onions, the radishes, and the turnips growing, and the children cultivating them while they did. I could smell once more the wild fruits, and the grand aromas that attended the harvest festivals.

So much came back to me as I sat there—even the Kettle Dance, with the men dancing forward and back, forward and back, and the leader plunging his hands in for the dog's head while the women clapped their hands in admiration over their open mouths. I saw everyone praying in unison, including the little children. There were the social dances and the giveaways, the Stick Dance and the Night Dance, and I saw the Sun Dances with piercing too.

Now we were being asked to put on the sacred Sun Dance, our highest honor to Grandfather, just for the tourists, and with restrictions as to how it would be done. The agency wanted it to be just a social dance, and it struck me now that all the Sioux had accomplished meant nothing to the non-Indians, except perhaps for Longneck and the white settlers who helped us. No one else really cared or gave us credit for how well we had adapted to a life-way totally different from our natural one. The non-Indians still did not know or care that Sun Dances were put on by people who had made vows and sought visions, and that it was for this reason they had to fast and sacrifice their bodies. Moreover, they wanted us to do it according to a yearly schedule, and to reduce it to something as empty of power as a Grass Dance.

I cried, and finally drew a deep breath. Then I began asking Grandfather which of the other sacred dances the whites would want the Sioux to re-create as social performances. Would we again do the Ghost Dance, Eagle Dance, Bear Dance, and the Prairie Dog Dance with the same kinds of restrictions? If so, to do this would mean we had lost, without our even realizing it, the strength to resist and defend our traditional ways.

I wanted to know where things had begun to go wrong. *Wakan-Tanka* answered that. He told me then that it had started when the young men went off to fight in World War I. It had been their first real exposure to the outside world, and to what money could do. The losses of the families whose sons were killed or handicapped had surely weakened the Sioux nation, but the worst damage came with the worldly and selfish attitudes the survivors brought back. Now money was paid them for compensation and other veterans' benefits. Moreover, the families on the reservations had added their produce to the war effort, been paid well for it, and money was desired by them for the first time in our lives. Where money is, liquor follows. Many of our young people were getting drunk and fighting one another. Had I not noticed that now and then cattle and horses were missing from farms, stolen to be sold for whiskey? It was known that one young man had even argued and fought with his father, a thing unheard of in earlier days.

When he finished speaking to me, I could see what *Wakan-Tanka* meant, that bad things often lie on the other side of good things when people are not equipped to handle them. If our leaders in the earliest reservation days had been able to read and understand any of the papers they signed we might have been prepared, but they couldn't, and the white people, with only a few exceptions, did not bother to explain the various possibilities to them. We did not know that bad as well as good could come from programs. Furthermore, I realized then that some of the consequences might have been seen by anyone who had taken the time to look, including myself. Self-respect had been fading away, as well as respect for the elderly and for the law. The time had come for me to admit openly what I should have known was happening: To obtain money, people were selling their horses and cattle to non-Indians; obtaining money for pleasure was all that mattered. Soon now the Sioux would lose nearly everything they had.

The word "jealousy" came to me, and Four Horn came to mind again. I recalled how greatly we had admired him when he became the first large-scale Indian farmer. I remembered that after he went to visit relatives and saw non-Indians farming in a big way, he wanted so badly to be the first Oglala to do this. He couldn't read or speak English, but that didn't stop him. He bought his seeds and he paid a non-Indian to plow a lot of land for him. Then he planted oats, barley, wheat, and beans, and more corn and potatoes than the rest of the people in the district put together. The agent had them harvested for him, and he made money selling them; big money, which at first brought big admiration, and in the end big jealousy.

These were the keys: money and jealousy. If you can't control money and the desire for it you can't control the people. So if we Sioux were going to hold onto our traditional way of life, we would have to fight to protect it. We would need to fight against the idea of people becoming more concerned about spending money than they were about their religion, families, homes, and farms. If we did not do this, if happiness was to be based upon having as much money as one could get his hands on, then we Sioux were becoming far less red and far more white.

We should have known better. We had had our first lesson when the slaughter of the huge buffalo herds began after 1875. At that time the government encouraged the Indians to join in and make money on it too. Well, more than a few did, and soon the buffalo herds were gone. Now the government was moving to do us in again, only this time with a plan that we knew even less about and could not begin to handle well.

This time their weapon was programs! Between the years 1920 and 1930, they decided to give each person on the reservation a certain income with which to purchase supplies and clothing. This method, which was intended to replace the rationing system, might have been all right if the people had known how to manage their funds. Also, the people were not earning this money, so they were losing their sense of achievement and freedom. In almost no time at all, many people were in trouble. Some had no alternative but to steal, and this was completely against our traditional way. If a man had a good horse he had to guard it day and night, just as our ancestors once did their camps and herds against enemies. In fact, people were now obliged to watch everything they owned, and all because of the desire for money. What, I wondered, did the future hold for us, and how long would we Indians last? What comes next? Where are we heading? And who in America will help us?

The government had also revised the way in which the districts were served. They placed a white man in each district to manage it and to consider the Indian needs. Now he, instead of the Sioux leader, would discuss this with the head agent. Both of them being white, and Longneck being gone for some time by now, many of our requests were ignored or denied. We saw less and less of the agent, and it was a different kind of a man from Longneck who pressed us to have the Sun Dances for curious whites. His name was Roberts, and when I tell you later on about him and the Sacred Pipe, you will learn what sort of a man he really was.

I could hardly believe it! The whites, who had years ago forbidden the Sun Dance, wanted now to show us off to people who would purchase tickets to see us sing and dance! We were to become a Buffalo Bill kind of sideshow, performing so strangers could stand in a circle around us and view us as they did rodeos and wild animals, while we performed with sincerity what supposedly was the most important dance of our traditional and sacred way of life! *Wakan-Tanka* told me there was no question but that the Sioux would have to fight as best we could against this and other changes, and he told me to bring that answer home.

I left the holy mountain thinking it is amazing what can happen when we become occupied with personal matters and forget whatever else is going on. For the three years since my impressive beginning as a chief and my dreams of glory for the people, I had been a blind leader. When I arrived back at Porcupine I began to travel across the reservation, and the change was so plainly there I was stunned I had not seen it before. I guess it was partly because it had come so gradually that its full consequences only surfaced with time and *Wakan-Tanka*'s message to me at Bear Butte.

There were hardly any milk cows, chickens, ducks, or pigs left. The once beautiful gardens were nothing but dry brush, and the chicken coops were broken and falling down. Even the corrals had weeds in them, because the horses were gone. Gone also were many of the farm residents. Stores and schools were being built by the government, and the people were abandoning their farms and settling down around these. Towns were coming into being. But what pitiful towns they were. The government had taken advantage of us once more. At the same time, problems were coming from another direction. The white population around the borders of the reservation was growing and expanding. They decided we owned more land than we needed, and they figured out a way to get it. It was easy. They encouraged the destitute Oglalas to sell or to lease their allotments to them and then to move into towns, which they did, for the money, naturally!

So people left their once fine log homes and storage cellars and settled down in tents and shacks. They exchanged their freedom for money and liquor, and as it turned out there would be no end of this curse. The flood had begun, and the traditional life-way dam was so weakened it could not hold it. I had always prided myself in being a strong-minded man who could weather anything. But after I made my visits to the vacant farms and talked with those who were still there, I returned home feeling like an old man. What, I asked Fannie, are we going to do?

Four Horn, war, money, liquor, I said to myself. Jealousy, hate, and revenge. And the only way we had of combating them was through traditional education and religion; through morals, ethics, prayer, and sacrifice. Yet the government wanted to reduce our power even to do those things to nothing. I made up my mind that I would not lead the tourists' Sun Dance yet. I told them I wanted to wait a bit, and to discuss with my people exactly what was going on. Actually, I had an urge to just go away for a while and think, and the opportunity to do so was not long in coming.

CHAPTER 12   THE INTERCESSOR

In 1927, I went touring with other Indians in a Wild West show, and that summer found us in Madison Square Garden in New York City. The show included Indian, black, Mexican, and white cowboys, many horses, and some buffalo. One afternoon, while I was still fully dressed in my buckskin ceremonial costume, the show manager talked me into riding a wild buffalo. That turned into some kind of a ride for me and for the audience, because while it took every ounce of strength I had, I rode it till it quit bucking and running. It was the most furious ride of my life, and while I was asked to do it several times after that, I always refused—or suggested they do it instead.

While we were in New York, people told us that close by Jack Dempsey, and some other fighter I don't remember, were having a world championship boxing match and would make thousands of dollars. We shook our heads in amazement to hear that two grown men were fighting for so much money. And it made us even more aware that the white society did everything for the dollar. We didn't even consider going to the fight, because we had fought people and the weather nearly all of our lives just to live. Furthermore, physical combat was against my nature and calling as a holy man. I did not like fights, and I didn't want to see that one, big an event as it was.

We remained in New York City for two weeks, and camped in tipis inside Madison Square Garden itself. Fannie and my daughter Marie were with me. We were given our meals, travel expenses, and pay. I received ten dollars a week, and the rest of the Indians were each paid eight dollars a week. Huge crowds came to see us, and we made additional money by posing for pictures. People would pay us from twenty-five to fifty cents for each photograph they took. During our stay there, Abraham Yellow Bull and I were taken to see the Statue of Liberty and also to the top of the tallest building in New York. That was really an amazing experience.

To make the trip even more exciting, we had our first rides on motorcycles, and then rode in a big boat out to the Statue of Liberty. I remained at the base thinking about what the word "liberty" really meant to an Indian, but Abraham climbed up the inside stairway to the top as most tourists do. At that time there was an opening where the right arm joined the shoulder, and I remember looking up in surprise to see Abraham peeking at me out of the opening. We returned to Madison Square Garden on motorcycles, and I recall asking myself which of them I thought was more dangerous, the motorcycle or the buffalo. I concluded that they were both dangerous, especially in those days. But while the buffalo could probably knock me out, the motorcycle could kill me. I didn't ride one again!

I found the number of people in New York City to be beyond belief. Masses of humanity were everywhere, and as overwhelming to me as the endless number of tall buildings. I think that what impressed me even more, though, was their rude behavior. We Indians had given them corn, turkeys, deer, tobacco, and more. They were living on our land. Yet we found no appreciation at all. They just swept past us like running buffalo in their rush to get someplace. We even gave them cigarettes while we were there, but none of them ever offered us a smoke or asked whether they could do anything for us.

Our stop at New York was but one of several we made on a trip that took us to New Jersey for two weeks; to New Haven, Connecticut, for two weeks; to Boston, Massachusetts, for a month; to Jacksonville, Florida, for a week; to North Carolina; and on the way home we stopped off at Washington, D.C. The man in charge of this eastern tour was named Bill Penny. He was a white man, and he was very good to us, watching out for us wherever we were.

In our Wild West shows we Indians rode, sang, and danced. The dances were social performances, though, and never sacred ones. We did try to include a variety of steps, concentrating on one type in one city, and changing to another style at the next stop. We would also ride ponies, chase buffalo, and compete in horse races. Now and then the people who ran the shows had us make an attack on a speeding stagecoach. Being the chief, I always had on my full costume and wore a double-tailed ceremonial bonnet. My main job was to oversee the other Indians, and while they performed I rode around the arena on a splendid horse, checking to make certain they did everything right.

While we were in Washington, D.C., I received a telegram from our reservation agent, in which he asked me to go to the Indian Bureau to see what was holding up the agencies' request for a bigger hospital. The number of Oglala who were ill at that time on the Pine Ridge Reservation was such that the existing hospital, doctors, nurses, and the medicine men together could not care for them. The Oglala people, the agent said, wanted me to see about this. Fortunately, I had with me my signed credentials, which identified me as the leader of the Porcupine District, so I made at that time my first visit to the Washington BIA office. They had a Yankton Sioux interpreter there, and I outlined to him our need for a larger hospital building, and for more doctors, nurses, and medicine. Eventually we did get some of what we asked for, but never as much help as we really needed.

Our touring group arrived back home to find something new going on. The agency officials had talked our people into having district fairs with exhibits, a rodeo, and a powwow. These were to become annual events in which we would display our finest livestock, produce, costumes, and craftworks. They even wanted us to make bows, arrows, lances, and various displays that would show how the Sioux had lived in the old days.

I was somewhat pleased with this idea, since I felt that it might in time turn the people into productive families again. Yet no one could know what it might actually accomplish, because so many families had left their farm homes and moved into the villages. And the final irony in it all was that we would now have to pay to see in a fair what we once did gladly for nothing!

Nevertheless, the annual fairs did bring back an atmosphere of cooperation for many of the Sioux at Pine Ridge. And once again, if a farmer came to the fairs with big potatoes and healthy corn, people asked him how he did it. If a man had a healthy cow or calf, others wanted to know what made it fat, and what they might do to produce one like it. People were even asking why some chickens looked alike while others were entirely different from one another. The possibility of self-improvement and the value of meeting challenges were stirring at least a little among us again, and I was glad. I remember sitting there at the fairground one day and thinking about these things. As I did so I was reminded of Black Elk, and our memorable trip to Cheyenne in 1916. He had predicted then that the fairs would come to pass at Pine Ridge, and now they had. He was a very special holy man, and *Wakan-Tanka* foretold many things through him.

My thoughts that day were abruptly ended when I was confronted by a small group of white visitors who wanted to know whether I was Frank Fools Crow. When I answered that I was, they assaulted me with a flock of questions, asking me about my work, visions, medicine, married life, where I lived, and what I owned in the way of livestock. But I did not answer many of their questions. A person must have a vision or be chosen by a medicine man to acquire such knowledge about sacred things, and most of the rest was none of their business either.

You, and Dallas Chief Eagle, were at Lower Brule in August of 1974 when I split the storm that was ruining their Trade Fair. I wish I had had in 1928 the power to stop the different kinds of storms that were menacing our Teton Sioux people. Child deaths became daily occurrences on the Pine Ridge Reservation in the twenties, and in 1928, Fannie and I lost Grace. She was our second child to go, and together with everything else that was happening it really hit us hard. We decided to have the traditional giveaway, and invited the poorest people in our district. Of our 183 horses, we gave away nearly half. We had 42 cows, and we gave half of them away. We gave away all of our poultry. We gave away our clothing, including most of the ceremonial costumes and beadwork we had worn as we traveled to different places for the contests and shows. All we kept of our furniture was the kitchen stove and the cooking utensils.

Then Fannie and I went into mourning, and we remained alone for a while. As is our way, my father kept my pipe for me while we did this, and returned it to me when we were finished. Those who understand our traditional customs know why we had to mourn and have the giveaway. Our desire was to suffer and to do penance as an expression of our love for our lost children, and in the hope that Grandfather would take pity on us. Actually, we were not worried about the material things. We knew that others would return the favor when they had problems, and that in time their giveaways would supply all we needed to get back on our feet. This proved to be so.

Not long after Grace died, a friend came to us and told us that Colonel Miller's 101 Ranch in Oklahoma was looking for Indians to tour with a show.[17] He said that a number of our relatives and friends were going, and wondered if we might not do well to accompany them. It would give our spirits a lift. So we accepted the invitation and went. We took our little daughter Marie with us. We stayed with the 101 Ranch group for 9½ months, and traveled to many large cities in the Midwest and East.

You asked how, as leader of the reservation, I could be away so long from people who needed me. My answer is that I had to do it because I had a broken heart. Fannie and I were terribly saddened and suffering from emotional pain. Our people understood this, and it is the Sioux custom to let the bereaved do whatever they feel is best. When it is possible, the traditional Sioux still follow this custom today, and when the mourners return to the reservation their friends act as if they have never been gone.

In the late spring of 1929, I received a letter of great consequence from my father. In it he told me that he was very happy, and had been thinking about me. He was writing now from the Rosebud Reservation to let me know that, in response to the agent's urging, the Brule had put on there a spectacular Sun Dance without piercing in 1928. It was a great success, and over five thousand Indians had attended it. The next Sun Dance was to be in Pine Ridge in July, and everyone—my relatives, my friends, and the other medicine men—was thinking of me in connection with it. We could do everything we wished except the flesh offerings and the piercing. We could pray in the old way, we could have the sweatlodge, and we would be permitted to fast.

If, he wrote, we were happy in Oklahoma, doing well, and loved the life we were living, we should stay there. But if not, everyone would like to have us with them, for at last the great Sun Dances could be held in the open and without fear of arrest. He ended the letter by saying again that it ought to be my own decision as to what I did. The people did not want me to return just to please them. I should only return if I truly wished to be with them for the promising event.

How could I say no to my father and my friends when they felt the way they did? I returned to Pine Ridge, and I joined in doing the Sun Dance with them. But I still did not like to do the dance without piercing, or for a crowd of white spectators, so all the while we danced I prayed from the bottom of my heart for more understanding and a change of attitude on the part of the agency officials. I also prayed that the Sioux children who were being educated in the ways of the white man would learn how to search out the opportunities being given to them and to reject that which would harm them. I prayed that the Sioux in general would be able to weave our traditional culture into whatever the whites permitted us to do, so we would not lose our traditional culture.

The Sun Dance was held at the town of Pine Ridge. Spotted Crow was the intercessor. He asked me to assist him, "because," he said, "from then on your role will be that of intercessor." I did not at once accept the invitation, but my father, Eagle Bear, said, "Look: Spotted Crow is an old man now, and he has asked you to help him. He is in pitiful condition, and you must go and assist him."

I did as my father asked, and since then, whenever the Pine Ridge Sioux have wished to have a Sun Dance, I have served as the intercessor. Those who are organizing the dance notify me several weeks before a dance is to be held, and it always takes place the last two days in July and the first two days of August. I also lead Sun Dances on other reservations, and I have conducted at least seventy-five of them.

My previous Sun Dance training had come from Stirrup and what I saw at the secret dances. Spotted Crow used the 1929 ceremony to teach me the rest of what I needed to know about the details of the ritual. He taught me how and why each thing was done, everything except piercing. I had to teach myself to do that later on.

We did not like doing the Sun Dance without piercing, and after the Sun Dance of 1929, we pleaded constantly with the agency superintendents to let us pierce. Finally, in 1952, I was called to the agency office and told that I could pierce the male pledgers. But there were certain conditions I must meet. They wanted to know whether I had medicine to treat those who were pierced or gave flesh offerings. When I told them I had, they told me that if there was any infection or any other bad effect the responsibility would be mine, and not that of the agency or the local doctors. So I said I would agree to that, because I was not worried.

So in 1952 I was given a letter that permitted me to pierce, and I pierced eight men that year. Since then, I have pierced pledgers every year as a regular part of the Sun Dance.

We have only one Sun Dance on the Pine Ridge Reservation each year. At Rosebud there are several, but we only have one, which is the way it was done in the old days before the white men came.

I would like now to tell you about the meaning of the Sun Dance, and how it should be done. It is our religion, our most important ceremony, and it is not possible to know and understand our traditional way of life without knowing and understanding the Sun Dance.

Much has been said about the role of the sun in the Sun Dance. Some people say we are sun worshipers. The sun knows everything. To us it is like the Sacred Pipe. They are both instruments used by *Wakan-Tanka*, and they are the greatest instruments of service he has, next to the directions. But the sun is not God. The sun is something he created for the rest of creation. We respect it and pray to it because it watches over the world and sees everything that is going on. It also serves God by bestowing special gifts that it has upon the world. But the sun is not God. There is only one true God, and we Sioux have believed this for as far back in time as we can remember.

People also say that we stare continually at the sun while we dance. But we have never done that. Part of the time we have our backs to it and we are staring at the cloth banners that are tied to the top of the Sun Dance Tree. We do face the sun and pray to God through the sun, asking for strength to complete the Sun Dance, and that all our prayers will be heard. As the pledgers and I continue to do this, we are able to see the sun with our eyes completely open. It doesn't blind us, and in it we see visions. No one should be surprised about this. Wonderful and mysterious things happen at the Sun Dances to prove that *Wakan-Tanka*'s and Grandfather's powers are active in our midst.

You want to know now how I understand the difference between the high power and the highest power, what the exact differences are among *Tunkashila,* Grandfather, and *Wakan-Tanka. Tunkashila* is only slightly lower in power than *Wakan-Tanka.* "Great Spirit" is not a proper translation of *Wakan-Tanka. Wakan* means "holy," *Tanka* means "big" or "great." But "Big Holy" doesn't do it either. A better translation would be "Holiest of Everything." I think that is as close as we can come, since he is everywhere, even across the sea and sky—the "Holiest of Everything." Perhaps you have noticed I have told you twice now that *Wakan-Tanka, Tunkashila,* and the spirit powers make a trinity, just like the Father, Son, and Holy Spirit do in the Christian religion. It is good to say this often, since so few white people seem to know what we really believe.

In the old days, every pledger was required to go on a vision quest before he did the Sun Dance. But that is not an absolute requirement now. Some of the men work and do not have time to do it. Some are afraid of ghosts, and hate to be left alone in a lonely place like that. But others do vision-quest, and may do so as much as a year before their Sun Dance is held.

Whoever wishes to make a vision quest now as part of the fulfillment of their Sun Dance vow comes and tells me. If in my judgment they are sincere, I have a sweatlodge purification ceremony with them. Then I take them out to wherever they want to go to vision-quest. They choose their own place, and I help them build the questing square. After this I return to the sweatlodge, and I remain there in deep meditation and prayer, giving them support until they are through. We may stay only one day, or as much as four days. They tell me in advance how long it will be. Then when the time is up, I go and get them.

Both of us fast while we are there. I share fully in what he is doing, and whatever he sees in his vision, I see too, I see it and when I go to him I can tell him exactly what he saw. The reason some medicine men are not able to do this is that after they have placed their pledgers they get into their automobiles and go shopping or get a bottle and have a party. They only return when it is time to get the pledger. I don't do this. The vision quest is too sacred, too holy. I want to share completely with them and give them my full support. I want us to be of one mind, and I want to feel and suffer with them.

To make the vision-questing place I set four tall cherry-tree branches in the ground to mark the corners of an eight-foot-long by six-foot-wide rectangle. It could be a square; it wouldn't make any difference. I remove the leaves from the branches, and I tie to each branch one of the four sacred colored cloths to mark the cardinal directions.

There is no pipe rack. I cover the rectangle with sage, and if the pledger brings his pipe he places it on the sage. I also place there a saucer of *wasna*. Then I prepare a string of 405 tobacco offerings for the good spirits, and I wrap this around the four branches, beginning at the west, where the black cloth is. I bring it completely around and tie it at the west. I do not tie the string to the other branches.

When the pledger is within the enclosure he faces in whatever direction he is praying to. He will look up when he prays to *Tunkashila* and *Wakan-Tanka,* and he will look down when he prays to Grandmother Earth. If he stays there several days he will follow the sun and turn clockwise as he prays, whether he sits or stands. He can lie down at night and part of the time during the day, depending on how tired he is.

If the pledger has decided he will stay for several days, but has his vision on the first day, he must still complete the full number of days he promised.

When a pledger is finished, I already know what he has seen in his vision. But some men may have questions about how their visions should be interpreted. If so, I answer the questions for them.

About a week before the Sun Dance will be held, a group of people, including the Sun Dance pledgers and their families, gathers to build the Sun Dance enclosure. Depending on how many dancers there will be, the enclosure is a circle that is from 70 to 150 feet in diameter. A 10-foot-wide shade arbor, under which the spectators will sit, encloses a center circle, called the Mystery Circle. This shade is made of two rows of cottonwood tree trunks, with branches laid between them to join them together, and pine boughs are placed on the branches to make a roof. The main entrance to the circle is at the east, and an opening is made there for the dancers to enter. There is no roof over the dancing circle; it is open to the sun and sky. In the exact middle of the circle a hole is dug to hold the sacred tree.

After this, some of the men and I build one or more sweatlodges of willow branches and cover them with blankets. The number depends on how many men and women will be dancing. One lodge is enough to hold the purification ceremony for eight people, and if there are sixteen dancers we use the same lodge twice to take care of them. For fifty or more dancers we build several sweatlodges. Each sweatlodge has a small fire pit in its center, called the altar or rock cradle. Sage is spread on the ground on the inside of the lodge. The entrance is at the west. Just in front of the entrance I build a small dirt mound, called the mole hill. My pipe and pipe bag are placed on this, along with the sweetgrass we use to purify the heated rocks that are used to make the steam for the sweatbath. The rocks are heated in a large fire pit that is dug about ten feet to the west of the sweatlodge. This is just a pit; it has no meaning attached to it.

The first thing we do when the Sun Dance is about to begin is to get the cottonwood tree. Others go out first to find a selection of several forty- or fifty-foot tall trees that might do. Then they take me to these on the day before the dance and I make the final choice. We form a circle around this tree, and we pray. Then I wipe the tree trunk with a braid of sweetgrass, after which I light my sacred pipe, smoke it, and offer it to the six directions. Then I touch the tree at the four cardinal directions with the mouthpiece of the pipe. I light the sweetgrass and smoke the tree on all sides to purify it. Then a young girl, who must be a virgin, takes an ax and chops the tree once at each of the four directions, beginning with the west. Following this, several men cut the tree down with saws and axes. They then remove the leaves from the lower part of the tree, but not the leaves at the top. The tree must always have a fork about halfway up.

It is all right if the tree touches the ground when it falls, but we make a litter of wooden cross-sticks to carry it to the truck that we use to transport it to the Sun Dance ground. We use the same litter to move it from the truck into the mystery circle.

The Sioux consider the tree to be an enemy, and in the old days warriors rode up to it and attacked it with their bows and arrows and guns. When it was chopped down they killed it. But what they killed was not, in spiritual thought, the tree, but its growth. That was done to destroy an enemy to the people. It stood for our victory over death.

We kill the tree to stop its growth, so that it will remain exactly as it was at the moment of cutting while we pray to it during the four days of the Sun Dance. The Sun Dance is, among other things, a ceremony of renewal and restoration. So the dying of the tree, followed by its death four days later, represents the time period between the casting off of our past ignorance, sin, hopelessness, and, at the end of the four days of dancing, the bursting forth of new growth, knowledge, forgiveness, and hope. The tree is an enemy in the sense that everything stops while all of life is changed and redirected through the doing of the Sun Dance.

The tree is brought to the Sun Dance ground, removed from the truck, and carried on the litter of cross sticks to the east entrance of the mystery circle. I walk beside the tree and we stop four times to pray. I pray to the two higher powers and to Grandmother Earth, saying that this tree has come from her. We have taken it from her to use for a special purpose. In our humble way we will help her make it holy. Then I pray for all of the people in the world, that beginning today and for the four days following we will ask the powers to give us their special attention. We want them to hear our prayers and to grant our requests, because we are all people who need divine pity. I pray like this: "From the earth, from you, Grandmother, we have been given this tree. And you have given us many things from yourself [and I name some, including minerals]. These come from you. Make our hearts feel good, give them rest, make us happy and contented without ill feelings. We have taken things from you, but only because we feel you have given them to us for this special occasion. May it be that from this point on all the people, including the children, will walk the one good road together." I pray the same prayer each time we stop.

In the old days, as the intercessor walked beside the tree, he made the sound of a coyote or a wolf. Even today some intercessors do this, but I don't. The people do not want me to, because as the tree is brought in they are lost in thought, and the sound would surprise and disturb them.

The day before the Sun Dance begins, the same day we get the tree, I give flesh offerings as a prayer to *Wakan-Tanka* for good weather during the dance. I was told in a vision to take these offerings from my forehead, the palms of my hands, and the soles of my feet. First I put herb medicine on the places where I intend to cut. Then I lift the flesh with a needle and cut the pieces off with a razor blade. I wrap each flesh bit in a piece of cloth and put all of them in the hole where the sacred tree will go. God gave me a special healing medicine I apply before and after I cut the pieces. When I use this medicine I feel no pain, and the cuts heal quickly. Also, there are no scars, while others who give flesh offerings have scars and even black spots. These do not happen to me. I have good medicine.

The only other items I place in the hole are sage and a little saucer of *wasna*, which is a mixture of different kinds of meats and berries. Whatever I put down there is going down into Grandmother Earth, and is taken by the good spirits. When the tree is removed after the Sun Dance everything is gone, including the saucer. It just disappears, and is never there when we look for it. Before any of the things are placed in the hole I smoke the hole with burning sweetgrass to purify it.

The *wasna* under the tree is an offering; it is given in honor of the people of all nationalities who have died and left needy dependents. It is a prayer that God will watch over them, and feed the dead and their widows and children.

After the items are placed in the hole, I make a large bundle of cherry branches, and in the middle of it I place a small hide medicine bag containing a cherry tree root, fat or tallow, and dried meat and sage. The bag cannot be seen from the ground when the tree is up, but this does not matter, since it is an offering to God in thanksgiving for what he has done and will do for us. Then I tie the bundle to the tree, where the tree forks.

When the cherry branch bundle is in place, we tie the ropes, those the pledgers will pull on, to the tree, just below the place where it forks. I also tie to the upper branches an image of a man and a buffalo. Both of these are made of rawhide, and are cut from a piece of buffalo hide that has the hair removed. The man holds the hoop of the Sioux nation in one hand, and its sacred pipe in the other. He is painted red on both sides, while the buffalo is painted red on one side and green on the other—the same as the buffalo skull is painted for the altar. The red is for fire and the Lakota people, and the green is for growth. In ancient times, some of the images had an erect reproductive organ, but the green color is used now as a prayer for reproduction and healthy growth.

There is something very special about that man hanging up there above the buffalo in the Sacred Tree. While we are dancing, even though he has no eagle-bone whistle, we hear the sound of a whistle coming from him. And the buffalo, he's pretty smart up there. He remains silent, but sometimes he sits down, sometimes he lays down, and sometimes he stands up. The pledgers watch for this, and they see it. As for the bundle of cherry branches, on the first day of one Sun Dance we all looked up and saw an airplane land on it. It was puzzling, but it was quickly explained the next day when Ed Magaw, the pilot, flew in in an airplane to do the rest of the Sun Dance with us. There are many things to be seen up there, but the crowd seldom notices them. They might look up there for a moment, but most of the time their eyes are glued on the pledgers.

What makes the real difference is that the pledgers are dancing, praying very hard, concentrating, and calling for God's pity. People forget that, but what we do brings us great power.

When the man and the buffalo are secured, I then tie four cloth banners to the tree. The highest one I put there is white, the next lower one is yellow, then comes red, and the lowest banner is black. This is to help the pledgers and the people, as they pray and see visions in the tree, to move up from the black, which stands for sin and ignorance, to the white, which stands for purity and enlightenment.

Now the tree is finished, and we drop it in the hole and raise it up. It is very heavy, and it is hard to raise.

On the last night before the Sun Dance begins, we hold a purification ceremony for the pledgers in the sweatlodge, and then each of the four days begins and ends with all of the participants sharing in a purification ritual.

I use twelve heated rocks for the Sun Dance sweatlodge fire pit. I paint a red circle on the one that will be the seventh passed into the lodge. This is to show that in the lodge we will be seated in a circle, and our hearts will be as one.

As the heated rocks are passed by a helper, called the custodian, into the sweatlodge, four of the rocks are placed in the altar at the four cardinal directions, beginning with the west. Then there is silent prayer. After this a rock is placed near the center of the altar for Grandmother Earth; then one is put there for Grandfather, and the seventh rock with the painted circle on it is placed at the exact center for *Wakan-Tanka,* the highest power. The remaining five rocks are piled on top of the first seven as we all pray quietly.

As I said before, the entrance door of the Sioux sweatlodge always faces west. I enter it on my hands and knees and crawl around the outside edge in a clockwise direction. I seat myself on the sage on the south side of the entrance. Then one of my helpers comes in and sits on the north side. The others enter on their hands and knees and are seated on the sage around the edge of the lodge in the area between us. My helper has either a piece of forked elkhorn or a wooden branch, which he uses to arrange the hot rocks in the altar. He also has a pipe, and as each rock is passed in from the outside by our custodian, my helper touches it with the mouthpiece of the pipe. This is to bless the rock and to fill it with *Wakan-Tanka*'s power. When all of the rocks are in place, we first of all bow down and pray in silence, each person in his own way and with his own thoughts.

The custodian closes the door flap and seals out all air and light. Then everyone stops praying and raises up. I have with me a bucket of water and a wooden cup. I fill the cup and pour the water on the hot rocks, first on the west, then the north, then the east, and finally the south. Then I pour some to each of the higher powers, and finally to Grandmother Earth. The steam rises, and we all stretch and clear our throats, because we will soon be singing. There is a brief pause, and then I pray about the powers that will be in the lodge with us. Then I sing this song to them: "You are coming, you are coming among us. We have prepared everything for you and we are waiting."

I repeat this song three times, and then I sing the same thing three times to *Wakan-Tanka* and Grandfather. Then I do the same for Grandmother Earth. After this I sing again, but my song this time is: "You are all here. You are among us, you are with us, you are in our presence!" Then I make my little "whoo" sound to the spirits. By this time the spirits are answering me with the same sound, and we hear it everywhere, inside around, above, and outside the sweatlodge. The spirits are there!

I open the sweatlodge door four times during each purification ceremony. The total length of time a ceremony lasts after I have completed my part is determined by the length of the individual prayers of the pledgers. Each man offers a prayer that tells why he is participating in the Sun Dance. He ends his prayer by expressing his gratitude to the powers for what they have done and will do for him. Any expression of need and thanksgiving is all right. For example, one man or woman might be concerned about personal illness or an illness in their family, and another person about financial problems. Whatever it is, they ask for help, and then end the prayer by expressing their belief that the request will be answered.

The last thing I do before the purification ceremony ends is to pray: "Well, God, I am going to be outside pretty soon. But before I go, make everything well. When I leave here and these people leave here let us do so with a clean heart, soul, and body. Let us be pure and keep us that way. And show us the good road we must all walk in unity and as close friends, whether we are red, white, black, or yellow." Then I shout "Ho" four times, and the custodian knows we are finished. "Ho" means, in Lakota, "we are through now." The custodian opens the door flap. If there is any water left in the bucket I give some of it to the pledgers. They can drink it or rub themselves with it. If there is still some left over when I have done this, I pour it on the rocks. The water must be entirely consumed. Then we leave the sweatlodge on our hands and knees in a clockwise direction.

Each man shares in a purification ceremony after the tree is first put up on the day before the Sun Dance begins; then we have one each morning before sunup and one at sundown on each of the first three days of the dance. On the final day, we have a sweatlodge ceremony at sunup and one when the piercing is finished. This is our last sweatbath. The principal reason we do this one is to avoid the crowds and to be alone with our thoughts. Once we are inside the sweatlodge, people understand that we are in deep prayer and remembrance and should be left alone.

After the sweatlodge is over each morning, the pledgers are painted and get dressed in their Sun Dance costumes. Other medicine men assist me by painting each male pledger according to his vision. If a man has received a vision of a buffalo, his body is painted black from the waist up and red from the waist down. If he has received a message through a thunder being, lightning lines are painted on his arms, legs, chest, forehead, and the sides of his face. As I told you when we talked about the Kettle Dance, lightning lines are usually forked at the end, and only those who have had thunder-being visions should use this design. The elk- and deer-vision men are painted from head to foot with white spots. There is no base paint on the body, just the spots.

In the old days, men who had visions of buffalo wore curved eagle feathers on their heads, and those with elk or deer visions wore the horns of the animals wrapped with fur, such as otter skin. Nowadays pledgers do not wear the curved feathers or the horns on their heads.

In addition to their body paint, the male pledgers have either one or two red circles drawn on their chests to indicate how many times they wish to be pierced. I am not told how many circles there will be before the dance. I learn this when I see later how many red circles there are on each man's chest. If he is to be pierced on both sides, there is a circle on each side. I have an old earth paint that the medicine men use to make the circles. An uncle of mine named Bear Comes Out brought it home from Utah in 1908 and gave it to me. The supply is getting low now, but I have a little left—probably all I'll ever need.

As the first day of the Sun Dance gets under way, many thoughts are running through my mind. I am thinking that everything must be done right; that I must make no mistakes. I know the things we will do during the four days by heart, and I have done them over and over again down through the years. I am ready. But for the sake of all concerned I must now fill the role of intercessor perfectly, even in the way we offer our prayers to God. I also think about those who are sharing in the dance with me. I wonder what they have on their minds, and my hope is they are agreeing that we should follow the good road with one heart. I pray constantly, and I concentrate fully upon leading the Sun Dance as it ought to be led. As I do so I feel good in knowing that I am there, that I am in good health and able, through *Wakan-Tanka*'s power, to help the people fulfill their vows.

The sweatlodge purification ceremony begins before dawn and is finished by the time the sun has risen completely. Then the crier calls out several times to the people to come. While he does this the pledgers and those who are assisting me get painted and dressed. Then we line up in single file. The man who carries the buffalo skull goes first. Behind him, side by side, comes the Keeper of the Pipes and the intercessor. Then come the male pledgers, then the female pledgers, with each pledger carrying their own pipe, which is already filled with sacred tobacco.

We start from a place near the sweatlodge, which is located to the west of the mystery circle, and we walk outside the shade arbor toward the west cardinal point. We stop at this point when we are directly west of the sun pole, and we pray in silence to the west wind and its powers. We do not ask the powers to come, though, because we don't want the Sun Dance to be disturbed by their wind forces.

Then we move forward a short distance to the north, where we stop again and pray to the north wind and its powers. Then we move again, stop, and repeat the same prayer to the east winds and their powers. The last pause for prayer is made at the east entrance to the mystery

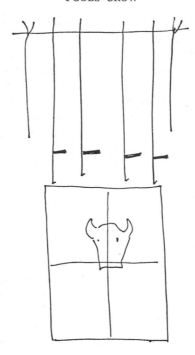

Fools Crow's own drawing of the Sun Dance altar and
pipe rack.

circle, where we pray to the south. Then we enter the circle and walk
clockwise, passing behind the flags at the west and turning back to a position directly in front of where the altar will be, facing the sun and the
sun pole. The singers sing four songs, and while the pledgers dance in
place and offer their pipes up to the sun, I make up the Sun Dance
altar.

To make the altar, I draw a grooved line in the ground to mark a
two-foot square. Then I cut out the square of dirt and turn it over.
After that, I draw two shallow lines within the square in such a way as
to divide it into four equal parts, like a windowpane, so there is a cross
within the square. Then I fill these shallow grooves with sacred tobacco
that has first been offered to *Wakan-Tanka,* Grandfather, Grandmother
Earth, and the four cardinal directions. Over this I sprinkle powdered
red paint, and then shiny white mica dust. It only takes a minute to do
this. If any of the pledgers want to, they can place a downy eagle
feather at any of the points where the altar lines come together. It is not
necessary that this be done, they only do it if they wish to make a special prayer through the eagle. Sage is then spread over the altar square,

and the buffalo skull is placed in its center, facing the rising sun in the east.

While some intercessors do not paint the buffalo skull used for the altar, on the day before the Sun Dance begins I paint it in the traditional Oglala way. I draw a dividing line down the middle of the skull and paint it red on the left side and green on the right, including the horns. The red symbolizes the Lakota people and fire, and the green stands for fertility and growth. The earth is covered with green, and children are just like the earth's covering. They grow. So green is good for the earth and good for growing children. I also put the balls of sage in the mouth and eye openings for purification.

The small pipe rack, made of three cherry-wood sticks that are painted green, is set up to the immediate west of the altar square, so that when the pledgers' pipe stems are leaned against it the bowls will be even with the westernmost line of the square. The pipe stems of the intercessor, assistants, and sometimes that of the dance leader are leaned against the buffalo skull on its south and north sides. A pipe rack can hold about a dozen pipe stems, so when there are more pledgers than that, the men shared the pipes. They do not all carry one, and a large pipe rack is not needed.

When the altar is complete the leader of the dancers may place his pipe on the north end of the pipe rack, with the bowl on the ground and the stem leaning at an angle on the rack's horizontal bar. Then the other pledgers place their pipes next to his side by side, moving from north to south. After this, they return to their place in line, put their eagle-bone whistles in their mouths, and blow sharp, piercing blasts on them while they dance in place and the singers sing three more songs.

If you remember the story of Calf Pipe Woman, this placing of the pipe is exactly what she did. She entered the circular tipi in a clockwise direction and placed the pipe bundle on the ground. She also gave the Sioux seven bags for the seven powers, and there were four colored flags in the lodge. We put our pipes down in memory of this, and the four and three songs, which make a total of seven songs, are done in memory of the seven bags.

The words sung by the singers for the first seven songs are mostly melody, but the words they do sing are, "*Tunkashila*, Grandfather, have pity on us. We have come here and are doing this so that everything will be right with us." It is a very sensitive time as we begin the dance, and as the singers sing it is common for some of the pledgers and their relatives in the audience to sob openly. We feel no shame in this; it is a wonderful moment.

While the last three songs are sung, I go to the four cardinal directions, and ten feet or so inside the edge of the mystery circle I set up,

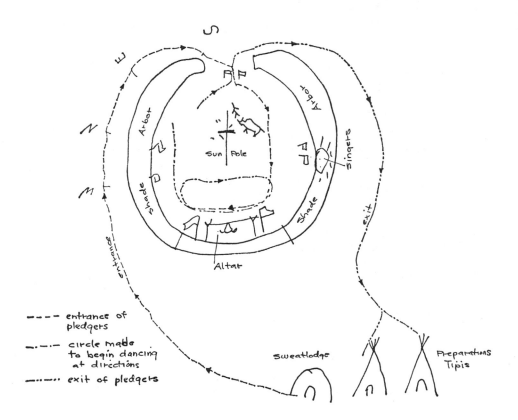

entrance of
pledgers

circle made
to begin dancing
at directions

exit of pledgers

Fools Crow's drawing of the Sun Dance Mystery Circle.
Hand lettering by author.

spaced about four feet apart, four pairs of flags, which are tall sticks
with cloth banners tied to them. Two black flags are set at the west, two
red flags at the north, two yellow flags at the east, and two white flags at
the south. The dance circle becomes now the mystery circle, and it is
filled with power. After this, no member of the audience can step, without my permission, inside the boundary of the circle marked out by the
flags, and if any of the sun dancers wish to leave the mystery circle,

they must exit through a pair of flags and come back again the same way.

Once the flags are set up, the circle becomes holy ground. Even the other creatures, such as birds, know this. If someone makes a mistake and steps over the boundary line or walks in or out without passing through a pair of flags it is a bad omen for that person. Trouble will follow him, and his life will be plagued by suffering, tragedy, or hard times. It might even be that lightning will strike and kill him. But it won't hurt the dance or affect the power that is loosed. The bad things will strike the offender after the Sun Dance is over. Tragedy for that one is assured. The power of God and the spirits in the mystery circle is so great they must not be disobeyed or offended. This is why, as intercessor, I rely so heavily on my pipe. Once those flags are set up and the dance begins, power is within the mystery circle in a very special way. It also is in the audience. A very careful observer will notice that we now and then point our pipes toward the audience as we dance. This is to make certain they too receive the full blessings of the ceremony, and that their prayers will be heard by *Wakan-Tanka* and *Tunkashila*.

I have told you that I take seven flesh offerings from myself, for the seven bags, before the Sun Dance begins. When I bring the pledgers in on the first day, some of them will also have given flesh offerings. I collect all these bits of flesh in a cloth and take them to the sun pole, where I dig a little hole at its base and bury the offerings bundle in it. I pray with it to *Wakan-Tanka* and *Tunkashila* before I cover it up with dirt.

Flesh offerings can be given by anyone, even a spectator. Those who wish to do this take their shoes and stockings off and come barefooted into the circle between the flags. Once the flesh offerings have been taken from them, they go around the tree clockwise and then exit the circle through the same pair of flags. They can do this any day during the four days. We wrap their flesh offerings in little pieces of cloth and bury them at the base of the tree together with those of the pledgers.

After this is done, I move the dancers from the west to the east cardinal direction. To move them, I take hold of the left sage wristband of the leader of the dancers and lead him in a circle around the altar. The pledgers come behind us in a single line. We follow the sun, walking past the north this first time and going directly to the flags at the east because the sun is fairly high now. Four more songs are sung here while the pledgers dance in place. Then we move to the south and dance again. When the four songs are finished there, I give the leader of dancers his pipe, and he takes it forward and presents it to one of the singers, who waits between the white flags to receive it. Then the dancers leave the mystery circle and rest. While they do, the singers smoke the pipe. This completes the first circle, and we continue to circle throughout the day, changing the direction we face, toward or away from the sun pole for each circle, and until all of the pledgers' pipes have been presented to the singers and smoked.

In dancing, part of the time the pledgers' arms are down, and other times they are held up to the sun or the tree. Whether they raise one or both hands they are appealing to *Wakan-Tanka* and *Tunkashila*. They also appeal in this way to the tree and the sun. When they do this, some of them feel a special power in their hands. And they may see the answer to what they are looking for up there in the sun or the tree—an eagle, a buffalo, a bear; things like that.

If they want to talk with me about what they have seen, we discuss it in the preparations tipi at night. Some of the pledgers know the meaning of their visions, others may have only a question or two about theirs, and some need a lot of help. I interpret the vision for these pledgers in private. No one else hears what we say.

It is at least three o'clock in the afternoon when we are done, and we are all very tired from dancing in the hot sun. Some of the pledgers will be in agony, because they are not supposed to eat food or drink water until the Sun Dance is over. In an average dance we have fourteen pledgers, and fourteen pipes to present. But some Sun Dances have many more. At one Sun Dance in Green Grass we had seventy-two pledgers, so four men at a time took their pipes forward. Even then we finished each day just as the sun went down about 9:00 P.M. It was an exhausting experience.

To end the dancing for the day, I move the pledgers to the west, where they form a line and dance in place. While they do this, I go and pick up the flags, and the person who brought in the buffalo skull picks it up. Then I lead the pledgers out of the mystery circle and to the preparations tipis. On the way we stop four times: twice before we get to the east entrance and twice shortly thereafter. The singers continue to sing until the last pledger is outside the mystery circle. Once we reach the camp area the women go to their tipi and the men go to theirs. They change to their regular clothing, and then go to their individual camps. Except for the sweatlodge ceremony, which is held at sundown, they will stay in their own camps for the night.

The second day of the Sun Dance is almost like the first day, but some things are different. We begin with the sweatlodge ceremony; the dancing and basic procedure are the same, but the sun pole is different in that we see it differently. It not only looks different to us, but also sometimes we see eagles flying among the branches, or even an airplane in there. Everyone sees these things, and we see different things each day.

You are wondering whether fasting has anything to do with what we see, whether it causes our minds to wander. I'm not sure. Our pledgers can smoke, because smoking is associated in the Indian mind with ceremonies, and the spirits have never told me to deny the men cigarettes. But they are not supposed to have food or water for the entire four days. Nevertheless, some are unfaithful and secretly drink water. Some have even had friends sneak them a hamburger. I neither say nor do anything about this. It is their problem, and God will handle it. Their offense does not affect the rest of us.

During the second day I select, according to what I know about their worthiness, certain of the male and female pledgers, and I place them around the sun pole in four groups of equal number, with a group at each cardinal direction. Then at my command they go forward together to place their hands on the sun pole. They do this four times, twice in the morning and twice in the afternoon, while the rest of the dancers remain in their places and blow their whistles.

To tell them to go forward I say *Ho Ka Hey,* and the first three times they only act like they are going to touch the pole. The fourth time they do touch it, and remain there with both hands on the pole, praying for about a minute. The special thing is that when they do so, the tree feels exactly like human skin.

Before the dance begins on the second day I use lipstick to paint two red lines around the tree trunk about five feet up and eighteen inches apart, and this is the only paint I put on the tree. I use lipstick because other medicine men would want to borrow real medicine paint from me if I had it. The lipstick becomes a medicine when I pray over it as I put it on the tree. The pledgers place their hands on the area between the lines, and that is where it feels like human skin. The rest just feels like the bark of any cottonwood tree.

What makes that part different from the rest is that when I paint the two lines I pray very hard about it, that this area will be holier and different, and when I finish, it is.

Once, when I was intercessor for a Sun Dance at Crow Dog's place at Rosebud in 1974, the seventy-four pledgers said as one that when they went forward to touch the tree in the area between the red lines it felt just like warm human flesh. They really had to believe in what they were doing to have felt that. So the tree, even though its growth is stopped, becomes a living thing for us. It becomes human, and it dies for us like Jesus died on the cross for everyone. When the men finished at Crow Dog's, twenty-four women pledgers went forward and touched the tree, and had the same experience. They came away chattering like women at a party, saying it was a human being.

During that same Sun Dance, a small, oblong black stone fell out of

Fools Crow's drawing of the stone that fell at his feet
at Crow Dog's place at Rosebud in 1974.

the sky and landed at my feet. I don't know where it came from, but
there it was. I picked it up, and on its surface was printed "WEJOT
68." I do not know what language that is or what it means, but I am
hoping it is a sign that the treaty of 1868 will be renegotiated—and we
will either get back our Black Hills or receive proper payment for them.
A Roman Catholic priest, who was one of the pledgers, was dancing
right beside me. He saw the stone fall, so I offered it to him. But he was
afraid and wouldn't take it. So I put it in my shirt pocket, went on with
the dance, and when I looked for it later it was gone.

The even more amazing thing is that when I was leading the Sun
Dance at Pine Ridge six years earlier, in 1968, I kicked a rock, and
when I picked it up found the same thing printed on it: "WEJOT 68."
But this rock was reddish in color, flat like a disk, and not much larger
than a nickel.

One more thing about the Sun Dance at Crow Dog's in 1974. The
same meadowlark who danced with us at Pine Ridge in 1972 was back,
lifting its little wings and dancing with us again. Later on, I will tell you
about the 1972 meadowlark.

Early on the morning of the third day, those who wish to be pierced
let me know this. After we enter the mystery circle, I separate them
from the rest of the pledgers and place them at the cardinal directions,
from which they go forward four times, touching the tree and praying
the fourth time. After they have gone forward, I go to the tree and push
my head in among the pile of colored prayer cloths that are hung on its
trunk. Several times I quietly make the hoot of an owl. That places
the spirit of the owl in there so the pledgers will hear it when they go to
the tree later on. Then I proceed with the piercing.

I place a layer of sage on the ground on the west side of the sun pole.
On top of this I put down a buffalo robe, hair side up. The head is to
the north and the tail is to the south. There is no paint on the robe.

For the skewer sticks that are inserted in the pledger's chest we use
cherry wood, and the sticks are about the size of a four-inch-long
wooden pencil, sharpened at both ends. Cherry is a very strong wood.

The sticks are not greased with anything to make the insertion go easier.

The pledger lays down on the robe on his back with his head toward the north. He bites down hard on something—his pipe or some sage—to fight the pain. I take a special medicine that *Wakan-Tanka* has given me for the purpose, and I rub it on the man's chest where the circles are. This medicine crumbles up fine and looks like dirt after it is applied. Then I grab the skin, pull it up, and push the stick through. If this is done right, the pledger doesn't feel a thing. I do not cut parallel slits in the chest before I insert the stick, as is sometimes done at Rosebud.

The use of eagle claws instead of the stick is common at Rosebud today. But eagles handle dirt, snakes, and small animals, and I feel the claws might carry germs. So while I have pledgers who would like to use claws I won't permit it at Pine Ridge. When I'm serving as intercessor elsewhere and they want to do it, I let someone else insert the eagle claw.

You say that several authors, writing on the Sun Dance over the years, state that in the old days the skewer sticks were inserted under the muscle. Never have we put the sticks under the muscle, never! The skin itself is very strong. If I put the stick under a muscle the pain would be unbearable and they couldn't pull it loose in a year. I just grab enough skin to get a firm hold, so that I can stretch it, and then I push the stick through the skin. Then I wipe my medicine on their chest a second time.

Each pledger carves his own sticks. He makes his own decision as to their diameter and length, and he brings them with him when he comes to the Sun Dance.

When the skewer sticks are in, the rope is tied to the skewer. In the old days the main rope, whose one end is tied to the tree, was cut from a single buffalo hide, and a smaller deerhide thong was tied to the main rope's loose end in such a way that the two ends of the deerhide extended out in a V shape to be tied to the skewers. We don't have buffalo hides for the main ropes anymore, so most pledgers use commerical rope such as clothesline. But I still use a small deerhide thong to tie the main rope and the skewer sticks together.

When the tying is done I help the pierced man to his feet and take him out some distance from the tree to a place previously marked out for him. I never touch him because he is very holy now, except that when he is in place I once more wipe my medicine on his chest to control the bleeding. Some men do not bleed at all, and if others bleed a little it stops before the ceremony is ended that day. Very little blood is shed in my Sun Dance.

Beginning with the lead dancer, all of the candidates are pierced in turn, and then they all pull on the ropes at the same time. Before they start to pull back, I have them go forward and back four times to the tree, and when they touch the tree on the fourth approach they hear the owl hoot, the spirit I put in there. They will not have known I did it, yet they will always hear it and they tell me about it. This means they are very sensitive and open now. They can be taught and made wise.

The piercing takes place about 10:00 A.M. so that we will be done with the first group by noon, and again about 3:00 P.M. for the second group, so that we will finish about 5:00 P.M. Pledgers do not pierce on one side in the morning and on the other side in the afternoon. Each man must finish at the time I select for him to be pierced. The piercing of the second group ends the third day.

This is a good place to explain why the Sioux pierce in the Sun Dance. Many people think it is such a terrible thing to do, and some of the other tribes who do the Sun Dance have never pierced. The Sioux received the Sun Dance from *Wakan-Tanka,* and we honor him by doing it as he told us to. Since the white man has come to us and explained how God sent his own son to be sacrificed, we realize that our sacrifice is similar to Jesus' own. As to how the white man feels about what we do, there was a far more terrible thing done by Jesus Christ. He endured more suffering and more pain. He was even stabbed on his side, and he died.

The other Indian tribes must speak for themselves, but the Sioux feel a special closeness to God in the dance and in the piercing and flesh offerings. We even duplicate Christ's crown of thorns in the sage head wreath the pledgers wear. In any event, the pledgers seldom lose any of their flesh if they are pierced and tied properly. And even if they do, it is considered as a thank offering returned to the God, from whom it came in the first place.

The fourth day is the same as the third day, except that if some of the pledgers wish to, they can perform their sacrifice by pulling one or more buffalo skulls suspended from their back. I divide the number who wish to do this equally. If there are eight, four will pull theirs in the morning, and four will do it in the afternoon. The buffalo skulls are turned upside down so that the horns will dig into the ground, and one end of each of two ropes is tied to the two skewer sticks placed in the man's back. The other end is threaded through the eyeholes of the skull and a little hole which is next to the eyehole. When they are stretched out, the ropes look like two parallel clotheslines. I have had pledgers pull as many as three skulls at one time. These skulls are placed single file, one behind the other, about two feet apart, and then they are tied together.

When such a pledger is pierced on his back to pull the skulls he kneels down on the hide. He has circles painted on his back similar to those put on the chest so I know how many sticks to put in. Then I pierce him in the usual way.

We also do feather piercing on the third and fourth days. To prepare the feathers, which are always tail feathers from a golden eagle, we bend the end of each quill back to make a loop, then insert with a needle a thread tie through the loop and through the pledger's skin. Any pledger who wishes to can have this done. The traditional number of feathers used is twelve, six equally spaced and running from the right shoulder down the right arm, and six running from the left shoulder down the left arm. None should be placed on the back or on any other part of the body.

The piercing on the fourth day ends the Sun Dance. The only things we have not talked about are the healing ceremonies we do each day. All such rituals must be done before the dance ends, within the four-day period. The people who wish to be healed come forward to the flags at the east, and the pledgers and I bless them. We do not give the people medicine. We just lay our hands on them and pray for them, because they could have any kind of illness, ranging from headaches to appendicitis to paralysis or heart trouble. We might make a mistake and give them the wrong medicine. Then too, not all of the problems they come for are illnesses; they could be alcoholism or family strife or something similar.

Sometimes, *Wakan-Tanka* tells me what is wrong with certain people who are at the dance. Also, some of the pledgers who have real dedication and faith become different as they dance, and they receive special insight and extra power. They too might know what ails some of the people who appear before them. But we still do not give them medicine. If people want healing they must come to me later and bring a pipe. Sometimes I do make exceptions, as I did at Green Grass in the case of a boy with the bent leg. Later on, I will tell you how I did that.

We have talked enough now about the Sun Dance. The last thing I want to say is that I am past eighty years of age, and like Spotted Crow was when I assisted him in 1929, I am ready to have someone take my place as intercessor. So I am teaching several young men: Philip Brown Eyes to be a lead dancer; Dawson No Horse, John Attacked Him, and a fellow who works at the Pine Ridge hospital to perform various tasks; and I am teaching Everett Lone Hill and Silva Young Bear to be lead singers. Most of this training takes place during the Sun Dances. If they overlook something, try to do things differently, or make a mistake, I go to them at the end of the day and I discuss it with them.

At other times during the year they either come to my house individually, or they all come as a group. Then I talk with them about the Sun Dance, and I answer any questions they have.

They have learned a great deal already, and these young fellows are very good. So when the Sun Dance is in progress I express my gratitude to *Wakan-Tanka* for that. I do this at night, when everything has gone well, when all is quiet and the camp is at peace, and I also thank him that we've had no arguments, no conflicts, no bad winds, and no rain to disturb the ceremony.

It is not supposed to rain on a Sun Dance. But sometimes it does because something has gone wrong. The last Sun Dance at Porcupine is a good example. It rained on the second day because someone present was impure. Either a pledger or someone in the audience was not cleansed properly, so the thunder spirits brought rain down to help cleanse us. There was even thunder and lightning, but they didn't harm anything. The lightning did not strike the sun pole, and we all remained happy because we understood what the problem was. We finished the dance and went home happy and pleased as we usually are when a Sun Dance is over.

CHAPTER 13   WALKING STANDING BUFFALO AND THE RUNNING HORSES

The year 1929 was a good one in some ways, a bad year in others. Many of the problems that would trouble us thereafter became known for the first time then.

We had been given the right to vote in 1924, and as we began to exercise that privilege, it caused us some surprising conflicts. For example, we could now vote for the man we wanted to be our Great White Father in Washington, D.C. However, since he would be the very one who chose and directed our agent who would be forwarding our requests to him, as we saw it, we were voting for two important men at the same time. A mistake could be costly, and we wondered how to avoid such mistakes. We realized that by now we ought to know what to do in such matters, but we didn't. In going along with everything the officials had told us to do so far, we had become so mixed up we had even forgotten why we had done certain things, and what we believed our advantages would be in doing them.

We could hardly remember by now what promises had been made to us each time the government people asked us to accept their new laws. And when in consequence we Sioux failed to claim our rights, the government simply put in new programs without even consulting us. We had no voice in the lawmaking or understanding of the problems, and whatever information we were given about the new programs was carefully designed to favor the white man's purposes. How, and indeed why, we wondered, was a person to act or to vote sensibly in a circumstance like that? It was only much later that we learned that our votes would not be important anyway. There were too few of us to matter. So the government people simply did with us as they pleased.

The period between 1920 and 1930 was a trying one for the Sioux for many reasons. The white doctors and the Indian medicine men were confronted by waves of sickness that swept continuously over the people. In fact, from 1915 on the Sioux were struck with a succession of diseases that killed hundreds of people, both young and old. From 1920 to 1930 it was particularly bad. Even though living conditions were relatively good, people died of pneumonia, extreme headaches, and diarrhea. Diarrhea took a lot of people. I remember thinking how fortunate we were that our old form of burial was no longer being used. Because of white religious influences, and because we were not able to travel freely about our original territory anymore, we had, by 1880, begun to employ the white man's method of burial in cemeteries.

In former days our people believed in tree and platform burials. When a person died those who buried him put up four tall posts, each with a fork at the upper end, and then fashioned a platform on top of these with branches. They laid the body on it wrapped in a robe, which could be buffalo, bear, or elk. If the deceased was a man, they would bring his favorite horse to the site, kill it, and place it on the ground under the platform.

Then his mother, or a close relative if he had no living mother, prepared his favorite meal and placed it under the platform. They did these things because it was believed the deceased was going to another world. He would need the meal to sustain him on the trip, and the horse to ride when he arrived at his destination, because the hunting would always be plentiful there. Of course, what went with him was not the actual meal and horse, it was just their spirit.

Anyway, there were so many deaths occurring during these years that I thought it fortunate we were using cemetery burials. If we were still doing it in the old way, there would have been so many burial platforms they would have covered the whole reservation, and all of us would be walking under them. As it was, men were at times digging graves both day and night. The cemeteries we used were Roman Catholic, Episcopalian, and Presbyterian, since they were the first to erect church buildings and provide burial grounds.

Whites and Indians were buried side by side in the church cemeteries. There was no separation of races. The bodies of the Indians were placed in rough wooden boxes. They might be dressed in a fine, beaded outfit, but dancing garments, the pipe, and eagle-feather bonnets were not placed in the boxes with the body. The pipe and the eagle are sacred, and should not be buried. It would be as wrong to bury these as it would be to bury a Bible. So pipes and feathered things were kept by the family or given away. This was true of platform burials as well. The custom of leaving food on top of the grave has been continued until today.

It was in 1929 that my lifelong wish to see our Sacred Pipe was almost realized. And this is a good time to tell you about some of the experiences I have had regarding it.

I have heard people say that the Sacred Pipe has never left the place where it is kept at Green Grass. But this is not so. In 1929, at the time of our public Sun Dance at Pine Ridge, the Keeper, who was an old man then, brought the Sacred Pipe bundle from Green Grass to Pine Ridge.

As I have told you, I was not the intercessor, or leader, for that dance, but was the assistant to Spotted Crow. The Keeper of the Pipe was Walking Standing Buffalo, who told Spotted Crow and me that he had received his name from his grandfather, who was also a Keeper. He also said that on the next day he would open the bundle and show us the pipe. However, he had financial difficulties, and wanted to know whether we could help him out with food and clothing. He would appreciate even a dime. And, if we would do this, I could go to Roberts, the agency superintendent, and ask for his permission to let the pipe bundle be opened.

So I went to Roberts and asked his permission. Roberts and I were good friends, and he would like to have said "Yes" for my sake, but he couldn't. He just stared at his desk for a while before he raised his head and spoke. He said, "That pipe is very sacred, very holy, very powerful. I am afraid of it and other people should be afraid of it too, I don't want it shown."

He went on to tell me that he had heard that not long before this, two foolish police officers had gone to Green Grass and taken the Sacred Pipe away from the Keeper. Within days thereafter, lightning killed one of them and the other went stark, raving mad, tearing at his own body and killing himself. Roberts didn't know whether or not the account was true, but he didn't want to risk the consequence of having the pipe shown.[18]

Roberts added that if I would agree to leave the bundle closed, he would take Walking Standing Buffalo to the commissary and give him a quarter beef, a slab of bacon, dried prunes and peaches, flour, sugar, coffee, and baking powder. He would also give him forty dollars. So I brought the Keeper to Roberts, and when we both assured him that the bundle would remain closed, he gave Walking Standing Buffalo everything he had promised.

Actually, we could have opened the bundle, for the pipe is only dangerous to people who are unholy and do not believe in it. My anticipation had been so great that I was bitterly disappointed, and many more years would pass before my wish to see the pipe was fulfilled.

Walking Standing Buffalo and I did have an opportunity to visit for several hours before he left for Green Grass. That night he came to my tipi, and we talked till the fire burned low. It was then he told me the story of the coming of Calf Pipe Woman as he had learned it, and I will tell that story to you now.

About eight hundred years ago a small band of Teton Sioux were in Crow Indian country, at the eastern foot of the Teton Mountains. Their food supply was low, so two young men went looking for buffalo. They climbed to the top of a high mesa from which they could look in all directions, and to their amazement they saw a woman coming toward them. As she came closer they discovered that she was very pretty, with long black hair that hung loosely down her back and over her shoulders. She wore a red cloth dress, a red cloth shawl, red cloth leggings, and her moccasins were covered with red porcupine quills.

On her back she was carrying a buffalo-hide-covered bundle, suspended by a buckskin loop that passed around her neck. The bundle was the same size as the pipe bundle is now, and tied in the same way. It is about forty inches long. The buckskin thong securing it is looped around it six times and connected with half hitches. The loose ends were used to make the neck loop. The outside cover was not painted.

When she was quite close, one of the young hunters said to the other, "Look at that beautiful woman! I'm going to have sexual intercourse with her." But the other youth replied, "No, don't say that or even think anything like it."

When the young woman came to where they were, she was smiling. But she looked at them and said, "One of you is thinking bad thoughts. Whichever it is, why don't you come over and do what you are thinking?" So the delighted young man threw off his buffalo robe and went to her. But as he did so a white cloud, filled with undulating streaks like heat waves, descended and covered them both. When this happened, the other young hunter turned and fled.

Before long he stopped and looked back, just in time to see the cloud rise up again. The young woman stood as she was before, still smiling. But only the bones of his hunting companion remained, laying on the ground, and from the bones came all of the different kinds of snakes that exist on the Plains. Before that moment there were no snakes in the Teton country. After that, the snakes spread out and soon were everywhere.

The woman beckoned to the young hunter to come close. He did so hesitantly, being ready to run at any sign of danger. But she only smiled, and told him that things like that would only happen to people with evil thoughts and who did evil things.

She then instructed him to go to his camp and to tell the leader, the first Walking Standing Buffalo, to prepare a huge lodge in a special

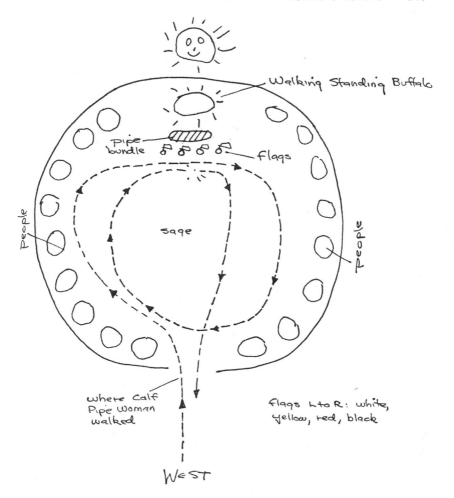

Walking Standing Buffalo

Pipe bundle

Flags

People

sage

People

where Calf Pipe Woman walked

Flags L to R: white, yellow, red, black

West

Fools Crow's drawing of the lodge when Calf Pipe Woman brought the Sacred Pipe to the Sioux. Hand lettering by author.

way, after which the best people of the band were to be invited to an important ceremony.

The entrance of the lodge was to face west, and the ground within the lodge was to be covered with sage. Four feet in from the lodge wall and on the east side four tall sticks were to be placed upright in a row. Black, red, yellow, and white cloth banners were to be tied to the sticks to make flags, and the camp leader was to sit behind the row of flags.

When the lodge was ready, the leader and the invited guests entered and sat down to wait. Indeed, the entire camp waited, and an awesome hush settled upon the place. Even the children knew the holy woman was coming, and when she entered the camp circle, the dogs, usually so noisy, laid quietly on the ground.

Calf Pipe Woman went directly to the tipi, entered it, made a complete circle in a clockwise direction, and then continued on for another half circle until she stood directly in front of Walking Standing Buffalo and the four flags. Then she removed the Sacred Pipe bundle from her back and laid it on the sage behind the flags and at Walking Standing Buffalo's feet.

"Walking Standing Buffalo," she said, "today I bring you this pipe from *Wakan-Tanka,* from God. He asked me to bring it down and to give it to you. Use it whenever you need guidance and help. There was a young man who had evil thoughts, and a terrible thing happened to him. But it won't happen to you if you use the pipe correctly. Whenever you need anything, make your request through this pipe and you will receive it.

"If anything evil happens to you, if people are not treating you well, if bad things are taking place, tell God about it through the pipe and let him take care of it. Leave revenge to him; he will take care of it. You are to hand this pipe down through succeeding generations. Take care of it, and never make fun of it, for it is holy and sacred. If it disappears or is destroyed so that its power ceases, the world itself will end."

In addition, Calf Pipe Woman gave Walking Standing Buffalo seven bags—each an understanding of the powers of the four directions, Grandmother Earth, *Tunkashila,* and *Wakan-Tanka.* She did not give him the seven sacred ceremonies, as is commonly thought. She told the people that these ceremonies were coming, but they were actually given to us later on through the powers. For example, as recently as two hundred years ago the Sun Dance was given through the Thunder Being, a great bird who lives in the storm and the cyclone.

After the bags were given, Calf Pipe Woman walked in a quarter circle and left the lodge, saying, "I'm going to go home now." She made her way once again through the quiet camp, and when she was about one hundred yards beyond it began to flip from side to side, changing as she did so into a young but fully grown buffalo cow—not a white one, just an ordinary color. It played around a little, and then it took off running until it disappeared from sight in the distance. That is the end of the story of Calf Pipe Woman.

As might be expected, the people were very impressed with her visit. The Sacred Pipe was handled with great reverence, and according to Calf Pipe Woman's instructions, it has been handed down from Keeper to Keeper over the generations. Yet I feel that the end of its use is very close. Even now there is an increased amount of disturbance in the little building where the pipe is kept at Green Grass. You can hear the buffalo spirits making noises; they even shake the building. Although it is far away, I know when it is happening. I feel it. Sometimes the Keeper calls on the telephone and has someone bring me a message to tell me it is going on. But I already know and I pray about it with my pipe, since as I do so the Sacred Pipe bundle calms down.

I am not happy about discussing the design of the Sacred Pipe itself, or about revealing the details of the building in which it is kept. I am, in fact, afraid to do this. But I will tell you a few things about the building now, and if I feel all right about it, more about the pipe itself later on.

The wooden frame building in which the pipe is kept is little more than a shack, ten feet long and seven feet or so wide. It has a single door on the east side and one small window on the south. Sage is spread on the floor. The pipe bundle itself rests on a bed of sage on a small, thirty-inch-high rectangular platform, which sits on four forked sticks, to which cloths of the four sacred colors are tied. The scaffold and the bundle are set in an east–west direction, and a large buffalo hide is draped over the entire arrangement, hair side up. On each of the occasions when I placed my hand on the pipe bundle, the buffalo hide was first removed, and my hand was laid directly on the inner coverings of the bundle.[19]

As we entered the 1930s, we thought conditions were about as bad as they could be. The Great White Father in Washington, D.C., and his representatives at the Pine Ridge agency were changing our way of life so rapidly we could hardly keep up with what they were doing. But the worst was yet to come. Soon the terrible droughts commenced, and before long we were wondering if, for some reason, *Wakan-Tanka* himself had decided to do his part in punishing the Sioux too. Fannie and I had just begun to rebuild our home and property. We had purchased as many chickens, turkeys, ducks, and pigs as we could, plowed up our land, and put in a garden.

And what happened next, or maybe I should say what did not happen next, was something to remember. There was no rain at all, and nothing grew—not the gardens, not the wild fruits, not the crops in the fields. Every year it got worse. The grasshoppers came in swarms, the grass didn't grow, and tumbleweeds were everywhere. Always the wind blew, and the air was thick with dust. It got through everything, sifting into our homes and even our clothing. Most of the horses and cattle starved to death, and the poultry and the pigs shriveled up and died too. Bad as it was, you would think that common sense would prevail at such a time. But it didn't. Instead, our frightened people began to behave in strange ways, and the government officials didn't do much better.

A program called the ERA was started. I came to think of it as meaning "Endlessly Running Around," because we had to travel somewhere to get whatever we got, and as much as thirty miles just to pick up our little share of the cattle-issue part of the program. The worst part was that very few people had the horses to ride the thirty miles to the distribution point. So I loaned mine out until I was down to only a few head. Then we decided we would all go together to get the cattle and have a cattle drive. If I remember correctly, the government brought these cattle to the reservation from Texas, Oklahoma, and Kansas. Once we got the herd back to the districts, we divided it up. Each individual in a family received one head. My friends really appreciated the help I had given them, so those I'd loaned my horses to got together one day and decided they would each give me one head of cattle from their family's issue. As a result, I received twenty-seven beef from them.

Another thing we did after that particular cattle drive was over was to try to determine what ERA really meant, so that we could figure out what might come of it. Here again we experienced the helplessness of being subjected to programs that were not explained to us and that we hadn't the education to read about and understand for ourselves. So we were forced to turn to the "squaw men" for advice. These were the white men who came to the reservation and married Indian girls as a trick to get in on the government programs. There were a lot of them during these years, and as a result there are scores of mixed-bloods still causing problems on our reservations today. It did not take us long to learn that the squaw men were not to be trusted. They recognized immediately our lack of understanding, and took full advantage of it to strengthen their position while keeping us weak. By the time we found that out, though, it was already too late.

As I have said, there was little food to be had then. The drought had wiped out our produce, and even the flour, coffee, and sugar were scarce. In no time at all the cattle that had been given out were being stolen. Many of them just disappeared and were never seen again. Then the mixed-bloods made the situation far worse by convincing a lot of the desperate people that ERA meant "Eat Right Away before something happens to it." They told people they were supposed to eat whatever was available immediately, and then they would be given more to replace it. Like I said, foolish things were done. Amazing as it seems, before long people were butchering beef nearly every other day, and sometimes taking only the good parts, like the hindquarters. Understandably, the beef-distribution program was quickly brought to an end by disgusted agency people.

Soon thereafter, we were told that a man named John Collier, the new commissioner of Indian affairs, was coming to see us from Washington. Charles Red Cloud and I were selected as spokesmen to talk with him, and the agency people went to Rapid City to pick him up. He arrived at Pine Ridge with another new program in his hand. This one was called the Wheeler-Howard Reorganization Act, or IRA. Collier explained that it was at last the answer we needed for our reservation problems. It would entirely reorganize our manner of government, and its main purpose would be to teach us to be self-supporting.

"Money," Mr. Collier said, "comes before everything else." So we Sioux would need to learn again to farm and to raise cattle and horses. But this time we would do it in such a way as to convert our produce into money. Then we would be taught how to put our money into a bank and how to live on a budget. I recall thinking at the time that we had been living on less than a budget already. "For the most part," Mr. Collier went on, "everything else will be as it was, except that the Sioux will not receive food or clothing rations from the agency." Also, "you cannot make requests to the agency. This will be handled by an organized government of your own, called the Tribal Council."

And, oh yes, the law-and-order system would be changed in one respect. The old liquor law, which sentenced any Indian caught drinking on the reservation to a year and a day in jail, would be dropped. The Sioux still could not purchase liquor on the reservation, but it could be brought in without the severe penalty that had been the only thing that had kept the people in line.

Soon after that, young people were drinking freely on the reservation. What else would they do with nothing but time on their hands, and especially when so many of the Sioux had been separated by white teachers from our traditional life-way without at the same time being prepared to enter the white man's competitive world?

Once again, though, we all had little choice but to go along with Mr. Collier. Many families were down to eating their starved horses and their dogs. Hard as it was to believe, from a happy and prosperous way of life the Sioux had sunk to suffering, sickness, and this. Poverty of the worst kind was our daily companion.

It took a while for the Reorganization Act to get going, and we lived miserably until it did. Finally it started. The boarding schools were remodeled, and more teachers were brought in. The hospitals were enlarged, and several doctors were added to the staff. A few nurses were set up in district offices. New school buildings were erected, and school buses were put into operation. The government inaugurated work programs called the CCC and the WPA. Now the men were put to work at $1.25 an hour, which was good money for poverty-stricken people. Of course, things were still pretty cheap then.

As was the usual case, being a holy man and a traditional chief, I was not offered a job in keeping with my position. The non-Indians took over the top positions, and the supervisory and hiring posts went to the mixed-bloods who could read, write, and speak English. At the same time, pressure was increased upon parents to send their children away to boarding schools. This was still a hard thing to swallow. But again, what could we Sioux do? We were a people defeated by deceitful acts and clever words. I have always said that being beaten in war was bad enough. Yet being defeated and placed in bondage by programs we could not understand or handle is worse, especially when it is done to what once was one of the most powerful, independent, and proudest of the Indian nations of North America.

Once the new reorganization program got rolling, we were told that some of us could borrow money and return to our farms. We could use it to buy livestock and poultry. And, they said, with good management, we would make enough money to pay back the loans. This would "make men out of us," because when we paid off our loans, others could borrow and do the same. Most everyone thought this sounded great, and grabbed everything they could of this "New Deal," as it was now called. But I was against it, because I could feel the sharp winds blowing on top of the hill again, and I was certain that this program, like all of the others, would assure continued trouble for my people.

So I resigned from my job as district leader, and walked away. When I did this, the superintendent, which was the new title for the man who ran the agency now, called upon me and asked why I had done so. I told him I was a beaten man, that it seemed my traditional way of life and its solutions to problems were no longer useful to my people, adding that many of the elderly shared my feeling. Our family structure was crumbling because independence and irresponsibility were being encouraged among the young people. Bootleggers were after the Indian's money, and were hauling cheap wine and whiskey onto the reservation by the truckload. Our young men were being persuaded to sell liquor for them, and as a result it was not long before drunken people were trading every worthwhile thing they had for liquor. Even the young women were drinking now, and this assured a future tragedy of the worst possible proportions.

The years from 1930 to 1940 rank as the worst ten years I know of, and all the Oglala as old as I am will agree. In that one single period we lost everything we had gained. Fewer and fewer ceremonies were held, and even the social dancing dropped off because of problems caused by intoxicated people. Most of the elders knew that the good spirits would be terribly displeased with such shameful behavior, so they did what they could to avoid becoming part of it. But that was not enough, and I knew it was past time for those who still cared to do something. I had walked away, yet I knew deep down inside as I did so that I could not really desert my people. So I gathered the traditional medicine men and civil leaders together for a conference. We discussed many things, but in the end concluded that the solution was not in our hands, that all we could do for the moment was to fall back on our prayers.

I decided to go again to Bear Butte to fast and pray. I would pray for an end to the liquor problem, for a change in the attitudes of the youth, for crops, wild fruits, and for the grass. I would also pray that the agency people we had to deal with would give far more consideration to what was really best for us. We believed that most of our difficulties were caused by white indifference or mistakes, yet in my prayers I would ask *Wakan-Tanka* to help the Sioux correct the errors we had made, and to meet the agency people halfway.

For some reason I couldn't pin down, I felt that before leaving I should go and talk to one of the Jesuit Black Robes I had gotten to know well. He was a fine man who seemed to understand the problems of our people. I did so, and when I told him what I had decided to do, the priest replied that he would pray for me while I was on the butte, but in his own way, according to the way of the Roman Catholic Church. I really appreciated this, and it gave me added comfort to know that one white man at least would be joining me in sincere concern for a just and lasting change for the Sioux.

I spent another four days and four nights at Bear Butte, and do you know what happened? *Wakan-Tanka* and *Tunkashila* gave me the same answer I was given on my trip there in 1927. The Sioux should go back and pick up the good things that our grandfathers, grandmothers, aunts, uncles, fathers, and mothers had taught us. Our only hope was to fall back upon our traditional way of life. It was the only foundation we had that would give meaning and purpose to us. I brought this message back to the elders, and we all went to work on it by improving our ceremonial life and daily productivity. We started to live the traditional life again, and not long after that some things at least began to change for the better. I am sorry to say that the drinking problem was not one of these. That has gotten worse with every passing year. Whiskey and wine are the most terrible things the white man ever brought to the Indian people. Alcohol is the bitterest curse we have, and it has done more to weaken and destroy us than anything else. We had no strong drink, no such thing as whiskey, before the white man came to our country. We didn't need it then and we don't need or want it now. The best thing the government people could do is to come and take it off the reservation. Once this is done we might be able to build a worthwhile life again.

As our situation worsened, mental illness began to trouble our people for the first time. This too was virtually unknown among us until the 1930s began. In the ancient days mental illness was a rare thing, and until 1930 the only instances I experienced personally were those connected with the veterans of World War I.

Earlier you said something about the fact that I have claimed I could cure every physical illness, and then you asked what I have been able to do about mental illness. You wanted to know whether anyone was ever brought to me for that.

About 1931, a young man was brought to me who was wild-eyed, sweating, and having fits. His problem was that he had some tiny worms with red heads in his brain tissues. I prayed about this and was told by the spirits that it was a mental problem. So I put a black cloth hood over the patient's head and one over my own head while assistants made the room we were in completely dark. Then I could see sparks coming out of the top of the man's head, and afterward came the little worms with red heads. The other people in the room did not see them, but with the spirits' help, I did, and then I cured the patient. I will not say how. There are some things I should not tell and that must remain secret.

There are other healings I remember from the 1930s, and I will tell you about some of them.

In 1936 or 1937, while I was two miles or so away from my house and out looking for some of my horses that had strayed, a woman came running across the field to get me. She was not crying, but I could tell by the anxious expression on her face that something was badly wrong. Gasping for breath, she said that a young mother was not able to deliver her baby, and the entire family was crying and afraid because the child just wouldn't come. The girl was not ill, but they believed she would certainly die if something was not done quickly. I knew they were correct. Actually, she was close to death. So when the woman said they were waiting for me at the house now, I mounted one of the horses I had found and raced toward the house, praying as I rode. On the way I passed by a pond and saw there at its edge a certain beautiful plant. It was a long weed and it had no blossoms, but it was beautiful. I leaned down and snatched it up. Then I rode on.

Arriving at the girl's home, I boiled the plant, and prayed all the while I did so. Even though there were many people present, there was complete silence. A few watched me, fascinated at what I did, while the rest looked away into space, praying with me in the hope I could help the anguished girl.

As soon as the broth was ready, I had her drink a cup of it. By the time it was finished, the child started to come. It came out without trouble, and was a beautiful baby boy. Since then I have used that same weed to heal childbirth cases several times.

You ask whether there were any deformed children born in the days before the white men came. No, there were not. But this is no longer the case. Intermarriage and disease has caused some of our babies to be born with misshapen heads, bodies, arms, legs, and even without limbs. So many kinds of sad things are seen now.

In the old days the Sioux had clan rules carefully designed to prevent intermarriage, but now, due to the government's unwise policy of shifting people about on reservations and the loss of information regarding families, we have had considerable intermarriage. As a result serious physical defects have become common. I just the other day saw a young boy at Eagle Butte on the Cheyenne River Reservation who had a mass of long hair growing right out of the middle of his forehead and just above his eyes. It made me sick to see it.

I have healed people with deformities. In 1941 a boy was brought to me who had a deformed right leg. It was swollen at the knee, and his right foot was shaped like a club. The boy was not able to walk because of it. To treat it, I sterilized a needle with a match and pierced the knee in two places. Lots of water came out. Then I did the same thing just below the ankle, and more water spurted. It appeared to me then that the skin shrank, and that even the bones grew smaller. Finally, at both the knee and the foot, the bones seemed to collapse. At this point I told the boy and his parents he would be all right, and they took him home.

Four or five months later, the boy came back to see me. He was walking well, and the leg was growing normally. The muscles and flesh were not yet as heavy and strong as those on the left leg, but progress was definitely being made.

As the 1930s came to an end the rain started to fall again, and the government sent us new supplies of food and cattle. We were happy to see an end to hunger, and to know that the hospitals would no longer be overflowing with the sick. We could at last put our shovels down and rest from burying the dead.

It was not long after that that feasts were being held for birthdays, weddings, and for the naming of children. As our outlook for the future became brighter, more people began to attend the mission churches, and men and women also prayed more with their pipes. Somehow the word got around that I had gone to Bear Butte to pray about our former troubles, and it was believed that my prayers had something to do with the change for the better. So several white people came to ask me about this. They wanted to know what I was shown, whether I fasted, and what exactly a person must do to obtain such answers from *Wakan-Tanka*. But I did not answer them, because Black Elk had advised me against it a long time before, and because of what had happened once with a certain man from Switzerland.

One day the agency superintendent persuaded me to tell a little about myself as a holy man to a man from Switzerland. He had come to Pine Ridge seeking information about our sacred ceremonies. The superintendent knew that I did not like to do this, but he asked me to give the visitor at least a little information about my Yuwipi ceremony, a couple of my other ceremonies, and something about the way in which I treated my patients. At that time I had three men who helped me with my sweatlodges. They prepared the lodge, heated the rocks, and obtained some of the articles I needed to treat patients. So I sent for them and we performed a sweatlodge ceremony for this man. He put it all on wax records. When we were done, he gently placed the records in a leather container. As he did so, we heard a crackling sound. Startled, he reached in to see what had happened, and found that the records had crumbled into little pieces.

As it did with everyone else in the United States, World War II dominated the lives and consciousness of the Sioux from 1940 to 1950. Our sweatlodges at Pine Ridge were overworked during that awful time, first as the armed forces began to take away the young men and women, and then as those who survived came limping home. From the time of Pearl Harbor, and during the entire war with Germany and Japan, there was no end of crying and praying on the reservation.

I remember well the behavior of people then. As the scope of the war increased, more and more of our youth were called up by the armed forces, and the families and relatives at home became more and more conscious of their need for *Wakan-Tanka*'s help and of their need for humility before him and their fellow men. The Sioux fulfilled the commitments that their leaders had made to the government, but it was a painful thing to do. Every so often a family received a telegram informing them that a son or a relative had been wounded, killed, or was missing in action. Now and then as we went about our tasks in the evening, the crisp air would carry to us the voices of elderly people singing plaintive war songs about young people who would not return home alive.

Sometimes we gathered together and sat up all night talking about war, and about how the world might be coming to an end as our forefathers predicted it one day would. We were warned that when the end of the world comes, the entire earth would burn. And now strange things were happening. There were more and more people on earth every year, and the wars were more frequent and terrible. In some of those all-night talks it was argued that the United States was the cause of the war. It seemed logical to us that if we were unhappy with the United States Government for what they had done to us, other countries would be angry at the United States for the same reason. Still, we prayed that the pattern of what happened to us would follow the circle. As our way of life had changed, the bad things came first, then the good things, and then the bad things came again. Perhaps it meant that the good things would now return.

Whenever a Sioux veteran came home from war he was purified from its horrors in the sweatlodge. Before long, everyone started to come alive again, and we were a fairly happy group once more. The mournful war songs ended and victory songs took their place, although a few songs were composed for those who remained in lonely graves overseas, and who would not, except in spirit, return home again.

We medicine men used our pipes and sweatlodges constantly during the war years, because we were filling the same role served by medicine men after World War I. Our returning youth were never the same as when they had gone away. Some had mental problems and some came home without arms or legs or eyes. Others had seen the world and war, and could not forget them. They were all taken into the sweatlodge, where medicine men prayed with the pipe, sang, performed their ceremonies, and talked with them. Some of the veterans took their advice. Others didn't, and continued instead to drink so much liquor they died from it. If a person sits by the road and watches the passing crowd he sees many things. The elderly people of Pine Ridge saw in the Second World War an ominous cloud hanging over the future: the grim inheritance of lost sons, orphans, and widows, and a restless younger generation with a taste for new and non-Indian things and ways.

Nevertheless, we had to swallow those terrible years of war as did other peoples all over the world, and we knew it was vital to replace and confront the tragedies with something better and more promising. So the older people worked even harder to build up their homes and their communities. They raised as many cattle and horses as they could, and they farmed wherever they were able. They held annual fairs, rodeos, and powwows, and they put added effort into their ceremonies. By and large, it gained them little. The wounds of war were too deep, and the exposure of the young people to city life was too disturbing. Many of them shook their heads, then our hands, and told us they were leaving to live in the city. No matter what we said, they believed that their ambitions and hopes could be better realized off the reservation. They argued that the elderly who had died had taken most of the old way with them, that all we could do about it now was talk. Many of them said the real thing was gone, and could not be resurrected. They were wrong, but they would not listen. So they began to leave by the dozens, while those who stayed on the reservation continued on as best they could. At least, people were able now to turn their produce into money, and the government helped in another area by easing the burden of aid to the handicapped veterans and by caring for the orphans through the Veterans' Administration.

In 1950, I went to Bear Butte again, this time to seek a vision. First I purified myself in a sweatlodge, which I built in the little meadow at the base of the mountain where all our purification ceremonies are done. This meadow is actually about one quarter of the way up the mountainside, and it is a beautiful spot that is covered with tall green grass in the spring and summer.

For many centuries the holy men and medicine men of many Indian nations have made their camps and sweatlodges in this meadow as they prepared to seek visions. Bear Butte has always been a neutral ground for Indians. The Cheyenne and Arapaho have made much use of it, and the greatest of the Sioux leaders have quested at Bear Butte since the time we first entered the Black Hills country. Even the Blackfoot medicine men come down from Canada to this holy mountain.

When my purification ceremony of 1950 was finished, I climbed to the highest point on Bear Butte and made my vision-seeking place. I made my seeking place by sticking four cherry tree branches in the ground to mark the corners of an eight-foot square. Black, red, yellow, and white cloths were tied to these branches to mark the cardinal directions, and sage was spread over the entire square to make a bed. Then I began my fasting and prayers in search of a vision.

When my vision came I was standing up in the seeking place. First I heard thunder booming, and then a rich and pleasant voice said, "My friend, my friend, look up. Your friends have come to visit you." So I looked up, and from the west through swirling clouds came four riders on four running horses. The first horse was black, the second was a bright red sorrel, the third was the palomino or yellow, and the fourth was white. The color included the mane, tail, and hooves. The Indian rider of each horse was the same color as his horse, including his clothing. He wore only a breechclout, and was barefooted. Some of his hair was tied in a knot at the back of his head—about where the coup braid used to be—and the rest of the hair flew loose in the wind behind him as he rode. They swept over me with booming thunder and flashing lightning following behind them, going on until they disappeared in the distance.

Then the voice told me to look up again, and the same four horsemen came from the north and swept over me once more, with the sound of thunder and the flashes of lightning trailing behind them like the howling that follows a jet plane through the sky. Then the same four riders came over me in the same way from the east, and after that from the south.

When they were gone, the rich voice explained that the riders represented the four winds and the four storms. So they were the powers of the four directions. The reason the riders were shown to me was to tell me that I would be as strong with my medicine as they were, and that after this their colors would be my trademark when I did my ceremonies to heal the sick. That was why I should set out the black, red, yellow, and white flags whenever possible when I did a healing ceremony. Of course, I was already using these colors in my ceremonies, but now they would take on added meaning, and I would gain greater wisdom from them. People should know that our visions do not always bring us entirely new information. Sometimes they simply add to what we already know and are working with. Then we do what we do better, and have a greater effect.

CHAPTER 14   WE MEDICINE MEN

There are several medicine men who are living today and whom I hold in high regard. I will tell you who they are. Still, it might be best if we do not include their names in the book, or else those I leave out will be unhappy with me. What is important for everyone to know is that holy men and medicine men must be measured by more than curing abilities. They must also be measured by their manner of life.

I do not think well of those who drink, and who make a habit of fooling around with women other than their own wives. If a man really respects a woman, he will treat her like he would a cherished sister. A few present-day medicine men are radicals. They are violent, and like to fight. This too is not right. A true medicine man cannot act that way and he cannot do such things. If he does, he will not have much power to heal. Also, a couple of our Sioux medicine men have more than one wife, and that is contrary to the medicine man's role. So they have continual problems, and are not consistently successful at healing. No real medicine man uses profanity, either. I have never cursed in my life. Honesty and sincerity are absolutes for us, as is total faith in *Wakan-Tanka,* in Grandfather, in the directions, and in the Sioux traditions.

Of course, we medicine men have always had our problems insofar as what people think of us. Some people do not care for me because they think I am getting money from all over and using it for my own selfish purposes. Others are unhappy with me because I love the black, the white, and the yellow people, as well as my own red people, and because I want to get along well with all of them. But they are all human beings and God's children, and I love them and want to help them. So if people are against this, there is not much I can do or want to do about it.

Even the medicine men are jealous of one another today. And that is very bad. Years ago all of the holy men and medicine men worked together, and as a result accomplished great things. The medicine men shared their power in the healing rites and in the other ceremonies. Even when they paid homage to God they did so in such a way as to help one another. There was unity of purpose. They were as one, and the people were very happy about this. But this seldom happens anymore. Now the medicine men compete against one another, which only promotes jealousy. If one man is successful in curing someone, he will broadcast it everywhere in an attempt to build up his position. In the old days nothing would be said by him or the patient.

Perhaps the best way to illustrate how fully and unselfishly we holy men and medicine men once shared our secrets is to tell you about an unusual man who did the Eagle Ceremony. His name was Frank Good Lance. He was a stocky man, very good-looking, and a deep thinker. He owned over seven hundred horses, was well respected, and got along well with everyone. He lived at Wounded Knee, and died there about nine years ago. His wife passed away two years ago.

One day in 1950, I received word that I was one of four men who were invited to the Good Lance home. He did not say why we were asked to come. When I arrived, the other three—Poor Thunder, Black Elk, and Horn Helper (or Horn Chips)—were already there. We had a nice visit, and, just as the sun was going down, Good Lance told us his reason for inviting us. He said that he had been given power from the eagle. And he was very happy about this because it was such a privilege to be chosen. He was now the funnel through which the Great Spirit would use the eagle powers to heal people. So he wanted to show us how Grandfather was doing it through him.

The first thing we had to do was to share with him in the sweatlodge ceremony. After that he took us to his frame house. It was empty of furniture, including the lamps. The floor was covered with sage, and we were instructed to sit down on it. His helpers brought in four bunches of small tobacco bags and placed them in a circle. Then one brought him his pipe. We thought he might have some special medicine, but he didn't. All he did was take his moccasins off and sit down in the center of the room facing east. He had his regular clothing on, no feathers or anything else out of the ordinary.

Good Lance said, "My ceremonies are simple. Right now the eagles are gathering to the west between the clouds and the earth. Whenever I perform my ceremony they will do this, and then they will come. They are on their way now. Soon they will be here, and will be flying above us. You must take my word for this because it will be dark and you will only hear them. My entire ceremony is done in the dark. I have no

lamp here, no fire going outside, no light of any kind. In all of this you
will need to believe me, and that my commitment, obligation, and dedication to the sick are the same as yours. As for the medicine I will use,
the patients themselves take me to it. Even if it is late fall or there is
snow on the ground so that the plants are gone, they will take me to a
place where the medicine will be found. If there is snow, it will be the
only green thing there, and the ground around it will be clear. The
prayers I use are the same prayers you use. And the reason I have invited the four of you is because I respect you the most."

When he finished explaining this, he sang his eagle song, and he is the
only one I have ever heard sing it. Then he told his helpers to bring in
the food we visitors would eat with him. As the food was brought in he
took a little of each kind in his hands and prayed with it to *Wakan-
Tanka* and *Tunkashila,* thanking them. Then he held the food toward
the ground and thanked Grandmother Earth for providing it. Finally,
he held the food to the four winds and thanked them. Then he told us
we would hear something "out there." He threw the bits of food out the
door, and suddenly we heard a lot of people talking. We could not understand all that the people were saying, but they seemed very happy
that he had given them food.

Then to our surprise we heard eagles screaming, and making hum-
ming noises with their wings as they flew around. They were outside the
house, and some even came inside, where we could feel the wind from
the fluttering of their wings. It was awesome. When at last the sound
subsided and the ceremony was over, Good Lance told us to eat the
food and not to worry about how he received his ceremony, because we
were all doing the same work and were united in our concern for the
welfare of our people.

Good Lance explained at this time that, as we knew, he was the only
boy in his family. The rest were girls, so it placed upon him a special
sense of responsibility. And when he realized that eagle power as an instrument for healing was coming from *Wanka-Tanka* into his life, he
knew he would be required to change his ways, just as the four of us
had done. He would need to live the traditional life, to be an example
to the people, and to merit their respect. He knew also that he could no
longer seek material gain for himself alone. He mentioned a second time
that the eagles helped the patients choose their own medicine after the
ceremony was over. Then he said he knew we medicine men had noticed
when we arrived that he had a lot of horses, cattle, and poultry. He
even had a lot of puppies. "I am tending these," he said, "for my people, so that the animals will always be in good condition. Everything I
have belongs to them. I want you to believe this, and I know that you
do the same. I even consider myself to be lower than any condemned

man anywhere, and I will never exalt myself above anyone. I will be this way to prove to myself, and to *Wakan-Tanka,* that I am living the life of a true medicine man."

When Good Lance finished this speech, Horn Chips was the first to go to him. Horn Chips shook his hand and said, "You know, you are my nephew, and this has been a great honor for me and for our fellow medicine men who are here with me today. We want to thank you for inviting us, and in the future we will invite you to our ceremonies. We do have the same feeling you have toward the people, and I personally have heard of the many good things you have done for our people.

"Furthermore, I remember well the day when your father brought you to a ceremony, and was so proud that he at last had a boy. At that time he asked all of us, the medicine men, the leaders, and the people, to always remember you in our prayers, so you would one day become a man who would put our people ahead of himself. Now you have become what your father prayed for. And I am sure that, wherever he and all of the others who were present at the ceremony and have passed on are, they are all very happy.

"Don't ever forget that humility is a gift to be treasured, and you must guard yours against all temptations. Now we will be going home, and I am comforted in knowing that your sacred helpers, the king of birds, the eagles, are the most sacred of all birds to all Indians, and especially to the Sioux. Wherever they go they are the king. And we are proud and happy that you have accepted this great responsibility from Grandfather."

Then the rest of us congratulated Frank Good Lance, and ate the food that he had so generously provided. We left without asking him how he obtained his vision and received his power from the eagle, and he did not offer to tell us about it.

Not long after that, he invited me to attend a ceremony he was performing for a sick man who was thought to be dying. You remember that he told us his ceremony was simple, and it proved to be true. It was done at night in the one-room house where the patient lived. The furniture was removed, and all Frank Good Lance asked for at first was a cup of hot water. It was to be brought when he needed it, so that it would be very hot. He had his pipe, with two eagle feathers tied to it, but he did not have the usual medicine bag. Next he asked the patient's family for a few of the small tobacco bags in the four colors that are traditional for all medicine ceremonies.

I looked around for his singers, because all medicine men have one to three singers who do the singing while they perform their ceremony. But none appeared. Frank was just sitting alone in the middle of the room.

He asked now for a skillet filled with red-hot ashes. This was brought

in and placed in front of him on a flat rock. He put some medicine on
the ashes, and before long the place really smelled magnificent. It was a
different smell from anything I knew, and I have been to a lot of
ceremonies put on by medicine men. I think that all of us have our own
kind of plant to put on the ashes during our rituals, so as to have our
own smell.

The skillet was removed, and the kerosene lamps were blown out. At
this point Frank Good Lance sang by himself. He had sung also during
my first visit, and now I listened again to the most beautiful voice I
have ever heard. I have never in my life felt so good inside as when he
sang. I just relaxed and enjoyed it, and I could have sat there all night
listening to him sing.

When he finished his song he said he had to leave for a few minutes
to get the medicine he needed to cure the man. He told his helpers to
light the lamps, and then he took his pipe and went out the door into
the dark. He returned in a few minutes with a fresh-looking root. He
took his knife out, cleaned the blade off with a cloth, and chopped up
the root. He put part of it in his mouth, and then asked for the cup of
boiling water. He put the rest of the medicine in the cup, and then told
his helpers to put the lamps out.

Now Frank Good Lance started to sing again, and in the blackness I
could feel something flying around inside the room. Then I began to
hear bird noises; loud bird noises. I knew immediately what kind of
bird it was. It was the chirping of baby eagles. Many times I had found
their nests, and heard them make this same sound. Then outside the
house and above us I could hear the most wonderful and clear sounds
of screaming eagles. It was really something marvelous to experience.

When Frank Good Lance finished his singing, he told his helpers to
light the lamps. Then he walked over to the patient who was lying there
sick and dying. Frank Good Lance blew the medicine, which he was
holding in his mouth, on the palms of the man's hands and the soles of
his feet, and then gave him the medicine that was in the cup. "In a few
days from now," he told the man, and he gave him an exact date and
hour, "I want you to come over to my house because I have a nice
daughter who would like to feed you that day." Some of the people
there just looked at each other and marveled at his supreme confidence.
It wasn't that they doubted the cure (all medicine men cured people),
but they had to admire his confidence in setting a date for it. "And,"
Frank Good Lance said, "those of you who have participated in the
ceremony here tonight are also invited to the dinner. I want you to join
in a fine meal with my friend here. Incidentally, my daughter was the
one who set the date, and who said that he will be able to come to the
feast."

That was one meal I wouldn't have missed for anything. I arrived early, and exactly at noon when the feast was scheduled to begin, the dogs began to bark. Everyone looked to see what was causing this. In a moment everyone said, "Yes, that's him coming!" It was indeed the man everyone thought was going to die. He was walking and well, and we all had a grand time that day!

Frank Good Lance is the only one I knew who could do the Eagle Ceremony, and it showed everyone that there was considerable truth in their beliefs about the eagle—that he is assuredly the king of birds and very sacred in the service of *Wakan-Tanka*. I know one eagle song, and now and then when I go out to pray I sing it. Whenever I do, I see eagles flying above me, and I talk with them.

Later on, I invited Frank Good Lance to one of my own ceremonies, which I was doing in preparation for a Sun Dance. At that time I told him how I received my visions, and who my helpers were. He was astonished to learn that all 405 good spirits were my helpers, and he was pleased to discover that our sweatlodge rituals were alike in many ways.

Wakan-Tanka can do many things through a good medicine man. He can cure, he can prophesy, and he can make strange things happen—the kinds of things white people usually call miracles. We do not use this word to describe what he does, because he has told us that if we do exactly as he asks, these things will happen, and we should expect it.

On the south side of Rapid City, there is a long, high ridge. That is really a giant man lying there. At the east end of the ridge there is an outcropping of stone that is shaped very much like bare feet with toes. In the middle you can see the rounded form of a full stomach, and at the west end a head complete with its nose! In the early days, whenever medicine men came to Rapid City, they did not come by the easy flat way to the east; they climbed over that man because of his sacredness.

In 1916, there was a celebration in Rapid City, and four white men and some Indians, including two medicine men—Standing Elk and Chases the Spiders—came over that man to join in the celebration. These two medicine men were noted for performing feats of magic, and the crowd, delighted at their arrival, asked them to put on a show. The Indians asked what they would receive for their efforts, and after some negotiating a fee of fifty dollars was agreed upon.

Then Chases the Spiders (since spiders are thought of as evil, the name really means Chases the Evil Away) stepped forward, and the crowd formed a huge circle around him. He removed his beaded leather belt, tied his sacred medicine stone to it, rubbed the belt with sage, and placed the belt gently on the ground. In less than a moment it became a live rattlesnake, which started to crawl away while the crowd screamed and drew back. But Chases the Spiders caught it and picked it up, still writhing. It turned into a belt once again, and to the great relief of the astonished crowd he put the belt back around his waist.

Then Chases the Spiders pointed to a place some distance away and said he was going to go over there, whereupon he immediately disappeared. Everyone looked for him, and not finding him turned toward the place he said he was going. They saw a man there who was jumping up and down and waving his arms to attract their attention. He looked like Chases the Spiders, but they couldn't believe he was. So they sent a group over there to find out, and it was he. Those Indians went home with fifty dollars' worth of groceries.

I can do such things too. In either 1952 or 1956, I can't remember which, I was in Flagstaff, Arizona, for an Indian celebration. Medicine men were present from several tribes, including the Southwest, and one night a contest was held by them in a rodeo arena. A large crowd was present to see this, and they could still tell about its happening.

When the medicine men of the other tribes had finished some of their tricks, a group of Sioux, led by Jim Iron Cloud, took it upon themselves to say that one of their medicine men would perform also, and they volunteered my name. When the announcer made this known, I was surprised, but felt compelled to do something, so as not to have the Sioux lose face.

A small tree that had already been used by one of the southwestern medicine men was standing in the middle of the arena. I walked out to it, and having faith but not knowing what would happen, I prayed there with my pipe. As soon as I finished the prayers, little white birds that shone like bright lights swooped down from the sky from the west and passed over the tree. Then they came again from the north, then the east, and finally from the south. Finally they settled down on the tree, covering it entirely and making it seem like a brilliant Christmas tree, while the crowd uttered shouts of sheer delight. After a minute or so the birds flew up and away, and something that looked like fire blazed out from the tree without burning it to end the performance.

You ask me to explain, especially when I did not know what would happen, how this could be done. I just prayed to *Wakan-Tanka* to bless me and to let me enjoy my powers for the sake of the moment. When Chases the Spiders did his magic at Rapid City, he told some of the people there that he needed food, and had been praying all the way over for it, asking God to let him have some fun that day so as to earn what he needed. God honors us in such instances, so long as we do not abuse the privilege.

I do not ordinarily perform things like that, and I had nothing to do with starting it that time at Flagstaff. Jim Iron Cloud and the others volunteered me, and I had to do something. In fact, I don't like to do such things because it reduces my healing power; it saps it, so to speak. And healing is far more important than having fun. I could do many things to satisfy and astonish curious people. I could even take a baby and make him dance or do some of the other things only adults can do. But I don't really want to. I would rather confine my power to healing. I have met numerous people who have asked me to do feats of magic or miracles, but most of the time I have not chosen to do so.[20]

CHAPTER 15   KATE

In the spring of 1954, Fannie became very ill. There was no time for me to treat her, so we took her to the hospital at Pine Ridge. She died there on Easter Sunday morning, and I felt like half of my life had been torn away from me. She had been my partner for so many years, and together we had survived an endless succession of changes without giving up our traditional ways. Now I had lost four children and a wife. Only one daughter, Marie, was left, and she was married and busy taking care of her own family. There was not much for a district leader to do at the time, and I needed to get away, so I spent part of the next two years traveling with groups that publicized cowboy and Indian movies. We covered much of the United States, and also went to Alaska.

In 1956, my father passed away at the approximate age of ninety-eight. I think it was from gallstones, because he turned yellow. There were over one hundred automobiles in his funeral procession. But I was so overcome with grief that, even though I was over sixty years old, I ran barefooted behind the hearse all the way to the Episcopal Church cemetery where my father was buried.

Afterward, I took my pipe and went out alone onto the prairie to fast and pray. I was there without food or water four days and four nights, and would have stayed longer, but my relatives came for me on the morning of the fifth day and made me come home.

In 1958, I went with some relatives to a celebration at Pine Ridge. The powwow was to begin at 1:00 P.M., so we prepared to eat our lunch at noon. Just as we were sitting down to eat, a young lady named Janet came to our camp and said she wanted to talk to me. We had a brush shade built in front of our tent, so we put a chair there for her. Then everyone else left, because they knew that when someone came to talk to me it was a private matter.

She told me it had been four years since my wife, Fannie, had died, and that it had been a little bit longer than that since her father passed away, leaving her mother a widow. There were only a few children in the family, and she was greatly concerned for her mother. So she had discussed these things with her mother, and had asked her how long she had known me. Her mother had answered that she knew my family all her life, and in fact was a close friend of mine. Then she asked her mother why she had never remarried, because she knew her mother was really lonely. Many times she had caught her crying. Her mother seemed to be aging more rapidly now, and Janet was very concerned. So she had asked her mother's permission to talk to me, and to suggest that her mother and I get married.

This was quite a situation for me, since during the time that I had been living alone after my wife died, I had not been in the least interested in another woman. I respected all of my wife's unmarried women friends, but her memory was too much to allow me to court any of them. Still, I appreciated the fact that Kate had given Janet her permission to come and talk to me, and so I admitted I was lonely, and often felt as her mother did during the years after Fannie passed away. So I said that if this was what she and her family wanted, it was what I wanted too.

Kate and I were married shortly thereafter in 1958, and that is when I moved from Porcupine to her property on Three Mile Creek, where we are living today. It was now I learned, to my great surprise, that Kate had never left the reservation. And she was sixty-three years old. So I asked her if she would like to go somewhere, and when she said "Yes," we began to travel to different places as time permitted. This changed her outlook in a dramatic way, and brought new enthusiasm to her life. Everyone noticed that. We went to several big cities, where she met both Indian and non-Indian friends, and where she met people of many nationalities. And, we went also to the mountains and the lakes, so she could see what the rest of the country looked like.

As was the case during the marriage with my first wife, my years with Kate have been good ones. She is over eighty years old now, and her eyesight is bad, but she still cooks and takes care of our home. And she still likes to travel, but conditions are so bad at Pine Ridge that we never go very far or stay away from home for long.

Because my own marriages have been such good ones, it makes me terribly sad to see what is happening to so many families today. It is awesome to see what liquor and a little money can do. It can ruin a home in a matter of months. A number of young couples I once had high hopes for are going to court now, getting divorces, and fighting over their children and property. It is hard to believe that a once noble people like the Sioux would come to this, and would let their passion for liquor and material possessions do such a thing to them.

And I know that only our continued prayers to *Wakan-Tanka* can rescue us and give us the type of life that will bring an end to this and restore our respect for one another. He promised me he would do so when I was at Bear Butte, and so it must happen someday. We already know that a family whose members respect one another is always a strong family. This is because they learn that someone has to be first once in a while, and someone has to take second place once in a while. But knowing and doing are two different things.

There was not much I could accomplish as a leader in the postwar years, and so whenever an opportunity came I did some movie work, appearing in one film that, if I remember correctly, was called *War Bonnet*. Billy Fire Thunder, Daniel Dull Knife, Norma Shield, and a white man who went by the name of Gray Wolf had parts in that movie too, and I think the year we did it was 1959. After they made the picture, Gray Wolf headed up a promotional tour that took all of us to a lot of places.

We traveled for about two months, and on the day we arrived in Chicago, it was the twenty-eighth day of the second month, I became very ill. Something had happened in my stomach, and blood kept coming out of my rectum. I was put in a hospital, and the doctor wired back to the Pine Ridge Agency for someone to come after me. But no one did. So a fourteen-year-old white boy was hired to take me to the airport, get me on an airplane, and return with me to Rapid City. He was a fine young man, and he hated so much to leave me alone that he almost missed his return plane. He was the last one to get on, and they even waited for him. After several announcements he ran and got aboard. Since that time I get that same way every two or three years. I feel something happening inside, my stomach enlarges, and before long the blood is dripping.

I remember quite a bit about that movie tour. Wherever our group went they would arrange for me to be on radio and television shows both morning and afternoon. Naturally, I had to be in full costume, which meant changing clothes constantly. So they told me when to get ready, what time I would be meeting people, and to give brief speeches in Sioux. They even told me when to go to bed. Not surprisingly, I lost a lot of weight. As soon as we finished in one place, we would be on a plane to another city, and we never stopped to rest. We even went to a number of cities and towns in Canada. At one of these, I met some Sioux who were overjoyed to see me. They came to the hotel where I was staying, and I visited with them for about an hour.

Some of these people were the descendants of those who had followed Crazy Horse and Sitting Bull to Canada to escape the soldiers who hunted them after the Custer battle. They told me they had actually chosen Canada for a refuge because of a girl's vision. They said that an eighteen-year-old girl who was with Sitting Bull's group was making a vision quest near Interior, South Dakota. She had only been questing one day and one night when she was told that terrible trouble was brewing, and that her people had better move away from there immediately. A coyote would lead them to where they should go. So the people took down their tents and tipis, and headed North. And in accordance with the vision, a coyote came to them and led them. They traveled by night and slept by day, and he took them safely through the heart of the rugged Dakota Badlands, through the northern Plains country, across the Missouri River, and into Canada.

Later on, several groups of Indians joined them in Canada, and before long a large number of Sioux were living together up there. Even in 1959, many of them still lived in tipis and followed the old customs. They used animal hides for the tipi covers because canvas was not enough protection against the snow. I didn't see these tipis, but they told me about them. They said that their way of life was about fifty years behind ours on the Pine Ridge Reservation.

Some of the older people asked me whether any relatives of Sitting Bull, Chokecherry Seed, or Knife Chief were still living. I told them that my father, Eagle Bear, had just died, and that he was the only one left. Among those who came to see me was an elderly lady who carried a lard bucket. As soon as I saw her I went over to shake her hand. She said, "Grandson, Grandson, they have been telling us you were coming here. So we have been expecting you, and have come down to see you." Then she gave me the lard bucket, and it was filled with dried deer meat.

I had quite a bit of money, and she looked so poor I gave her ten dollars. I also had a lot of cloth, which had been given to me a short time before by white people who took my picture, and I gave the cloth to her as well. She was very happy, and promised she would bring to see me that evening a boy and a girl who were very anxious to meet me. She would also bring more dried meat, and some pemmican. But I was kept so busy talking and meeting people that I never saw her again. Late that same night the tour people took me to the hotel to sleep, and early the next morning we were on our way on an airplane again. I have heard from the Sioux in Canada since then, and they have asked me to come back for a visit, but I have not been able to go.

By the time the movie tour was done I was ready to settle down at home again. I returned to Pine Ridge to find many changes, and in some ways things were better than when I left. A lot of people had picked themselves up, were doing better, and were more cheerful than they had been in a long time.

It was during these days that I saw what may have been the last Sioux shinny game played. It was held at Porcupine, and was a lot like ice hockey, where the players use sticks and a puck. But our sticks were shaped like walking canes, and we used a ball. The goal lines were at least a quarter mile apart, and the goal posts were about four feet part. One district was challenging another district. The game started in the late morning, and began with the ball being thrown up in the air. Then the teams battled for it and tried to put it through their opponent's goal posts. Each goal a team made counted one point. There was plenty of betting going on, and people wagered horses, saddles, guns, other goods, and money. Each district provided food for the players. The winners got to eat first, and the losers had to eat the leftovers. The game lasted until sunset, and it was very interesting. Everyone was tired and happy when it was over.

Not long after I returned, Kate and I were sitting outside our home under the shade trees. We were talking about the old days, and how the pleasant customs seemed to be passing away one by one. Just then two young fellows drove up in a car. One introduced himself as Jim Zimika, and he wanted to know if I was Mr. Frank Fools Crow. I said I was. He said, "I don't know you, and you don't know me, but I'm from Wanblee [which is another district]. Is this pickup truck sitting here yours?" "Yes," I answered, "that's mine." "Well," he went on, "I want it, and that is why I came. I want to trade with you."

That really livened things up, and my response was immediate, because it was like a touch of the old days, when trading was common. Here, Kate and I had just been speaking of this kind of thing going away, and some of it had returned in this young man. So I entered into the spirit of it, and replied, "All right, you can have my pickup and give me whatever you want for it." After some bargaining, we agreed he would bring me two sorrel mules, which he said were a team and both broken to ride. He would also give me a male and a female pair of coon hounds, a .30-.30 rifle, and a box of shells. Then he took my pickup truck and left. Not long after that he returned and brought me everything he promised.

Even a trade like that was a boost to my morale. Old customs can do this for you. And it made me believe again that if the qualities of the old were still there in the young, we might well be able to revive some of the everyday things we once did. By the way, the mules' names were Jim and Bessy, and some months later still another young fellow came to my home and bought them from me for four hundred dollars.

Of course, whenever I speak of customs that might be revived, I mean not only the dances and ceremonies, but also the manners and morals. Most non-Indians just think in terms of the first two. We could, if we thought it best, revive most of the old dances and ceremonies. But the reasons for our doing many of them are not present anymore, and the attitude of many people about them is not right. The Sun Dance is performed, and we could do again the Ghost Dance and the Buffalo Dance. But Sioux people do not request these, because they figure it is best to leave them alone. The stone and the war-paint powder we once used in the Ghost Dance were taken to the University of South Dakota at Vermillion, and they are on display there. I suppose we could get them back if we wanted them badly enough. But there is no reason to do so.

The sweatlodge remains in constant use, and is popular with medicine men for many purposes. Kettle Dances, although some are being done poorly, are still held now and then. A number of people have asked me how and where I was given my special sweatlodge ceremony. They want to know whether it was during a vision. I only tell them that it was given to me at the same time I received the special medicine I use at my sweatlodge ceremony. But I do not say exactly when and where this was, although it was a long time ago. As we have talked now, I have, though, explained many things about my sweatlodge ceremony. I pray the sweatlodge will remain with us because it is badly needed by our people. The same is true of the Sun Dance, the Kettle Dance, and Yuwipi. I have always assumed that someone will take my place to assure that my ceremonies continue. In fact, it is my firm belief that someone will, just as they will take the place of every other medicine man as it becomes necessary.

In 1960, I made my next vision quest. This one came to pass because of a young Indian girl who had been in a terrible automobile accident. She was in very poor health and paralyzed. She was also brokenhearted and discouraged, and she asked her parents to bring her to the Sun Dance at Pine Ridge so she could ask me personally to treat her. When they brought her and I learned about her situation, I said that my main prayers during the dance would be for her, and that I would give her medicine. I finished by telling her I wanted her to be there the day after the Sun Dance was over, on the day that the powwow dancing would begin. Then I gave her the medicine, and went on with my preparations for the dance.

To my surprise, she came to the dance every day, and remained there all day long. When the Sun Dance was finished and the powwow got under way, I announced to the people that my prayers had been answered. I also told them I was going to walk over to where she was sitting in her wheelchair, and then would have her stand up and walk with me around the edge of the dancing arena. I went toward her, while the crowd held their breath and watched with complete fascination. But I was not afraid. I knew that my prayers had been answered, and that she would walk.

I took her hand, and said, "Well, you can walk now. Will you walk around the arena with me? From this day on you will regain your health, and you will be in good physical condition." Then she stood up and walked alongside me around the arena. The people were really amazed. I saw that their mouths were hanging open, and that they watched the girl every step of the way, wondering if she would fall down. When we were almost back to the wheelchair, I shouted to her mother, and said, "Take a blanket or quilt or anything and cover that wheelchair. Then get it out of her sight, because she doesn't need it anymore." She did as she was told, and the girl, whose last name was Dubray, walked away from the dance arena on her own.

Only a year or so later she was well enough to join the armed services. I don't remember which branch. But when she finished her term of service she got married, and I was invited to her wedding. Now she has two children. I saw her recently with her family, and she is happy and beautiful, with handsome children and a fine husband. She walks as though she had never been paralyzed.

Immediately after the Sun Dance I sensed that it was time to go to the holy mountain and commune with *Wakan-Tanka* and Grandfather, so once again I made the long trip to Bear Butte. I felt the need to fast, and I wanted very much to thank *Wakan-Tanka* in a special way for healing the girl. I hoped also to find answers that would help control the terrible drinking problem we had with young people on the reservation.

Daniel Dull Knife and Sonny Larvie went to Bear Butte with me. Both of them brought their own sage and the four cherry branches and cloths they would need to mark the corners of their seeking places. They also had their *wasna* wrapped up in a saucer, and 405 tobacco-offering bags tied on a string. Each man carried all this in a sack, but when we reached the top of the butte they gave their tobacco strings to me. Then when I prayed for them, I used their offerings.

The most unusual thing that happened on this trip had to do with a buck deer. When we had finished our sweatlodge ceremony in the meadow and were beginning our climb up the trail to the top, a deer appeared directly in front of us. We stopped in amazement. He just stood there for a while looking intently and unafraid at us, and then he turned and led the way up the trail, staying only a short distance ahead of us all the way to the top. Then he disappeared. We made our three vision-questing places with the squares about two feet apart, and in a row. I was in the middle, Sonny was on my right, and Daniel was on my left, with all of us facing west. Each of us wore a buffalo robe for warmth and sacred power.

We spent three days and three nights there, and then the spirits told me we were through and to go home. Just then that same buck deer showed up again, and promptly jumped over all three of us in three hops. Then he waited for us to get ready, and led us down the trail to the meadow.

Once we arrived there, the deer went off a short way from us and rolled in the grass like a frolicking horse does, twisting and turning himself in all directions. Then he jumped up, leaped, bucked around, took off, and disappeared. He was obviously a spirit deer; a holy animal. He was there to tell us that Grandfather would lead and watch over those who entrusted themselves to him, and that we should be happy and bouncing around because of this. I am sorry to say that I received no answers on that trip about the drinking problem. So I knew it would go on.

CHAPTER 16   THE DAYS AT HOME

After 1960, my life began to settle into a consistent pattern, which it has followed until now. I concentrated more on my ceremonies for healing, I led the Sun Dances, I spent more time each day in prayer, and I became more active in tribal events. I was invited with increasing frequency to participate in ceremonies on all of the Teton Sioux reservations, and the Sioux generally began to think of me as their Ceremonial Chief. Requests for help came also from the eastern Sioux, the Sisseton, Crow Creek, Yankton; and the Santee of South Dakota, Nebraska, and Minnesota. I have also received invitations from the Omaha tribe of Nebraska, and I have been called upon to perform ceremonies for several other Indian tribes.

Visitors, both Indian and white, continue to come to my home seeking information and advice. I have made appearances at public events every year, both on and off the reservation. I make personal appearances at many different kinds of gatherings, I make some radio and television appearances, and I have often given talks at reservation-school graduation exercises. I have made several trips to Washington, D.C., to seek help for my people.

Of course, most of the time I am at home with Kate, and the way I live then is quite different from the way it is when I have visitors from outside the reservation, or when I am traveling to tribal events or to cities. When I am at home, my day always begins and ends with prayer. About the time the sun comes up I take my pipe outside and I pray with it. No matter what the weather is like I do this. When I pray I will often see visions about the future, and many times animals will come and talk with me in Lakota.

When I finish, I return to the house, and Kate prepares my breakfast.

My favorite foods are eggs, sausage, and pancakes. These are what I like best. If I can afford to have them I do, and Kate eats the same.

Of course, I cannot always afford these. Right now I am fortunate. I have two dozen red hens, and I am able to have eggs every day. As for the sausages and pancakes, I only have these when there is money to purchase them. I have often gone a week or more without them, but in good periods I have had them every other day. Over the course of a year I have all of my favorite foods an average of twice a week. When the favorite foods aren't available, Kate and I eat beans, rice, oatmeal, cornmeal, and cornflakes.

For lunch and dinner my main diet is meat, usually raccoon or porcupine, which I hunt for myself and shoot even today. Along with the meat we eat an Indian bread that Kate bakes. Wild turnip soup is a great favorite of ours, and we usually have on hand several long strings of wild dried turnips. Sometimes we have potatoes, and now and then Indian fry bread. Dessert is something we only have when company comes, and then the company usually brings it. We seldom can afford to have it when we are by ourselves.

Back in 1972, things were going very well for us. We had at that time more than three hundred goats. But when the Wounded Knee seizure happened in 1973, and the Indian and government people began to come by the dozens to our house for discussions and meetings, we fed them all in an attempt to put them in a good and peaceful mood. We did this until all of our poultry and livestock were gone. Then we had nothing like that until two weeks ago (October 1, 1976), when a man who leased my land gave me the two dozen red hens as partial payment.

I do not regret having given everything away, even though I have received nothing in return. That is part of my life as Ceremonial Chief. Many of the visitors listened to me and did not go on to Wounded Knee. I feel all right, and I have never expected anything from anyone. I also get along well with the white people who live around here, and if I should be in desperate trouble they will bring me food; whatever they can. I also realize that I won't be here on earth very long, I will soon be going home to *Wakan-Tanka,* so I won't need very much for very long.

Several years ago I had reason to think I might one day live in a better home and eat well all the time, but I don't think this anymore. Back then, three members of the Pine Ridge tribal council came to tell me that since I was the Ceremonial Chief, arrangements were being made to get me a decent house and to guarantee me a regular food and wood supply. They seemed sincere, and I felt very good about it. But they have forgotten, I guess, since nothing further has been said or done about it. Even our old house that was burned cost me sixty-five dollars, when I should have gotten it, as is the custom when tribal property is given, for one dollar. Even the dollar is only necessary to make it a legal transaction. I had to sell part of my ceremonial costume to get the sixty-five dollars.

Throughout the ordinary day at home I help Kate with whatever she needs, including the household chores. I chop wood, and since our water comes from a creek, I haul in as much as is needed for the day. My old car needs constant attention, and I frequently drive it the few miles to the garage at Sharp's Corner to have it looked at. Sometimes I have to arrange for them to come to my home to get it going. I have no telephone, so in such cases I walk some distance to a neighbor's home and I ask him for a ride to the garage.

I receive from one to four letters a day, including some from Europe. Everett Lone Hill, Kate's son-in-law, reads them to me, but not being able to write in English, I am not able to answer them. I feel badly about this, so once in a great while, Everett writes people for me.

In the evening, just at sundown, I go outside again and I pray with my pipe. In a usual prayer, I thank God for many things: for the good health I have enjoyed that day; for being able to work and move around; for blessing the day for mankind; for bringing me along the good path of life until this moment. I always end my prayer by asking that things will continue this way for me and Kate, and that we will sleep well through the night.

Parts of some days and evenings are given over to making costume items that can be sold, such as bustles, roaches, and arm bands. Kate and I work together on these things. She does the beading, and I do the rest. The trouble is we are both so old that our eyesight is failing, making the craftwork more difficult year by year.

Indian friends often visit us in the early evening, ordinarily staying for only a little while. I talk with each of them briefly, and then I go to bed around 10:00 or 10:30 P.M. Most of the time we talk about how life used to be and how it is now. Comparisons are made, and we discuss how we would really like it to be today.

Sometimes they ask me to tell them a story. The kinds of stories they prefer may surprise you, because many people ask me about this extraordinary holy man who lived way back, Jesus Christ, who did such spectacular things as walking on water and changing a few fish and loaves of bread into enough food to feed thousands. So I tell them stories from the Bible as the priests have told them to me. And these really interest my visitors. Even today, the middle-aged and older Sioux are not able to understand and deal with Bible stories until they hear them told by an Indian and in their own Lakota language. Then they are able to sense the greatness of them and to feel their impact on their personal lives. Along with Bible stories they ask me to tell them about such things as the salt in ocean water and to explain why this is so. Why they expect me to know all of these things escapes me, but they ask me questions about hundreds of things white people learn as children and grow up taking for granted. I guess they enjoy having it explained from the Lakota viewpoint, and with the drama and emotion I use in giving the answers I am able to give. Perhaps they think of me as being like the storyteller was of old.

Sundays are a little different from the other days of my week. I pray as usual in the morning and at sundown, but I also pray a special prayer at all three meals. I pray more than just my short grace, adding longer prayers for that Sunday. I praise the day in prayer. Sundays also bring more visitors, and people of all ages come. Depending upon the weather, we might have a sweatbath, during which we pray and sing our ceremonial songs.

After the sweatbath, we all go into the house, where Kate has the table set, either for dinner or dessert. We share what we have and what the visitors bring. Children and adults sit together around one or more tables, and I say grace. It goes something like, "Father [*Wakan-Tanka*], Grandfather, thank you for this food," etc. It is a grace like that which the white man uses. Then everyone takes a tiny bit of the food and carries it outside to place it on the ground as an offering to *Wakan-Tanka* and Grandfather.

When that is done, everyone returns to the house, forms a circle, and sings a song. I will sing a typical one for you:

> God have pity on me,
> God have pity on me,
> God have pity on me.
>
> God you have given us a good day,
>   a happy day.
> Give us more of these so that we will
>   remain happy.
>
> God, don't forget to always have pity on me,
>   and always keep us worthy of that pity.

This song is really a plea for God's continuing concern, and you should notice that when old-timers and children come to visit, God is included even in the joyous, or social, songs.

The first song is followed by more songs, which have no specific words. These are "sound" songs, with drum accompaniment. The melody is harmonious and easy to catch, so everyone can join in by making their own sounds. Those who wish to dance do so. Others will shake hands to show their happiness at being together. These acts add to the happy occasion, and bring us even more joy.

I have talked much about spiritual things, and just now about their place in my daily life. I must, though, be honest about spirituality as it exists among the Sioux today. Non-Indians who find our old spiritual life-way meaningful often wish to believe and hope that much of that ancient kind of religious life still exists among our people. We have talked about customs that have been carried on, and about the new interest in tradition that presently exists. But it is important for everyone to know what the present situation is in the daily life of the average person. The fact is that my kind of prayer life is not by any means common among those who live at Pine Ridge. Only a handful of the young and the old pray as I do each day.

Sometimes it seems I am the only one left who lives completely that way. Years ago, in the time of my youth, there were a lot of them. But now, even though there are others, including a few medicine men at Pine Ridge and Rosebud whom I have taught how to live holy lives, and how even to do some of the ceremonial things that I do, there are only a few. Some have tried to live completely spiritual lives, but the attempt is as far as they get. So many drink, you see, and haven't the strength or the dedication to live that way. They just give in and give up. I am not pleased to say this, nor am I boasting when I say I do better. I wish for the sake of the people that there were hundreds immersed in constant vision-seeking and prayer. But I think I am one of the very few left.

My wife, Kate, prays with me nearly every morning and evening. Whenever she is able, she puts aside the cooking or whatever else she is involved in and comes out and stands beside me to join in the prayers. Even during the day, if she looks out and sees me praying she will come and join me. My first wife, Fannie, also did this, and she was really good at it. Kate helps with the prayers, but not with the songs. She has never sung. But Fannie would sing right along with me.

In addition to our social visits at home, we do things as a community. Twenty or more times a year, the word goes out to the old-timers around the town of Kyle and Porcupine to "bring your buckets." This is an invitation to a community affair to be held either at someone's home, or in some instances at a community building. It is not really a public function, but if any person who missed the invitation hears about it and wishes to share in the happiness, he is welcome to come.

The expression "bring your buckets" means that each person or couple is to bring their choice of pemmican, coffee, bread, soup, a pie, a cake, cookies, or something else. That way there is plenty to eat, and leftovers are taken home in the "buckets." The invitation also means that people are to bring their own dishes and silverware. It is taken for granted that those who come will leave their troubles at home and enjoy themselves. Ill feelings and bad attitudes are frowned upon and not welcomed.

It is during evenings like this that we spend part of the time telling fun stories and making up tales that are not true. Several of the old-timers will see whether they can tell a preposterous story and make everyone believe it.

One of the stories I remember from a social evening is that of a young couple who were just married and needed something to eat. So the husband went hunting and brought home four jackrabbits. He asked his wife to prepare them for dinner. But she had no training in cooking, and probably was a half-breed. So she collected a huge pile of wood and made a roaring fire. The puzzled husband asked what that was for, and she said it was to singe the hair off the rabbits, as was done with dogs!

A story I always enjoy telling on such occasions is one about a brother-in-law who was given a large snapping turtle. He brought it home and told his wife they ought to have it for their evening meal. Not knowing what else to do, or how to kill it, she simply placed it alive in a big bread pan, salted and peppered it generously, and put it in the oven. She turned the heat up high, switched on the room lights, and set the table. Then she sat down in a chair to wait for the turtle to cook. Before long she heard a faint sneeze and wondered if someone was coming. But no one came. Then she heard several more sneezes, louder this time, and seeming to come from within the house. She knew no one else was in there, but looked around anyway. Now there was more sneezing, and she tracked it down, to the oven! In astonishment she opened the door —to find the turtle very much alive and sneezing away! There was no turtle dinner that night or at any other time.

A story I use to tease Kate at social functions is one in which her brother-in-law came to the house at noon with a large can of baked beans. He was hungry and asked her to cook them for him. But she didn't know what to do with them, and said so. He argued that he knew the white people ate them all the time, so they must be easy to prepare. So Kate was on the spot. She mixed fat into them, salted and peppered them, and put the beans in the oven. She turned it on, and then they visited while the beans cooked. Every so often she peeked at them to see how they were doing. Finally, after an hour or so she felt they must be ready and took them out. She poured them onto his plate, and they were like little rocks. Try as he would, he couldn't chew a single one, and has never, to this day, figured out why white people enjoyed baked beans.

Another story I like to tell is the one where I explain how I made the world record for the longest home run ever hit. The fact that my life has allowed me little time for sports such as baseball makes it even harder to believe, and all the more fun to tell. This is how I happened to tell it the first time: One day, after I had returned to Pine Ridge from a promotional tour for a movie with Daniel Dull Knife and Billy Fire Thunder, I went to a local fair. A jealous relative of mine, angered by the attention I was getting, came up to me, jabbed a finger into my chest, and said loudly enough for all to hear, "You don't know nothing! You don't know a thing about football or baseball or any of those important things. You don't know nothing! All you know how to do is talk!"

Realizing I had to defend myself, I replied, "Is that so? You haven't always been with me. Let me tell you about the home run I hit while I was in Florida on this last trip." Then everyone crowded around us to hear the story, and I continued.

Two professional baseball teams were about to have a game, and one was short a player. So they looked over the people in the bleachers and finally saw me. They could see I was well built, and a natural athlete, so they offered me twenty-five dollars to play. I told them it wasn't enough, and so we dickered for a while and finally settled on fifty dollars.

They gave me a uniform, and the game got under way. I hit a couple of singles, and a few others got hits too, but by the ninth inning my team was behind by three runs. Then we got the bases loaded, and I came up to bat. The first pitch came in low, fast, and straight, and I hit it as hard as I could. Out it went, rising like a frightened bird, over the pitcher's head, over the second baseman, over the center fielder, over the wall, and into the open door of a boxcar in a train just passing by. They never did find that ball again. Perhaps it went all the way to California, and it was easily the longest home run in history. I turned to my jealous relative, laughed, and said, "And you say I don't know nothing!"

Of course, I didn't really play in any such game, but my jealous relative still thinks that I did.

Unfortunately, the quiet daily life and the social life are not all we must deal with on the reservation. I must say again that I am extremely concerned about the disintegration of families. It is a bad thing that so many Indians are adopting the evil habits of the white man, such as carousing and shacking up. Couples are even living separate lives part of the time so as to collect more money from the government. Such separations encourage fooling around. The white system has infected us, and the really terrible thing is that it has become for our people standard practice, a life-style.

The only worthwhile thing the white man has ever done for the Indian is to provide money, yet even then we Indians are not taught how to handle it. So it causes awesome problems, and it especially hurts the children. Our little ones are really suffering, because the parents use the money for pleasure rather than sensible purposes. This reminds me of the years when our people were told by the agent that they would soon be agriculturalists. We were going to grow everything, be able to stand on our own two feet and be independent. But they neglected to show us how to be agriculturalists, so we never became what they hoped.

Take the young people who have moved themselves into my house. I won't give them any money. If someone hands them even five dollars they will buy cheap bootleg whiskey. Then they will get drunk, begin arguing, and might even kill themselves. So giving money to people like that is not, even though they are my relatives, a good idea. If something bad comes from what they do, people will blame it on the one who gave them the money, and I don't want that to happen to either me or my friends.

The older men on the reservation are more responsible than the youth I am talking about. Granted, the older men cannot do as much, but they help their wives wherever possible and do their part of the hard work. Yet you have seen how it is at my house. There are those two young men there who are strong and healthy. The doors and windows and other things are broken and need fixing, but they do nothing to help inside or outside. I chop all the wood, while they just eat, sleep, and play cards. If they aren't doing that, they eat breakfast in the morning, climb in their car, and are gone. Often, when they come home in the evening they are drunk. They only live and eat off of me. They are close to worthless. The girls have no parents, but are relatives of Kate's. She raised them, and by the time they were eighteen or nineteen they were married and running off on their own. One went to Seattle, had problems, and just now came back. The other married a soldier. He was killed in an automobile accident, and she received a settlement of five thousand dollars. Instead of taking three thousand of it and buying a good home, she purchased a four-thousand-dollar car. Then she left, wasted everything, and is back with a man who isn't her husband and four children. They are all living with us today, and will be for a while.

I have told them I am not pleased with them. They know exactly how I feel, but they just ignore me. They are warm and have food, and are certain I won't throw them out, since it would hurt the children. They feel so secure they won't even take the two school-age children out to the highway to catch the school bus in the morning. I do it for them, and they couldn't care less.

But if I were to say I would not do it again, that I would not feed them or the children, they would start crying, and Kate would cry too. She would sit there and weep and soften my heart. It is impossible for me to deal with that. Indians in general are like this about tears. No, I can't do that. Conditions like this will only change when the BIA Social Services Department takes a stronger hand and makes a worthwhile place for the transient and homeless people. The BIA should provide them with a place to live and make them go to work on government jobs. Once they were on their feet, and the women, infants, and children were placed in the WIC program, they should then be expected to make it on their own.

Such people are not able to obtain financial help from the tribe now, but some help is available from the BIA Social Services Department. They can draw food rations, and apparently are getting money, else they wouldn't have the funds to purchase liquor. But liquor should not be available on the reservation anyway. We can't keep anyone from drinking until whiskey is out of their reach. The last time I was in Washington, D.C., I told the government people who met with me that they should pass a law banning beer, wine, and whiskey from the reservation. Then they should clean it out and put police at the borders to keep it that way. Those who break the law should pay a five-hundred-dollar fine, and spend a year and a day in jail. That's the way it was in the old days. It's a terrible sentence, but it must be done. The Indians can learn to live with that. They certainly learned to live with liquor in a hurry.

The Tribal Council has not even tried to do something like this, and some of the councilmen themselves are heavy drinkers. So there really isn't much hope as things stand as they are. When men like Dallas and I aren't around anymore, the situation will become worse instead of better. When I am dead and people who believe as I do are gone, the first thing the rest will do is accept the government's financial-settlement offer for the Black Hills. Then they will waste it and they will soon have nothing. The Indian children will be living like the cats and dogs on the reservation. They will even be killed along the highways like stray animals. Is the white government able to live with that? Is it able to let that happen?

Among our youth there are some exceptions to all of this, some good ones. But these are such a small minority that whatever they attempt, even through the Tribal Council, is blocked and frustrated by the majority. The sad truth is that unless something dramatic happens soon to change the situation, we are headed straight for a worse kind of disaster than anything that has happened to us in the past.

CHAPTER 17   THE CLIFF
AT BEAR BUTTE

The year 1965 was the occasion of my greatest vision experience at
Bear Butte. Three white people—an older man, a younger man, and a
young girl—came to my home to see me, and wanted me to take them
on a vision quest. I held the sweatlodge ceremony with them, and took
them to Bear Butte. I got them situated in vision-seeking places at the
top, and came back down to the meadow, where I made my camp.

The Cheyenne had built a sweatlodge in the center of the meadow,
and the willow framework was still standing there. So I covered it over,
got everything ready, and went into the sweatlodge to be with the white
people in prayer and spirit. I intended to remain there for the four nights
and days, and to ask *Wakan-Tanka* and Grandfather to answer their
needs. But as I was praying on the fourth night, a voice interrupted me
and told me to come out. I crawled outside the lodge and stood up. I
was wearing only a breechclout and was barefooted; I had my pipe in
my hand. It was about 3:00 A.M., and it was quite cold, so I put my
buffalo robe over my shoulders and wrapped it around my body in the
ancient way.

The voice told me to walk toward the east, following a bright white
path that led up the face of the almost vertical rock cliff that is on the
east side of the Bear Butte group of peaks. Anyone can see that it
would be almost impossible to climb, especially for an old man. But I
did it easily with the spirits' help. I did this literally; it was not in a
dream or a vision that this happened. The white path was easy to follow
in the dark, and I kept walking along it, but actually I felt like I was
just gliding up the cliff toward an arrowhead-shaped hole that can be
plainly seen from the meadow below.

The voice told me to keep going until I came to a door. I was to knock on this door, say my prayers for that house, and the spirits would open it and let me in. When I arrived at the place, clouds formed overhead. Soon there was loud thunder, and the lightning began to flash. Then it felt like there was an earthquake. The whole cliff shook, and I was really afraid.

I looked around and saw no one. But I did as I was told. I prayed to Grandfather, saying I had come there as the voice told me to, and then I knocked on what appeared to be a wooden door in the face of the rock wall. The door swung slowly open and I could see inside. It was pitch black in there, and I was trembling. So I took only three or four nervous steps inside and stopped. The door closed behind me, and I began immediately to thank Grandfather for answering my prayers. I thanked him passionately for healing people through me, and for the confidence I had that he would help us find a solution to the drinking problem that was plaguing our reservation. I asked him to guide me and to keep me humble. I asked him to help me, because our people needed help. And still being afraid, I reminded him that I had a wife and a daughter to go back to.

When I finished my prayer, a voice answered in perfect Lakota, "When you go back, take some of your first meal, whether it is small or large, and throw some away. Do this to show how much you love your people and how willing you are to give yourself. We know you have never exaggerated or boasted, or kept anything from your people. You have lived the life that was planned for you. And we know when you are sad, and we know when you are happy. *Wakan-Tanka,* Grandfather, Grandmother Earth, and Grandfather Sun will always hear your prayers." Then the voice told me something very important about the end of the world, and I will tell you about this in a little while. He also told me that, if there was anything I wanted in life, I would first need to help my people by giving myself wholly to them. If I did this he would grant me whatever I asked. And I find this has been so to this very day.

I was about to turn to leave, but I asked the voice to sing me a song to help me remember this vision and to use it for healing. You see, each time I have fasted and sought a vision at Bear Butte, I have been taught a song that plays a big part in my healing ceremonies and in my prayers for others. So the voice sang me a beautiful song this time too. Then the voice, which I am sure was *Wakan-Tanka,* finished the meeting by telling me that the time would soon come when I should tell many things about my life to a person who would be made known to me.

I don't know how long I was actually inside the cliff—perhaps ten minutes, perhaps fifteen. Anyway, when I came out I heard voices of many people, both children and adults, laughing and talking in the Lakota language. They made very happy sounds. I did not see them, but I could tell their ages by the sound of their voices. I began to rub my eyes, and when I looked and listened again, there was nothing. Not even a sound could be heard now. I looked at the place where the door had been, and it was just solid rock. So I climbed with some difficulty down the cliff and returned to the sweatlodge in the meadow.

As impossible as it seems, I believe now that one day prayers about the liquor problem on the reservation will be answered. The closed and vanished door was a final thing, showing me there would be an end to it, and the happy people represented the Teton people, who will be joyful once again when the liquor is gone. That time has not yet come, but many Sioux detest drinking and liquor today, and we are making progress. While the voice did not identify himself, I know that it was either that of *Wakan-Tanka* or Grandfather. It was strong, but the voice of an elderly person. He spoke to me in Sioux, in the Lakota dialect, just as an elderly Sioux person would in sitting and talking with us today.

Another result of my 1965 experience at Bear Butte is that I now have seven small stones in my body. They were not there when I walked into the cliff, but they were there when I came out. One is in my back, just below the left shoulder blade, and the rest are just under the skin of my left arm and hand. One of these is on the outside of my wrist, another is on the inner side of the wrist, and there is one between each of my fingers and my forefinger and thumb.

Among other things, because of these stones in my body I am able to know when a bad incident is about to take place. They begin to move around. Then I pray that people's hearts will change and the bad will go away, so that good can replace it. Also, each day when I pray, the seven stones give me messages from *Wakan-Tanka* and the other powers. Some people might argue that the stones are just normal growths. But if this is so, how did they appear so swiftly while I was in the cave? And how could I move the growths so freely about as I do by simply pushing on them with my finger? Would not growths just be rooted in one place?

Another result of my vision quest that I have not spoken fully about so far is my ability to talk with animals, birds, and thunder beings. Since the quest of 1965, I am able to talk freely with pheasants, eagles, owls, prairie dogs, coyotes, and wolves. The coyotes and wolves really love me and help me. I ask them to give our people peace and to protect them. I ask them about many things. For example, I might ask what kind of a winter we are going to have, whether there will be a dry season, and whether there will be an abundance of cherries, plums, and turnips. If they say there will not be enough of these things, I ask whether they can help us in other ways: to work together, to care for our children, to keep us on the straight path, to help us improve all the time. I might also ask that there be no floods, or that the hardships endured by the Indian people might be made easier in some way.

I do not always ask, in my prayers and discussions, for only those things I would like to see happen, because no man can claim to know what is best for mankind. *Wakan-Tanka* and Grandfather alone know what is best, and this is why, even though I am worried, my attitude is not overcome with fear of the future. I submit always to *Wakan-Tanka*'s will. This is not easy, and most people find it impossible. But I have seen the power of prayer and I have seen God's desires fulfilled. So I pray always that God will give me the wisdom to accept his ways of doing things.

Sometimes, in our talks, the creatures just laugh at my questions, as a human being will do. Perhaps they think my questions are foolish, and that I should know better. Our conversations range over the whole of life. They cover healing, medicines, assistance, prophecies—many things. When we talk, they come and sit down by me. I have a special song that I sing. And then we visit. The birds might fly above me when we talk, or they might land. In 1972, when I was leading the Pine Ridge Sun Dance, a meadowlark came and sang and danced with us. The people saw it dancing around and singing, gracefully hopping on one foot and then the other, and stretching out its little wings like arms. Then it danced over toward the east entrance of the enclosure and flew off. The people were very happy about this. They knew it was a good sign, that the spirits were with us.

All of these animals speak to me in Lakota. If another person who believed was there with me, he too would hear them, but I would be the only one who would know what they were saying. Unbelievers will see the animals' mouths move, and will hear the sounds and the creatures laughing. But that is all.

I also have a special song that has been given to me to use when I want to talk to the winds, clouds, and thunder, to stop the rain, or to split the clouds. I pray to them with this song, and the spirits of the winds, clouds, and thunder hear me and respond in Lakota.

After my vision quest of 1965, my power to heal seemed to increase, and I have been able to heal every person I have treated. *Wakan-Tanka* has given me this power. You have diabetes, and I can cure even that.

In 1965, a woman named Agnes Red Cloud had sugar diabetes. The doctors told her that she had a bad case, and that was why she was losing so much weight. She was very skinny, and the doctors said they would have to start giving her insulin. But she said that she didn't want to take it, and immediately after that she came to me. I set out my four flags, performed a ceremony, gave her medicine, and today she is completely well.

I know I can cure any kind of disease, because I have treated most. No one has come to me with cancer, so I can't say I have healed that. In 1966, there was a boy about eighteen years old who was dying of cancer. The doctors at Pine Ridge told his parents he didn't have long to live, that he would in fact die in a week. So his parents cried, and they decided to take him out of the hospital and home to die. I arrived at the hospital just as they were bringing him out, and they were still crying. So I asked them if I could have him for one week. But they decided against it, and at the end of the week the boy died. I could have saved him if they had given him to me. It might have taken me two weeks, or even a year. But I would have cured him of that cancer. I feel and know that I could cure cancer, but I have never had the opportunity to do it.

In these last years more and more people have learned about my ceremonies and my ability to heal. Some are curious, and doubters have come to test me. About nine years ago, four white men and two white women from St. Louis, Missouri, came to visit me at my house near Kyle. They asked me if I knew how to conduct a Yuwipi ceremony, and even though I knew they already knew I could, I told them I did. Then they said, "Do you mind if we go to Pine Ridge and buy fifty dollars' worth of groceries and bring them here? And could we bring some of the nurses from the hospital and have you do a Yuwipi ceremony for us?" Then they even offered me a filled pipe, like an Indian would. So I accepted, even though it was clear by now that they had planned this all along to test me.

So they went for the groceries and the nurses, and when they returned I did the ceremony. We removed everything from our house, and there were so many people present they made two rows around the entire room. There were more than forty, but I can't tell you the exact number.

To prove how skeptical they were, one even brought a pair of pliers and some paper money. He said, "Frank, I have twenty-five dollars here—a twenty-dollar bill and a five-dollar bill. I'm going to go outside and find a can. Then I will put the money inside it, and stomp it and pinch it shut. After that I will hide it. You won't know where it is. But if you can tell us where it is during the ceremony, the money is yours." I replied, "I wish you would put fifty dollars in there." And of course they laughed about that because they were sure I couldn't begin to tell them where it was anyway.

The fellow found a can, put the money in, mashed it, and then hid it somewhere outside. He might have thrown it out in the brush; I don't know what he did with it. Then, when I was wrapped up in the Yuwipi bundle and the spirits were all in there with me, I told them about the white man's skepticism and the can. I asked them to help me locate it, and they answered, "Do you really want it?" I said, "Yes, because I really need the money." That was all that happened. Soon they released me from my wrappings, and the lights were turned on. There before me, lying on a piece of cloth, was a mashed can.

I asked the white man who prepared his can whether that was the can he mashed and threw away. He picked it up, examined it carefully, pulled his pliers out, pried it open, and there were the twenty-five dollars. He took the bills out, handed them to me, and said, "They're yours," while all of his friends sat in open-mouthed disbelief. I imagine those people aren't so skeptical about my powers anymore.

George Iron Cloud, who lives in the town of Pine Ridge, was a Sioux who didn't believe in the power of my Yuwipi ceremonies. So not long after the doubting white people were there, I invited him to attend one. I used all of my 405 Stone White Men powers, and made an offering string containing that many little tobacco packets. Then, as soon as the ceremony began, George Iron Cloud sat down and grabbed the string as tightly as he could with both hands. He made certain that no one was going to sneak it away from him by trickery of magic of any kind. He hung grimly onto the string for the entire ceremony, holding it fast in his clenched hands. When the lights came on he thought he still had it. But he didn't. The tobacco bags and string had left without his realizing it. He was sitting there with empty hands holding onto nothing but his imagination. What had happened was that the string of offerings left him right away, and had been gone nearly all of the time he was holding his hands like that.

But I am afraid that this is the way things are for many Sioux on the reservation today. Even Indians are skeptical about our ceremonies. They have too much white education. They think they know everything, when they actually know very little about the wonders of Grandfather and spiritual matters.

In 1969, I went to a dance at Batesland, South Dakota. A friend of mine, Dawson No Horse, was there. He likes to dance, and he attends most of the dances in the area. He came over to me and said, "I am going to be operated on. I have bad gallstones, and they are very painful. The doctors tell me something might bust on me, so they are going to operate on me tomorrow. Can you give me some medicine to keep me from having to go through this?"

So I went out onto the prairie and prayed for help and guidance. And there at my feet was a plant that I knew I was to take and use for the medicine. The spirits were encouraging me to do this. I brought the root back and cut it into four pieces. I told Dawson to take one piece, boil it for about five minutes, and drink the broth. Then he was to burn the piece of root he had used.

This was about three o'clock in the afternoon; at 5:00 P.M. he was to do the same thing with the second piece. At seven he was to take the third piece of root and do likewise. About nine-thirty he was to drink the broth from the fourth piece, and then go to bed. All this time I would pray for Dawson No Horse, and about the hour he went to bed, I felt a strange movement in my stomach. Dawson started at the same time to feel movement too, and at about 2:00 A.M. he had an urge to go to the bathroom. Then he went back to bed, and fell into a deep sleep.

While all this was happening, I had the distinct feeling that the gallstones were crumbling and coming out of his system. At about ten o'clock the next morning Dawson came to me and said, "I am well now, I have no more pain." Then he thanked me for my prayers, for the medicine, and for the assistance.

Even though Dawson felt fine, he still had to go to the hospital, because arrangements were already made to operate on him that day. When he arrived there he told the doctors he felt good now and didn't need an operation. They knew he ought to be in terrible pain, and so they took X rays to see what had happened. But they couldn't find any evidence of gallstones, or in fact that anything was wrong. So the doctors asked him how he could be well when he had just been in such pain and in need of an operation.

At first he told them he didn't know, that he just felt good and didn't know why. But the doctors kept after him with questions. They accused him over and over of having taken some Indian medicine. Finally he admitted it, and they wanted to know where he got it, and what it was. He told them he didn't know what is was or where it was found, but that Frank Fools Crow had given it to him. They didn't like that, but they had no choice other than to let him go. He never did have surgery.

There was a white nurse standing there listening to all of this. About four months later, she developed gallstones. So she came to me and asked me for some medicine to cure her. She wanted to give me money, but I told her no, I first wanted her to be well. Then, if she was satisfied, she could give me something if she wished to. So I gave her the same medicine, breaking it into four pieces and instructing her as to when and how to take them. She went home, and a week later came back to see me, completely well. She thanked me and made me take fifty dollars in payment.

In the winter of 1969, Louis Pumpkin Seed's wife was brought to me. She was paralyzed on the entire right side of her face and body. She couldn't feel a thing there. After I did my healing ceremony in the sweatlodge, she said she was able to feel a prickling sensation all over.

A few days later she had feeling on the paralyzed side, and was able to move her limbs slowly. It was hard on her for a while, but by practicing she was soon well and able to rebuild her muscles.

In 1970, I received a letter from a Cheyenne Indian in Montana, named Alfred Driver, who wanted my help in curing Driver's twenty-year-old son. Enclosed with the letter was a cigarette, and forty dollars for travel expenses.

So I left home about 5:00 A.M. one day with Everett Lone Hill, drove all day long, and arrived at the Driver home at about 6:00 P.M. I found that the youth had a badly swollen and painful knee. He had been working on an automobile and doing some lifting when his knee began to swell and become sore. As he continued to work, the swelling and the pain increased until the pain was unbearable. He went home and showed his parents. They discussed it, and fearing that a trip to the hospital would mean surgery, they decided to contact me.

I had my collection of herb medicine with me, and I went right to work. I built a small fire in the yard, set out my four flags, and prepared the containers I needed to make an herb medicine. Then I had them wrap my head with a black cloth, and I prayed to learn which herb I should use. When I received the answer, the cloth was removed, and I boiled that herb. At 6:30 P.M. I gave the youth his first dose, and I also rubbed some of the medicine on his knee. At 9:00 P.M. I prayed again and gave him a second treatment. The third dose and massage were given at midnight, and the fourth at 2:00 A.M.

At 2:30 A.M. everyone shared in a meal, and then we rested. Later that morning Everett and I left and returned to Pine Ridge. Two weeks later the Driver family, including the youth, came to my house at Pine Ridge loaded with food and gifts. The leg had healed, and the young man walked as though nothing had ever happened to it.

I don't know how other tribes know about my healing power. I am not sure—word of mouth, perhaps. But their requests for help have been coming to me for some time. It was sixteen years ago that I received my first call from the Crows, and I have been to their reservation five or six times since then. An Arapaho family requested my services about two years ago, and I have been going to the Cheyennes for the past seven years.

I am laughing now as I recall a time when a pipe was brought to me from Montana. So I went there and cured a man of heart trouble. In payment, the fellow gave me a cow. But I had no way to get it home— so it is still there and waiting to be picked up. It might be fun for us to drive up there and get it. We could simply lower the carcass down through the sun roof opening of your car and bring it easily to Pine Ridge!

I have done a lot of healing these last years, and I will give you some examples:

It was during the summer of 1973 when Ellis Head got food poisoning. I did not give him anything to make him vomit, but during the healing ceremony I spewed medicine from my mouth onto the back of his head and neck. Then Ellis started to throw up, and he didn't stop until his stomach was empty. Then I cleansed his body in the sweatlodge to stop the poison that might be spreading through it.

In the spring of 1974, I healed Mike Little Wolf of Kirby, Montana, who, like Mrs. Pumpkin Seed, was paralyzed on the entire right side of the body.

In yet another curing I did, there was an eastern Sioux Indian woman from the Yankton Reservation who worked at the Indian Sanitarium in Rapid City. She had been cooking there for about twenty years. She had a terrible leg problem, swelling in both knees, and it was very painful. She had a difficult time walking and getting around. It was agonizing to do her work, but she could not afford to quit. When she finally came to me and made her healing request, the problem had become so urgent that I didn't have time to do either a Yuwipi or a sweatlodge.

After praying, I took some dried medicine and ground it to a powder. I built a fire. Then I took some fat, heated it, and put the oil and the medicine on my palms. Then I started to pray very hard, and while I did so I rubbed the lady's knees, first one and then the other. I kept this up for about twenty minutes, and then asked her to wrap wet cloths around each knee. She did this, and some friends took her out to her car and home. A week later she returned to see me and was completely well. There was no swelling in her knees at all. She is even dancing today.

CHAPTER 18   THE CEREMONIAL CHIEF

When first we began, you were told that I am the Ceremonial Chief of the Teton Sioux. I think I should explain more fully what this title really means. I became a medicine man in 1913, began to practice my medicine about 1920, and I was made a civil chief in 1925. The combination of these things qualified me to lead any kind of religious or civil ceremony. It was, however, only as the years passed that I became a holy man and the Ceremonial Chief of the Teton Sioux. This is not an elective office. A man can only become this when the people accept him as such. So now I can conduct ceremonies to make other chiefs, and I preside at ceremonies and functions everywhere. A certificate attesting to my own title is filed at the courthouse at Pine Ridge, in the superintendent's office. That is, it is there if they haven't burned it yet, or thrown it away. That's where it was the last I knew. In any event, the certificate is only a white man's way of recording it. The traditional Sioux consider me to be their Ceremonial Chief, and they do not require documentation, certificates, or any other form of written recognition. The certificate was only done to satisfy white people.

Please notice that it is the traditional Teton Sioux who recognize me. There are many mixed-bloods, such as Dick Wilson, the former tribal chairman of the Pine Ridge Reservation, who do not. They think of me as an enemy. They do not understand or support our traditional culture. So they refuse my title, are disrespectful toward me, and will not even admit that I am a leader. The reason I mentioned that the certificate might have been burned or destroyed is that I heard only a week ago that Wilson had burned some records at the courthouse. He has been charged with misconduct by the traditionalists, and may well be getting rid of anything that might expose him for what he is.

But this unhappy situation I speak of is changing. In October of 1974 I was invited to a mass meeting at the Billy Mills Hall at Pine Ridge. Even the mixed-bloods, who do not practice the traditional ways, wanted me to be there, and the purpose of the meeting was to overthrow Dick Wilson. I did not attend, and Wilson was not put out of office then, but efforts to remove him continued, and in 1976 he was replaced by Al Trimble.

All of the other medicine men of the Teton Sioux, with one exception, recognize me as the Ceremonial Chief. I am not certain as to why this man feels this way. Perhaps he is jealous of the recognition I have received. The press and the television people have given me a lot of coverage, and this was especially true during the 1973 incident at Wounded Knee. But if that trouble had happened on his reservation, and if he was recognized as a leader there and had helped settle it, I would hold no ill feelings toward him. On the contrary, I would respect him highly. After all, it was not my doing that the Wounded Knee confrontation of 1973 took place on the Pine Ridge Reservation.[21] Once it did, though, as the ceremonial chief it was expected by everyone that I would go there and seek peace. It was not my role to arbitrate, just to avoid bloodshed. I help all people, even those who do not believe in traditional ways. My vow, given in thanksgiving to *Wakan-Tanka,* is to assist anyone who sincerely wants my help. No one really needs to worry about their standing. It is, after all, *Wakan-Tanka* who determines the position of people, not us.

There are other traditional chiefs on the Pine Ridge Reservation besides me. Two of them are quite old. One is Charles Red Cloud, and the other is Eddie Iron Cloud, Sr. A few years ago I made Dallas Chief Eagle a chief of the Teton Sioux. He is not a ceremonial chief like I am, but he is a leader among the Teton Sioux. Charles Red Cloud is eighty-nine years old, and is the grandson of the famous Chief Red Cloud. I was among those who conferred the title of chief on Charles in 1928, and there is an official paper on file at Pine Ridge that proves this.

As Ceremonial Chief, whenever trouble occurs I am immediately involved. When it happened at Wounded Knee in 1973, I was there. As the Ceremonial Chief of the Teton Sioux, I had the solemn obligation to protect my people and to prevent a blood bath, which is what would have occurred if the hotheads on both sides had had their way. I am the chief of the Pine Ridge Reservation. In a sense it is my land. And I do not want violence on it, for I detest violence, and I think it is self-defeating. In fact, I wanted no confrontation of any kind at Wounded Knee, so I talked with representatives of both sides: the AIM movement, and the federal marshals. The people who recognize me as the Ceremonial Chief were happy I was there. It is well known here that once the siege lines were drawn, the marshals tried to keep Indians from entering or leaving the Indian stronghold. And the angry Indians did not welcome outsiders into their midst. Yet with the blessing of both sides I went thirteen times into the camp of the entrenched Indians. I talked with the leaders to learn their views and to give them advice. I performed numerous ceremonies for the heartbroken, for those in ill health, for the aged, and I comforted the young.

During the entire siege I prayed without ceasing for all of the people involved, both white and Indian. Still, I had not asked the FBI men and the federal marshals to come there, I had not welcomed them, and except for wanting to avoid bloodshed on both sides, I had nothing to do with them. The government spent a tremendous amount of money at Wounded Knee. Yet most if not all of the problems could have been avoided if they and the news people had just stayed away.

Finally, though, the federal officials had enough public pressure and were ready to make a peace offer. They sent word that a document would be presented to me at a place near the little township of Scenic, South Dakota. This place was right on the boundary line of the Pine Ridge Reservation. I guess the federal people felt it was best for them to be off the reservation when they made their peace gesture.

Perhaps whites who read this might wish now to answer a question: The federal officials who presented the peace document refused to cross the boundary line, although there were already federal marshals and FBI men inside the line at Wounded Knee. What does one make of this? Anyway, sixteen carloads of us Indians went to Scenic for the meeting, and the document was presented to me. It was from Washington, D.C., and my first reaction, since I did not know what it said, was to refuse it. So I asked the official offering it to me to read it. But my friends said that was not the Indian way to do this, so I took it.

Then the man who gave me the letter made arrangements for the two of us and my interpreter to be flown over the badlands in a small airplane. To this day I don't know why he did this. We just flew around while the letter was read and interpreted. I was still not happy with it, but I did feel better. The letter did not really give anything up, and it promised nothing of consequence either. It was simply a request that both sides put down their guns and forget their differences, and it included an offer to look into some of the grievances. But I liked its tone, and when we returned to Scenic, I shared this feeling with my friends. They were satisfied with it too. They urged me to keep it, and to present it to the Indians at Wounded Knee.

The next morning I took the document to Wounded Knee. As soon as I arrived I stood up with my ceremonial pipe and I prayed to God, asking for his assistance for one of his children who needed it badly this day. Then I presented the document to both sides, and everyone seemed to accept it. They were happy that peace on any terms was in sight. So I handed the document to the federal leaders, and they all signed it.

Just then a furious Sioux youth from Porcupine, wearing a colorful beaded band around his head, burst into the center of our assembled group with a rifle in his hands and shouted, "Let's wipe all of them out!" He shoved the hard gun barrel deep into my stomach and threatened to kill me on the spot. I was stunned, but in a moment I recovered saying, "My son, I have lived many years; more than enough"; then smiling, I continued, "If you are man enough, pull the trigger."

You can imagine how quiet it was, and how tense and anxious everyone became. The entire situation would explode again if he shot me. So I explained this to him, adding that it would hurt his cause if he killed me. Then when I smiled at him again, he broke down. His head fell and his shoulders drooped. He was a brave and reckless young man who was standing up for the rights and needs of his people. I appreciated that, and he saw it and knew now he had made a bad mistake. So he took his gun down and backed away. The federal marshals were greatly relieved, and they rushed up to me smiling and wanting to shake my hand. Within a few moments they were bringing me ice cream, coffee, and cigarettes.

The Indian leaders of the group that had seized Wounded Knee signed the document, and when they were done I again prayed with my pipe. No other sound could be heard. Everyone was silent as I thanked *Wakan-Tanka* for what he had accomplished for us that day. The two groups broke up and went home. People had been hurt, but all-out bloodshed had been avoided. I slept well that night for the first time in weeks. For the most part, it was young Indian people who were engaged in this bitter confrontation, and I did not want them seriously hurt. They are the future of our people. The terrible thing is that something like this will happen again. Not one of the things that caused it has been corrected. Everything is just as it was before.

I am asked now and then by Sioux people why Indians suffer as they do, whether there is a reason for it. Friends come to me and want to know what we can do to avoid such things as hunger, poverty, disease, alcoholism, immorality, family divisions, and jealousy. A long time ago the Sioux were sometimes hungry, and differences of opinion did arise now and then, but we were not confronted by the kinds of problems that plague us today. We had family unity, we had clan unity, we had social unity, we had band unity, and we had tribal unity. Then these terrible white man's curses were injected into our bloodstream, our culture, like diseases being planted in us, instead of the preventatives we should have been given. The whites have invaded us and changed our entire culture and life-style, and it has not been for the better.

The introduction of liquor is only one example of this. Most of our problems with Indian youth are due to it. But beyond this it was and is the white man who keeps us upset, uncertain, and hungry. It is the white man with his different drugs, methods, and foods who has caused new diseases among us. It is the white man with his materialism and capitalism, and his stress upon the total independence of individuals and families, who has made us poor. It is the white man who put us on reservations with poor land, and who located the reservations so far from the cities that no Sioux can work in a city and still live on the reservation. So we often have unemployment that is as high as 80 per cent. It is the white man who has taught our young people immorality, stealing, dishonesty, and disobedience. These things are contrary to our Indian way of life, and all of them have been forced upon us against our will.

Even though we have very little, family unity has been destroyed by the desire for possessions. People see what the outside world has. There is a disregard for parents and grandparents today, where once such a thing was unheard of. And there is jealousy. In the old days jealousy was despised by the Sioux, whether in a warrior society, a clan, a band, or a tribe. It was considered bad taste to envy anyone. Those who did were frowned upon, rejected, and avoided. Sometimes they were even cast out for just giving evidence of such behavior. Jealousy was detested and was unacceptable in our life-style. So the problems Indians have today are not really Indian problems in the sense that we caused them. They are the end results of our having been torn away from our culture and forced to live the white man's way. And, in the process, we have been made almost entirely dependent upon the federal government. We did not want any of this, but years of dishonesty by government officials, and even by some of our Indian leaders who joined in with them, have finally forced us into a corner where we must struggle to survive and to retain the remnants of our culture. And, incredibly enough, we are expected to accomplish what the President and the BIA want us to do at the same time.

The things being done to the Indians today might best be called silent violence. It is not necessary to have armed confrontations or to destroy with fire and guns in order to have violence. The silent violence is what is crushing the Indian people today. It is this that has brought among us drunkenness, malnutrition, starvation, disease, suffering, and an endless number of deaths.

We are kept ignorant of our rights and of the benefits due us. There is no consistent attempt to correct unjust laws and to strengthen our social and economic structure. At present, the United States Government has but one interest, which is, in our view, self-interest. This creates for them a special blindness wherein the truth cannot be seen. No one sees any longer how we actually live. The system prospers by using us, and no one really notices.

This is, in fact, a disease that has now been passed on to and has contaminated even the Sioux. Among our own now, when a person attains a little power, he also turns into an exploiter and an intimidator. This can be profitable, therefore many Indians have sought leadership with this very end in mind. Some who did so gave up the attempt along the way, and some have gone to prison for political crimes. Others have achieved what they wanted, and accordingly pose severe problems for the rest of us today.

Wakan-Tanka has told me through the spirits that one day there will be a strong leader among us, one whose word is reliable and who will do what he promises. He will be a true part of our people, suffering with them and feeling exactly as they do. The people will listen to him and will be moved to co-operate and to grow in the good things once again. Such promises are also in the Bible, and we all look forward to his arrival.

Wakan-Tanka, God, is the supreme power. He is the holiest one. And he wishes to be honored through the sacred pipe, which is our way of homage and worship. It is bad enough that the white man does not know this, but so many of the Sioux children no longer know it either. Many adult Sioux do not know that there is only one path, the pipe, to *Wakan-Tanka,* to humanhood, and to understanding.

To avoid more tragic times than those that already beset us today, and to avoid economic disaster in the United States and the world, the government must purify its conscience by recognizing the 1868 treaty that was made with us in the name of God. Its provisions must be met. And there are incredibly bad times coming upon us, coming fast like an angry, charging buffalo, because they have not been met, and because far too many people do not believe in God. Therefore, people do not understand that treaties made in His name are not to be violated. Although the 1868 treaty has been ruthlessly violated, many of the current and future problems of this country could be solved if the federal government made things right with us today, and made it possible at last for us to live as brothers under God. But if the white leaders do not follow the pathway set forth by God and that leads to Him, and if they do not choose to honor their promises, then the godly people will soon disappear, and the entire earth will need to be purified by a great catastrophe.

When I was at Bear Butte in 1965, God told me what will happen.

The end will come by fire, and a fire so great in size that it will shake and consume the entire earth. This tragic moment is very close to us now. I am already preparing for its arrival by living in strict accordance with the Sacred Pipe and *Wakan-Tanka,* because when it strikes, there will not be time to gather up clothing or other belongings. The tragedy will be that sudden. We should all turn immediately to God, because this awesome thing could come about at any moment. So prepare yourself, and be humble. Not only the Indians will need God's pity; the whole human race will need it, because so few people are living in accordance with God's wishes.

If the federal government hopes to delay or avoid these bad times, it must correct the violations of the 1868 treaty. The whole country is in terrible danger. All people need do if they want to see the truth of this is to look to their own inner spirit and conscience. It will be to them like a mirror, and they will see the truth of it for themselves.

I have said that each morning I go out to pray with my pipe. And although I no longer see it every morning as I once did, I have seen as I prayed a huge white cloud rising up from the ground and a screeching eagle flying out of it. The white cloud is a symbol of purity and honesty, and the eagle that flies out of it is a protector of the Indian. If the wrongs are corrected, there will be unity among the people. Then that white cloud of purity and honesty will spread all over the world to enfold the whole of mankind. But with every passing day I grow less hopeful about its happening. I think this is why I am seeing the cloud less often these days.

So I again warn everyone that very bad times are coming. And they can only be delayed or prevented by the use of the pipe and by honoring the treaties made with the Indians. Indian parents must take their children and pray with the pipe to God. All nationalities must stop honoring false gods and must stop making the posession of material things their supreme goal. All people must unite in recognizing God and in paying homage to Him. There must be repentance for evil acts, and there must be harmony between God and creation.

God gave the Indians the pipe, and not many others know how to use it. So their role is to support our Sacred Pipe. They must beg the governments of America and of the world to aid us in our use of the pipe for the benefit of all. There is only one proper way to use the pipe, and we know it. And one must have absolute faith in it. Without this, requests to God will not be honored, and those making them are in danger.

People ask me whether the present world will meet its end in the way the Bible says it will. The priests and others have told me what the Bible says about it. In 1965 at Bear Butte, God did tell me that the end of the world, as we have known it, is coming close. But it will not end exactly as the Bible says. God is the only one who knows the true answer, and when it is time he will tell the Indian holy men about it first. So if the world is going to end while I am still alive, Grandfather will tell me. And if I am no longer on this earth, he will tell the holy people of the Indians who are alive. He will give them a message as to exactly when and how the end will come.

This very day there is a young woman, Calf Pipe Woman, who in the company of another young lady is walking about our country. These two can change themselves into red people, white people, black people, brown people, or yellow people. They can speak any language and become whatever nationality they wish to. I can think of no reason for their being here other than the probability that the end of the world is not far off. So prepare. I have spoken. And all of this is so.

But you still want to know where hope lies. You say that I am the greatest man that has lived among the Sioux for the past thirty or more years, a holy man of great renown. You say that I have stature and am respected. And you want to know how it happens that I do not wield more influence over the youth who drink. Why, being around me as much as they are, are they not influenced more by my spiritual life? That is not an easy question you put to me, and I do not think of myself so highly as you do. But I will answer it as best I can.

I have pleaded with hundreds of teen-agers in school and out of school. I have gone from classroom to classroom giving intense lectures on how Indians should live. But it just goes in one ear and out the other. The kids look for things that offer pleasure, such as outright drinking, and social activities that lead inevitably to drinking. Besides this, the youth are not able to speak enough Lakota. So when I talk to them they do not understand much of what I am saying. Even if they do catch the meaning of it they miss its impact.

The schoolteachers talk about the same problems. They discuss responsibility and preparation for the future with the students, but at present the Indian teen-agers are not listening to anyone who speaks of such things. It is with us here like it is in so many places in the outside world, except that the Indian youth seem to be turning bad at a faster rate than anyone else as far as personal conduct is concerned.

They are more curious people. They want to experience all of the fun things at once, and this is the way it is on all the Sioux reservations. Everywhere, our young people are searching for good times to help them forget the bad times. This is especially true of the young. They drink to excess, and when they sober up they are pathetic, hungry, and tired. Worse still, there is no repentance. As soon as possible they look for something else to steal, and then they sell it for enough money to buy the liquor that sends them back through the whole miserable process again. Theft is no longer considered a bad thing among our Indian youth. It is certainly not like it was in the old days.

Things do not look good at Pine Ridge and elsewhere. Our people are busy reviving traditional customs, and that is good, but it will not be enough by itself to change the dreadful situation we are discussing.

The kind of change we really need must begin with the Tribal Council, with the highest governmental unit on the reservation. And in each of our districts there are middle-aged and elderly men, including myself, who are willing to help, to add our thoughts and counsel. We can rebuild our philosophy of life and re-establish our culture if we can prohibit liquor and other intoxicants. I am not demanding this for the whole country, I only want it for our reservations. Then if an Indian craves whiskey, let him go off the reservation, get drunk for a week or two, and only be permitted to come back when he is ready to work and be responsible.

Of course, I do not know what chance there really is of getting prohibition when even Tribal Council members have been drinking to excess. If we aren't able to cure the leaders who are afflicted with the drinking curse, there is little hope for a positive program for anyone else.

We do have a new tribal chairman, named Al Trimble, and he is the kind of man who might change the situation. The former chairman, Dick Wilson, couldn't have cared less about the drinking problem. Changes like this were the farthest thing from his mind. And even if he had been asked to begin such a program, he wouldn't have done anything about it. After all, he was in office a long time and did nothing. All he cared about was the government money that came to him in a steady stream. But Trimble is a better leader.

I'm going to talk to him. I am going to Kyle and telephone him and make an appointment for a whole day. We will lock the door so we won't be disturbed, and we will talk about these things and see what we can do about them. Then he can set up a meeting with all of the district leaders and call them in, especially the elderly people. After this they can all meet with the Tribal Council to discuss and put into practice the ideas that come forth.

I think Al Trimble will listen. The Tribal Council still has some mixed-bloods on it, but Trimble owes his election to the full-bloods, who voted 100 per cent for him. He has a political obligation, and he will listen. I want to do this; I can start it off now. I have a few things I must do around the house tomorrow, but on Friday I will call Al Trimble to arrange an appointment for the following week. Working together we can build a good road for the people to walk on.

The tribal chairman before Wilson was a better man in my estimate than Wilson. His name was Gerald One Feather, and many of the things he started were completed by Wilson, who got the credit for them. But Gerald One Feather also ignored the traditional Sioux, and a chairman cannot do that without paying a heavy price for it.

About 58 per cent of the Sioux at Pine Ridge are traditionalists, and this figure would apply to all of the reservations. These are not all full-bloods, but they are people who practice the traditional ways.

You want to know whether the elderly leaders of the reservation districts have followed the custom of coming over the years to see me to discuss politics. Many elderly people do come to visit me and to tell me what is going on at the BIA and at tribal headquarters at Pine Ridge. Now that Trimble is the new chairman, some of the Tribal Council members also visit me and tell me what is happening. Each asks my opinion and position on certain subjects. Most Tribal council members during Wilson's term of office were mixed-bloods and did not consult me. Nor did Gerald One Feather or his Tribal Council. But three fourths of the members of the present Tribal Council are traditionalists, who believe in the Indian ways, so they come to see me regularly. But I have not tried to apply political influence. When Gerald One Feather and Dick Wilson were in office, I and the other traditional leaders simply divorced ourselves from what was going on, and there was never an organized effort to deal with it.

Naturally, we did talk a great deal about it when we were together, and about what needed to be done. But we did not do a thing except to vote as a group when the opportunity came. We finally put Wilson and his friends out of office—and for good, I hope.

You ask why, then, my house was burned, since I did not oppose Wilson openly. I feel certain they did it, although I have no proof I could use in court. One reason might be that Wilson at one time brought a pickup truck loaded with liquor onto the reservation. Some of the traditional Indians turned him in and raised a fuss about it. While I was not actually involved, nevertheless I was the first one he blamed for that.

Politics did not cause open trouble between me and Wilson until Al Trimble ran for office. He got together with me and asked for the support of the traditional Sioux. I helped him obtain it, and being united, we defeated Wilson. As you might expect, Wilson did not appreciate that.

There was something else that caused problems between us. Wilson did not like the advice I gave people in moral and ethical areas. Even here though, while I did tell the traditional Sioux how I felt, and while we discussed it, I did not recommend courses of action. *Wakan-Tanka* told me never to do this, because it would cause friction among our people. Even where Al Trimble is concerned, I will only talk with him. Any course of action will be left entirely to him. I will never allow any group to organize or seek action in my name here at Pine Ridge. I have led a few groups on trips to places like Washington, D.C., and the Custer National Monument. But that is different; there we confront the United States Government in search of our rights.

I did not go to the town of Pine Ridge for three years. It was not because I feared Wilson. I was afraid that if one of his followers did something to me it would start a civil war. So I just stayed away. Now that Wilson is out of office, he has left Pine Ridge. He and his followers have just disappeared. They are not seen anywhere around the reservation. We know that some of them moved to Rapid City. That is why I only go there when I must. I don't want to run into them.

CHAPTER 19   THE PIPE
AND POWER

During the winter of 1974–75, I was very ill, and in bed either at home or at the hospital for 42 days. Before this happened, I weighed 212 pounds, and when it was over I was down to 162. My illness started before Christmas, and although I was still quite sick, just before Christmas Day I walked out of the government hospital. I was uneasy and uncomfortable because they had moved me into the section where people are put when they expect them to die. Someone was dying there nearly every day, and people were wailing and weeping constantly. I didn't like it a bit, and despite the doctor's protests, I got up and left. I went home, and on January 3, I had a major heart attack. By January 5, I was back in the hospital, and was unconscious for 2 days and 2 nights. After a few more days I was released and went home to continue my recovery.

By February 15, I was considerably improved, and I was receiving visitors according to my usual schedule. Kate protested about this because family members had to pick me up off the floor twice and she was very worried But I was able to get around, and I did. By the end of February, my interpreter, Matthew King, and I were traveling to Chicago, New York, and Washington, D.C., for meetings and appearances. Since this kind of activity places me so often in the midst of whites, you want to know whether I regret not having an education in the white man's school, and as a result not being able to speak, read, or write English. I do not regret any of it. God has guided my steps to where I am today, and what might appear to be a handicap to others is actually a source of strength to me. God communicates with me personally, and I am wealthy in spiritual information and discipline. I practice these disciplines regularly, and I live a simple life. These free my energies for the more important things I know I must do for my people. Despite my recent physical illness, which, actually, is not unusual for a man of my age, I have remained mentally well. I give God and my simple way of life credit for this.

Simple living is less wasteful and more in harmony with nature because it permits us to share our resources with all other life. Therefore I use earth's gifts sparingly and with gratitude, attempting wherever possible to replace what I consume, and I try to preserve the natural beauty of the earth. My people only need the basic necessities of life, not the luxuries. The problem is that in these modern times under white domination we are so poor we are without even the necessities. Still, despite our painful and humiliating poverty, most Sioux accept their lot and take the sorrows and the sufferings as they come. So when I visit them in their homes and see how patient they are it only fills me with resolve to try harder and harder to help them.

No, I do not regret my lack of white schooling. Spiritually, I am far richer for not having left my people in any way, and I am one with them. I share fully their lives, conditions, needs, hopes, dreams, and anguish. I have made this commitment to *Wakan-Tanka* and to them, and I will die here in their midst because it is the role I have been given. Now this part of the story is told. I have done what *Wakan-Tanka* and Grandfather commanded me to do. The tapes and the papers have not crumbled. Black Elk will be happy. I am happy. This is *waste hcá* (very good).

The year 1976 was an eventful one. Once I was well again I went on with the practice of my medicine. So I will tell you now about some of the people I healed, and also something wonderful about the Sacred Pipe at Green Grass.

In March of 1976, a large man from Devil's Lake in North Dakota came to my house. He drove up in a car, and got out with a filled pipe in his hands. He brought it into the house, lit it, and without saying a word offered it to me.

I smoked the pipe with him, and when it was finished asked him what he wanted. He was about forty years old, and quite uncomfortable when he spoke. I think it was because he was not Sioux and didn't know how I would react to that. His father was paralyzed from the lower chest down, and sitting out in the car. "Will you heal him?" the man asked.

I told him to bring his father in, and the man carried him into the house and placed him on my bed. I had Kate wrap the black cloth around my head, I prayed, did my ceremony, and gave the paralyzed man an herb medicine to drink. The man and his son stayed at my house for four days, and we repeated the ceremony four times. Each day a little of the medicine was left over, and after the treatments there was still enough for an additional four days of treatment.

The man and his son went back to Devils Lake and continued the use of the medicine. Three weeks later they returned to my house with a large supply of food, and the father, who was well now, carried it into the house himself and gave it to me.

In the spring of 1976, my long and passionate desire to see the Sacred Pipe was realized. It was the fourth time I had gone to Green Grass, and while I was there, the bundle was opened by the Keeper, and I saw the pipe. Until now I have told no one about this except my wife, Kate. There were many people in the vicinity of the building at the time, including Kate and Everett Lone Hill, but I was taken inside, I prayed with my hand on the bundle, and then it was opened for me.

When I saw the pipe I really crumbled inside. I felt completely humble, pathetic, pitiful. I don't know how long I looked at the exposed pipe, and I don't like to talk about it. I am still afraid of its sacred power, and I am thinking again about what just happened to one of our medicine man who spoke of things he shouldn't.

I will not describe the pipe, except to say that it was a very good-looking pipe. I will tell you one more thing, and it will be the last thing I have to say about the pipe. When this lady (Calf Pipe Woman) came and gave the Sioux the pipe, she told them to go and kill four warrior members of another tribe. They were to remove a little hair from each man's head and to tie it to the pipe. Also an ear was to be removed from one victim and attached to the pipe. Then they were to get two tail feathers from a golden eagle and tie these to the stem. They followed her orders completely, and those things are there. When I saw the pipe, the hair, brittle from age, was breaking in places, and the two feathers were so worn away that only the quills remained. The ear was still in perfect condition, although it was as white as tanned deer skin.

After I looked at the pipe, the Keeper placed it back in its wrappings, and the bundle was brought outside to be seen by the other Sioux assembled there. Four flags with the four sacred colors were set up to mark the corners of a medium-sized square, inside of which a bed of sage was laid. On the bed in a circle there was a string of 405 tiny tobacco bags to invite the presence of the 405 good spirits who serve *Wakan-Tanka*. The bundle itself was laid on the sage in the middle of the entire arrangement, so that the people could walk around it and still be on the sage. As they did so they walked in a clockwise direction. They also prayed, and those who were bold enough bent down to touch the holy bundle. The people left gifts there inside the string circle, gifts of money, feathers, quilts, blankets, and clothing. When all of them had done this, I collected the gifts and presented them to the Keeper, Orvall Looking Horse.

Then the Sacred Pipe bundle was picked up and returned to its building, where it was laid on its platform and covered with the buffalo robe. I placed my right hand one last time upon the robe, and after a few minutes, I left. This day marked the crowning event of my life, and I could not have been happier.

In June of 1976, while I was the intercessor for the Sun Dance at Greenwood on the Yankton Reservation, I saw in the audience a boy about eight years old who was on crutches. His right leg was sharply bent so that the knee and leg were up in the air, and he looked very sad. The dance was already in progress, but I felt so sorry for him that I went over to him and brought him out to the Sun Dance pole in the center of the mystery circle.

By now everyone was watching us; even the dancers were looking to see what was going to happen. First I walked with the boy in a circle around the pole, then I stared twice at the crutches, prayed, and took the crutches away from him. I bent down and grabbed his right leg and straightened it out until he could touch the ground with it. Then I straightened his left leg, which was bent a little from favoring the right leg, and I told him to stand up and to walk over to his parents. He did. He walked over to them and sat down between them, and everyone was overjoyed. The sound of approval and thanksgiving ran through the crowd, and it became so loud that it could be heard above the noise of the singers and the drum. If the dance had not been going on, I think the people would have shouted for joy and pounded on the drum themselves!

The boy's father rushed over to me, his face beaming with gratitude, and asked me what he could give me. The mother came to shake my hand and also asked what they could do. But I told them I did not want anything, that I was pleased to have this opportunity to perform the healing where so many people could see it and know about *Wakan-Tanka*'s power. They insisted they had to do something, though, and several weeks later they came to my house with food and other gifts.

Patients and their families often come back in later years to express their gratitude. Sometimes they come and bring me things such as coffee and sugar. They tell me it is in thanksgiving for what I have done. At other times families ask Kate and me over to their house for a big feed, serving us good meat and cake. Whenever something like that is brought or served to me, I take a small part of it outside and offer it to *Wakan-Tanka*. I make a small excavation in the earth, and after holding the food out to the west, north, east, south, up to *Wakan-Tanka* and *Tunkshila*, and finally down to Grandmother Earth, I bury it in the hole. Then I return to the house and eat the rest.

I want you to know that I am very happy and that I appreciate your interest in these things. I am going to tell you about another recent healing. Ida Two Dog is about fifty-two years old and has had serious heart trouble. In fact, at times her body literally shook from it.

When I treated her there was time to do a full ceremony. So I took singers with me and went to her house in the evening. Enough of the living room was cleared of furniture to make a space for an altar in the center of it. I made the altar with four pieces of cloth in my sacred colors. Each cloth was four by six inches, and was laid flat on the floor so as to mark the corners of a three-foot square. The square itself was covered with sage, and on the south side four eagle feathers were laid side by side with their tips toward the west.

The spirits used the feathers to fan and purify all of the air inside the room. Then I told Ida to remove her shoes and to stand barefooted on the sage in the middle of the altar. I stood to one side of her, and the usual black-cloth wrapping was used to cover my head. Then I prayed, and as the singers sang the rain song, I could see that the woman was telling the truth about her heart. I could see that it was beating irregularly. So I removed the cloth, boiled an herb medicine for her, and had her drink a glassful. Then I told her to take the remainder home and finish it. Today there is nothing wrong with her. She is well.

Only a short time ago I had a patient, forty-two years of age, who had an ugly birthmark that began at his eyes and covered the entire lower part of his face. He had gone to doctors in Denver, Omaha, Rapid City, Sioux Falls, and Hot Springs to see if they could remove it. None could, and finally he came to me. I boiled an herb, and using a cotton swab dipped in it—I wiped the birthmark area. Then I told the man to repeat this procedure every evening, just before he went to bed, for the next three days. He did as he was told, and when he woke up on the morning of the fifth day, the birthmark was gone!

I am singing to you now my healing song, each part of which ends with a soft "whoo, whoo." In this song I pray to God to help me cure the person. Then I ask Grandmother Earth to help. Following this I appeal to the directions, to the day and the night, and to the four seasons. I tell them I want this person to be able to walk with straight limbs and body again, to be healthy and to have a good heart, with love for other people. In the song, I describe the patient as a friend, because all people are my friends. I finish the song by again asking the spirits to help the patient and to return him to good health, walking in a straight path. The "whoo, whoo" is my special sound to the spirits. It is an ending remark just between us, one that is gentle and affectionate.

In the fall of 1976, a lady was brought to me from the Cheyenne River Reservation. It was about noon when they arrived. She was suffering from terrible headaches and a continual nosebleed. Doctors had burned (cauterized) her nose in an attempt to stop the bleeding, but hadn't been successful. She had not stopped bleeding for four days when they brought her to me.

To treat her I built a small fire outside, near where the sweatlodge is, and set out my flags. Then I took a hollowed-out buffalo horn and with a knife scraped some shavings into the red-hot ashes to make smoke and incense. We stood together by the fire and I put a blanket over both of us—to capture the smoke and so that we were in darkness. I prayed, and soon the spirits helped me see that the swelling in her nose was receding, and that the drops of blood were slowing down. Pretty soon they stopped completely.

When she left for home I gave her the rest of the buffalo horn to take with her. As of now she has had no more headaches and no more bleeding.

You want to know why, since I have made such broad and positive claims, everyone does not come to me for healing. One reason is that I do not advertise for or encourage patients to come. So only a modest number of people here and there know what I can do. And those who are healed do not talk about it among themselves and spread the news. That is not the Sioux way. If a thing is holy and sacred, if it is a miracle, it is not talked about. It is too special for that. Visions we receive are in the same category. They are something personal between *Wakan-Tanka* and the seeker that affects the whole of his life. Even the person's family will not discuss it or tell their friends.

There are other reasons. Many people are cured in other ways. Some go to the hospitals. Some are cured by other medicine men, and by their own praying and singing of sacred songs. Some of the Christian Indians have been taught to have no regard for our medicine men, and will not go to them. More than a few have been told by their priests or pastors that medicine men are witch doctors.

You have also mentioned that at the time of our last talk together in Rapid City, Kate was a patient at the Indian hospital. She was being treated for pneumonia and had been in bed for ten days or so before we visited her. She was doing quite well though, and was expecting to go home in another week. You want to know why I had not healed her if I can indeed heal any illness? The answer is that I often know when people are becoming ill, and I knew it was happening to Kate. But she didn't bring me a filled pipe or tobacco of any kind and ask for my help, so I just couldn't help her! I must remain true to my rules. I cannot, even for those I dearly love, violate procedures that *Wakan-Tanka* has directed me to follow as a holy man.

You ask me whether I can lose my medicine power? Any medicine man can lose it by failing to do a ceremony properly, or by not doing something *Wakan-Tanka, Tunkashila,* or the spirits tells him to do, or

13. "I ran barefooted behind the hearse, all the way to the Episcopal church where my father was buried."

14. "He was a spirit deer, a holy animal."

15. "Then I knocked on what appeared to be a door in the rock wall."

16. "When we talk, they come and sit down by me, just as a person will do."

17. "Bear Butte is an absolutely spectacular place, and it is easy to see why the Indians would consider it sacred and choose it as a vision-questing place."

18. Fools Crow in his ceremonial costume at Bear Butte as photographed by the author in October 1976.

by bad conduct or bad-mouthing someone. However, he can regain the power by making things right again. He has to right the wrong. He must do more than apologize and say he is sorry. The Indian way is to show sincerity by doing things over a long period of time for those who are offended. One must show his remorse and continue to show it until his power returns and he can heal again.

You have to demonstrate your change of heart by thinking good thoughts and doing good works over a long period of time, and when God wants you to do something a certain way, you must do it just like that, or the gifts and powers will be taken away from you. Then to get them restored by *Wakan-Tanka* you are required to treat him like you would an offended person. There must be continual meditation, prayer, and sweatlodge purification, until at last your change of heart and desire are again proven. You know when you have your power back by your ability to cure again and by your inner feeling.

But all of these years I have tried to be a good man, and I have never lost my power. I am an old man now, and I am not even concerned about this. I don't even feel the threat of losing my power.

When a person is right with God he always has a special feeling. When I am curing I feel a charge of power and I am excited! I know about these things because they are going on inside of me. When people come to me for help, for an ailment or curing or whatever, as I do my ceremony I feel the strength, the energy, building up. And I know I can cure them. The spirits let me know it. They even come inside of me and give me confidence and strength. And I feel good about this as it builds up inside of me.

But that is enough about my healing and medicine powers. We should talk now about the problems that exist between the Sioux and the United States Government. Much of my time in recent years has been given over to this, and *Wakan-Tanka* wants the world to know the more important things I have done and said.

As you know, the Teton Sioux have attempted for many years now to get the government to return the Black Hills to us. We believe the Black Hills belong to us, and that the government does not have legal title to them. They have offered us money to settle the claim, but we do not really want the money, we want the Black Hills. That would give us jobs and incomes and a chance to live like human beings again. So I have gone several times to Washington, D.C., to talk about this, but it is only now that the government people have begun to listen. Therefore I am able to say more, and I want you to know what I say.

CHAPTER 20   WALKING A HARD ROAD

FOOLS CROW CONCLUDES

In September of 1975 I led a large delegation of Sioux to Washington in an attempt to see the President to get him to discuss the reservation problems. Usually I become involved in things like this by letters. In this instance the letters came from the two U.S. senators from South Dakota. They invited me to do this.

I was treated very well, like a baby. I slept in a fine hotel room and was even assigned two black security guards to remain by my door and see that no one bothered me or did anything to me. In fact, these guards were very thoughtful. Every now and then they would ask, "Fools Crow, do you want something to eat—sandwiches, coffee, anything at all?"

My room was on the second floor; some of the Sioux had rooms on the first floor, and others had to stay in the hotel basement. A number of them did some drinking, which didn't please me, and stayed in town longer than I did. They weren't satisfied with the results of the trip, and when they ran out of funds they probably had to find shelter and food in a church. I stayed only four days.

In the usual circumstance, when I am asked to come to Washington the government people have tickets and travel funds awaiting me at Rapid City Airport. That's the way it was done this time. And, contrary to what one Indian newspaper said, I did see the President, Gerald Ford.

I did not have a meeting with him, but the President arranged for a special assistant and his aides to meet with several of us and to hear and write down everything we had to say. The assistant's name was Theodore C. Marrs. He was White House Assistant for Human Relations, and he was extremely kind and attentive to us. We all sat around a long conference table, and several congressional people joined us. Just as the meeting was beginning, the door opened and a soldier came in followed by President Ford. Everyone stood up, and he walked directly to me. He shook my hand and said, "As long as I am here in Washington I will help you too." That's all he said, and there was no opportunity to mention the Black Hills. Then as he turned to leave he gave me a small stone, a desk weight, with the presidential seal on it.

When I had my meeting with the presidential assistant I was able to state my case fully. When it was over, Mr. Marrs told me that many Indian groups came to Washington to discuss their problems, but they always ended up arguing among themselves to the point that it appeared they might even fight one another. He was pleased now because this was not happening with me. Therefore I had been listened to with special concern and interest. The government representatives were very happy about it, and wanted to hear all I had to say. So, in addition to the statements I made at the meeting, I was taken to a small room where two secretaries recorded my thoughts in shorthand, after which I was told that this was done because the President himself wanted to know how I felt and everything I was concerned about.

When the meetings and note-taking were done, some of the government people and we Sioux had an expensive dinner together. The next day, some security people took me to the graves of John and Robert Kennedy, and to the tomb of the Unknown Soldier. I prayed over each of these. I was also taken to where the original copy of the treaty of 1868 was kept. It was a moving experience for me, and they gave me a chair to sit in while they brought out the treaty. I was asked to pray there with my pipe, and I did, that everyone would understand what the treaty really said and that its terms would be fulfilled.

The most memorable part of my trip was yet to come. With Senator James Abourezk of South Dakota making the arrangements, on September 5, 1975, I became the first Indian holy man to lead the opening prayer for a session of the United States Senate.

That was really an important trip for me. Then next one I should tell you about was made on June 25, 1976, when more than five hundred Indians went to the Custer battlefield in Montana to attend the one-hundredth anniversary of Custer's last stand. I was the real leader of the group, although AIM spokesmen did most of the talking, and I placed a wreath on the ground in memory of the Indian warriors who died there.

Sad to say, this centennial event attracted very little press or public attention, I think mostly because the Park Service played it down, fearing violence from us if they made too much of the ceremony. As Indian militancy has increased in recent years, the annual re-enactment of the battle, which featured local whites as Custer's soldiers and Crow Indians as the attackers, has been discontinued. But we did not disrupt the ceremony, although some Indians did take the stage before it began to explain their protest. Earlier, some Indians sang and beat a large drum in the distance, and the day after the ceremony we held our first victory celebration ever for the battle. The original Sioux warriors were too pressed by the soldiers to do it in 1876. There is no memorial to the Indians who died in the Custer battle; the place is known only as the Custer Battlefield National Monument.

In September of 1976, I met with the Lloyd Means Subcommittee on Interior and Insular Affairs, and at that time I gave a lengthy speech concerning the views of the Sioux regarding the treaty of 1868 and the Black Hills. Later on, it was printed in poster form and posted all over the reservations. The speech was entitled, "We Shall Never Sell Our Sacred Black Hills," by Frank Fools Crow, Lakota Chief, and Frank Kills Enemy, Lakota Headman. The subheading says it is a "Joint statement of Frank Fools Crow and Frank Kills Enemy on behalf of the Traditional Lakota Treaty Council before the Honorable Lloyd Means Subcommittee on Interior and Insular Affairs" (September 10, 1976).

This is what I told the committee:

"*Kola* [friends]. I am Frank Fools Crow, chief of the Lakota, and I am here today with Frank Kills Enemy, one of the most respected headmen and also an expert on Indian treaty rights. Before we begin, I would like to ask you why when we speak you do not listen, and when you listen, you do not hear, and when you hear us, you do not choose to understand what we say. This is one time that I ask you to listen carefully and understand what we have to say.

We have come here from Pine Ridge today to discuss this House bill [H.R. 14629], which permits the tribal councils and the people they represent to get interest on the $17.5 million award given by the Indian Claims Commission. That interest, I believe, amounts to $85 million. Our people have been holding meetings on this Black Hills Claim for many years and we have just held such a meeting at Porcupine on September 8 and 9, 1976. At this meeting, the people authorized us to come to this hearing today and speak for them. The people unanimously reaffirmed our long-standing position that the Black Hills are not for sale under any circumstances. We are therefore standing behind the resolution we passed at Fort Yates in February of this year. That resolution, my friends, reads:

RESOLUTION ON 1868 TREATY

WHEREAS, a meeting of all Sioux Tribes concerned with the 1868 Treaty was called by the Standing Rock Sioux and all elected and traditional leaders were invited, and

WHEREAS, during this meeting, presentations regarding the Black Hills were made by Larry Leventhal, attorney, traditional people and elected leaders, and it being the consensus of all present, the traditional people held a meeting and delegates of eight (8) Sioux Reservations were present.

BE IT RESOLVED, the delegates of the eight (8) Sioux Reservations have unanimously agreed that all land involved in the 1868 Treaty is not for sale, and all monies appropriated for such sale will not be accepted by members of the traditional people of each reservation, and

BE IT FURTHER RESOLVED, that the judgment of this Black Hills case immediately implement the overall and complete jurisdiction and sovereignty of and by Indian people of the Sioux Nation.

"Many people cannot and refuse to understand why the Lakota people do not want to sell the Black Hills and have taken this position. I am therefore going to explain our reasons, because the discussions surrounding this claim and the acceptance of it will have very far-reaching effects. I do not want our people, many years from now, to think that we have sold out. We will never sell out. I am eighty-six years of age and Mr. Kills Enemy is eighty-two. Our only concern here today is for the best interests and welfare of our people and future generations of our people.

"I have some comments I would like to make on what will be going on here today.

"On all our reservations today, there are tribal councils operating under the 1934 Indian Reorganization Act. These councils were placed on the reservations by the United States Government to replace our traditional councils. These puppet governments are oftentimes the most corrupt governments around and bring out the very worst in the white-man system of governments. Councilmen on these puppet governments always represent the view of the white man because they are indoctrinated by the white man to act like this. These types of people are on the council because very few of our traditional people vote in these white-man elections. I am told that only 30 per cent of our people vote.

These councilmen do not represent the majority of the people on the reservation. Naturally, many of them are here today to urge the acceptance of this bill, as they have been brainwashed to do by the white man.

"I want to repeat that there can never be an acceptance of this bill or the total Black Hills Claim under any circumstances. This is the wish of the people. We have a treaty and it requires three quarters of all adult male members to sign before our land can be sold. I believe that this provision was stuck in the treaty by the white man because Lakota do not sell their land. The white man claims that he is not bound by the three-quarters provision of the treaty. This *Lonewolf* v. *Hichcock* case has been explained to me and I have to laugh at the white man and his views. This case says only that the white man can break treaties with Indians any time he wants to. Let me tell you, my friends, that Mr. Kills Enemy has a book that tells that the United States commissioners who signed the 1868 treaty were in Chicago two or three days before they signed it, and they were passing resolutions that were designed to break it. After these resolutions were passed, the commissioners signed it. The treaty was broken by the white man before it was even signed by him. But we Lakota are more honorable men. We have signed the treaty and we will try to live by it and respect it. Even though this treaty may not be binding on the white man, it is binding on us until we vote it out. It says that three quarters of the Lakota adult male members must sign before land can be sold and the Lakota people can never accept any payment until this provision is fully complied with.

"The Black Hills are sacred to the Lakota people. Both the Sacred Pipe and the Black Hills go hand in hand in our religion. The Black Hills is our church, the place where we worship. The Black Hills is our burial grounds. The bones of our grandfathers lie buried in those hills. How can you expect us to sell our church and our cemeteries for a few token white-man dollars? We will never sell.

"We know the underlying policy behind the Claims Commission Act and we are not fooled. The government intends to clear title to the land illegally taken, to clear their own conscience, then terminate us. I see this come out in the testimony of government witnesses in past hearings. For example, on page 13 of the Senate subcommittee hearings on S. 2780 held on August 13, 1976, the witness answered Senator Abourezk's statement on how acceptance of the bill would be a disservice to the Indian people. The witness said:

> . . . by constantly bringing up the ancient wrongs which were supposed to have been settled once and for all by the Indian Claims Commission Act and having them litigated over and over again rather than forgetting the ancient wrongs and

let the very salutory effect of the doctrine of *res judicata* take
its effect as it does normally in any judicial proceedings in the
country.

"These wrongs only happened yesterday and are not ancient wrongs.
And I wonder where the white man ever got the idea that these wrongs
had to be settled in his courts, by his rules. Anyone can win a ball game
if he makes up his own rules. But whatever the rules, and whatever the
Claims Commission awards for the Black Hills, please remember that
we will never sell.

"There can only be one settlement for the Black Hills. The Black
Hills must be immediately returned to the rightful owners, the Lakota
people. After that, we can talk about compensation for damages done
to the fruits taken from the land. We should be paid for everything
taken from the land at the value they are worth today, since the land is
still rightfully ours today. But our people are a generous people and our
people are willing to accept one half the value of everything taken at
the value they are worth today.

"The Claims Commission, an agency of the United States Government, has stated that the taking of the Black Hills was illegal, and the
commission claimed also that it could have been by eminent domain.
We also understand that under the white-man laws, the rules of the
game that have been imposed in this claim, that land can be acquired in
only three methods: one, by discovery; two, by extinguishment of title;
and three, by sale. There certainly has never been any discovery of our
land by the white man. We discovered it first, because we have always
been here. The white man recognized this right; that is why they had to
enter into these treaties with us. These treaties recognized our title to
the Black Hills and other land and acknowledged our right to exist as a
nation without being terminated and placed under state jurisdiction. I
believe the white-man Constitution also recognizes this right. Also,
there has never been any conquest of the Sioux Nation by the United
States. It was the United States that came to us and asked for peace
after we continually defeated them in over twenty-three years of war.
With the exception of the Blue Water Creek and Wounded Knee massacres and maybe one small battle called the Box Wagon Fight in Montana, we defeated the United States in every encounter. We have not
been conquered by friends and instead have lived in peace with the
United States in accordance with the treaty as equals. And also, there
has never been a sale of the Black Hills, because there has never been
an acceptance of the government's offer to buy. What the decision of
the Claims Commission amounts to is an offer, although they do not
wish to call it that. By deceit, they are trying to get us to accept this

offer by telling us that we have no choice but to accept this offer, the United States can never have clear and legal title on their land because their titles are only as good as their government's. I would like to tell our IRA Tribal Council friends that this is the only reason that the United States is so anxious to get the Indian people to accept the award. They only want to clear their own illegal title in an underhanded method. We do not believe the United States Government has the power to eminent domain over us, anymore than we have the power of eminent domain over them. This is because we are equal nations living side by side. We are citizens of our own nations. But even if the government has this power, as the claims commission stated, and could have taken the Black Hills by eminent domain, the fact remains that it did not do so. Therefore, the Black Hills were taken by an illegal act and the government does not have any legal title whatsoever on our sacred hills.

"We understand that over 80 per cent of the Black Hills is still under the control of the United States. This must be immediately returned to the Lakota people and negotiations must begin for the remainder in individual ownership. We know the white people living in the hills now love it. We love it for many of the same reasons and more importantly because they are our sacred grounds. So these white people should understand why we will not sell. The Oglala Lakota have always been the caretakers of the Black Hills and it is appropriate that I have been allowed to talk here today defending the sale of these hills for my people and other Lakota people from our other Lakota tribes.

"Before I close, I have one statement to make about the attorneys representing the tribal councils. Naturally, at this stage of the game, they would rather get 10 per cent of $102 million rather than 10 per cent of $17.5 million. But they are the only ones who stand to gain from these claims. They testify only for their own self-interests.

"Most of these attorneys have worked hard for the puppet tribal governments that they represent. They do not represent us and the majority of the people on the reservations who reject the claims. They have never consulted us, the silent majority, to get our views on the sale. If they would have, they would have seen the majority of us are against the sale of the Black Hills.

"These tribal attorneys, many of them are of the Jewish people. They should look at their own history and hold their heads in shame for what they are trying to talk us into doing here. They lost their lands for almost two thousand years and have just got them returned. They lost many of their people throughout the years fighting for their homeland, but not as many people as we lost fighting for ours. Yet they stand here very eagerly trying to talk us into selling our land when they know the United States does not have good legal title. It is understandable that they do this because they too are white men. We wonder if they will be willing to sell Israel to the Arabs for $17.5 million plus interest.

"Also, we have been told that the passage of this bill today is 20 to 1 against passage. These odds are not good. I say this because I do not want to hear the attorney blaming us for the rejection of this bill after today. It is easy to use us as their scapegoats when they have to tell their puppet governments that the bill was defeated. I wish to emphasize again that our only concern here today is to restate our position that the Black Hills cannot and will not be sold under any circumstances and we are here today to protect our people.

"Before I go, I would like to attach to our statement a statement from the Standing Rock Lakota people. They have not been allowed the talk today, and I think what they have to say should be heard. *Hau. Hece tu yelo.*"

The statement from the Standing Rock people supported everything I had said to the Lloyd Means Subcommittee on Interior and Insular Affairs. These are bitter words though, and I am not a bitter or a complaining person. I don't like to be like this, but the situation on our reservations has become almost unbearable today. My people would like to just live our traditional life, but it so hard to do this with things the way they have been and are now. What else can I do but speak out?

Extreme political tension has added to our other problems and has led to an explosive situation that has shown no sign of coming to an end. And the circumstances at the adjoining Rosebud Reservation are little better. People on both reservations have been run down by unknown terrorists in automobiles. Cars have been forced off the road and their occupants pulled out and beaten. Readily available liquor only fuels the problem, and has given the ones who do this the courage to act. Therefore, even peaceful people dare not go far from home after dark without a loaded rifle in their car, and this includes the elderly people such as me. Even at my age I am forced to protect my family. The people at Pine Ridge live in a climate of fear and tension.

While official police figures show a much lower total, we Oglalas claim that more than one unsolved murder a week was committed at Pine Ridge in 1975, and that a total of eighty had been reached by mid-October.

Even Dick Wilson had to ask the U. S. Department of Justice for protection for himself and his supporters. When in March of 1975, along with at least thirty of his supporters, he received a subpoena to appear in Rapid City before a federal grand jury convened to look into recent incidents of violence and disruption on or near the Pine Ridge Reservation, he claimed that he had been shot at eight times since the takeover of Wounded Knee in 1973. He also charged that during the past three years he knew of at least one hundred incidents of shooting either at people or property by AIM members and their supporters. Notice that Wilson did not charge the traditionalists with the shootings. He knows that the traditionalists do not resort to violence or even to such common things as protest marches where their own people are concerned.

Nevertheless, in April of 1975, both my life and Matthew King's life were openly threatened by Wilson supporters. Soon thereafter, eight or nine rifle shots were fired into Matthew King's house. And after this, on May 3, while Kate and I were attending the first spring ceremony of the year at Eagle Butte on the Cheyenne River Reservation, our little house was ransacked and burned to the ground.

Frictions do not only exist among our Indian groups; an equally grim situation has come into being around the borders of the reservation as tensions and hatreds between whites and Indians have increased to the point where they are also explosive.

The whites have good reason to be alarmed and angry. Radical Indians have caused many problems in the towns located near the borders of the reservations of Pine Ridge, Rosebud, and Sisseton-Wahpeton. Automobiles belonging to whites have been burned and stolen, and a number of fires have been set in white-owned haystacks and grassland. At Sisseton-Wahpeton, the Indians have openly challenged the rights of whites to hunt and fish there. Many whites are worried now about driving through the Pine Ridge Reservation on the main highway they once used without concern.

But we Indians are so poor, so frustrated, and we have been so bound up in our circumstances that we feel we have little to lose. Even the questionable attention collected by AIM has given a much-needed boost to the Indians' dignity and self-esteem. The traditionalists do not like violent tactics, so we do not support AIM anymore. But they have accomplished things that our passive methods did not accomplish.

A century of Indian-white relationships have not benefited the Indian to any extent. In 1974, Sioux families on reservations had annual incomes of less than $1,900, an average of less than $400 per person. Unemployment ranged from 40 per cent to 80 per cent, depending on the season. Yet our expenses for food, clothing, auto fuel, housing, and utilities are the same, if not more, as for anyone else in the United States. Both the poverty and the crime rates at Pine Ridge are easily the worst in the nation. We Sioux feel deprived of our reservation land as well as our sacred Black Hills. Whites have been able, with BIA assistance, to lease or even purchase at very low rates much of the land originally committed to our Sioux reservations. White ranchers live on scattered farms throughout reservation land and do very well while the Indians suffer. Many of the businesses on the reservations are white-owned and -operated. Banks are run by whites, and because their loans are already committed to white ranchers, the banks will not take any risks by making loans to Indians who might compete. In our own country, we Sioux are more often than not treated either as second-class citizens or as foreigners. In the banks, the markets, the stores, and out on the streets, we are eyed and treated with suspicion.

I know that statistics do not move people; only involvement does. But a few government figures might help people understand what I am saying. A recent investigation by the Senate Permanent Investigations Subcommittee revealed such things as this: the death rate for Indians is forty times higher than it is for any other group in America. The best government-built houses, which the Sioux must buy if they want one, are the cheapest plywood, and have no insulation to keep away heat or subzero temperatures. Indians suffer sixty times more dysentery, thirty times more strep throat, eleven times more hepatitis, and ten times more tuberculosis than other Americans. Twenty-nine of the fifty-one hospitals maintained for Indians by the Department of Health, Education, and Welfare do not meet the minimum standard set by the government.

There are, of course, many Indians like me who care deeply about finding a solution to the reservation problems. We continue to believe that someone important someplace cares and will do something before our situation becomes impossible. Until then, we Sioux must express our grievances in every possible way. So we do everything from filing lawsuits to organizing protest trips to Washington, D.C., and other places, going wherever national attention might be gained. Since I am a Sioux leader, I am often asked by other Indians to join in these, and when I do, other leaders will also take part, because we all continue to hope that a time will come when we can again touch the happiness we knew in the old days, and which we see most of the people in America touching most of the time.

A leader and a medicine man walks a hard road and carries a heavy burden. I could even be praying and crying at my father's or mother's grave, and if someone brought me a pipe I would have to leave there and go. But that is my life, and now I have told you about it as *Wakan-Tanka* instructed me to do. I will continue to pray and to do my healing ceremonies until I die. And I will continue to love and to help all people, the black, the yellow, and the white, as well as my own. The last thing I would like to do is to tell you the prayer I gave before the United States Senate in 1975. It was a prayer offered to all of the people of America, and I would like them to hear it.

In the presence of this house, Grandfather, *Wakan-Tanka,* and from
the directions where the sun sets,
and from the direction of cleansing power,
and from the direction of the rising sun,
and from the direction of the middle of the day,
Grandfather, *Wakan-Tanka,*
Grandmother, the Earth who hears everything,
Grandmother, because you are woman, for this reason you are kind,
I come to you this day.

To tell you to love the red men, and watch over them,
and give these young men the understanding
because, Grandmother, from you comes the good things,
good things that are beyond our eyes to see have been blessed in
    our midst,
for this reason I make my supplications known to you again.

On this day, on this great island, Grandfather,
upon which I stand, I make this prayer to you,
for those of us who are in this house.

Give us a blessing so that our words and actions be one in unity,
and that we be able to listen to each other,
in so doing, we shall with good heart walk hand in hand to face
    the future.

This is what I want for all of us,
for this reason, Grandfather and Grandmother, I make this
    thanksgiving prayer.
You give me this Sacred Pipe with which I pray to say thank you.
So be it.

In the presence of the outside, we are thankful for many blessings.
I make my prayer for all people, the children, the women,
    and the men.
I pray that no harm will come to them,
and that on the great island, there be no war,
that there be no ill feelings among us.
From this day on may we walk hand in hand.
So be it.[22]

CHAPTER 21 A NOBLE LEGACY

Fools Crow had promised we would go together to Bear Butte and see where he vision-quested, especially where he walked into the rock cliff in 1965. So one day in June of 1975, after we had visited awhile and had lunch, we made preparations to drive to the Black Hills and Bear Butte. The party consisted of Kate; Fools Crow's son-in-law, Everett Lone Hill; Everett's wife, Ruth; Dallas Chief Eagle, and myself.

Just as we were about to leave, Fools Crow came out of his house with something in his hands. It was the ceremonial pipe Iron Cloud had given him in 1917, and which Fools Crow had used in every ceremony he had performed from that day until now. To my astonishment, he said that he wanted me to have it. For the moment I could not really believe it. I expected it would either be kept in his family or else passed on to the Oglala tribe, to a close friend, or to the person who would carry on Fools Crow's work. But he meant it, and after praying with it he handed it to me, using the traditional four gestures to do so. I refused it the first three times, to indicate I would be genuine in my use and the keeping of it. When I did take it on the fourth offering I was truly overwhelmed.

Later, as we were driving along, Dallas told me there were a thousand Indian and white people who would give anything to have that pipe, and that he too was stunned Fools Crow had decided to pass it on to me. Dallas felt that the pipe should really be given to me at Bear Butte. It would be the ideal location, since Fools Crow's life had been so singularly blessed in his vision quests there. We could also take still photographs and movies of the presentation, and thus have a permanent record of it. So we decided to do it that way.

Fools Crow, Kate, Everett, and Ruth went in Fools Crow's station wagon, and Fools Crow placed his loaded, high-powered rifle in the back. We would be returning through the area of Scenic after dark, and it was a remote and particularly hazardous part of the reservation. A number of automobiles had been fired upon there, and some had been stopped and their occupants dragged out and beaten by drunken young Indians.

Dallas and I went in my car, and we were on our way by 10:30 A.M. It was a beautiful day, and near Scenic, we stopped for a few minutes at the spot where Fools Crow had received the historic letter from federal officials at the time of the seizure of Wounded Knee. We had lunch in Rapid City, and it was another half hour from there to Bear Butte. We arrived about 2:00 P.M.

We approached the famous mountain from the south, and since we had followed a route that took us through a mountainous area, we could not see it until we were less than two miles away. From some approaches it can be seen from a distance of twenty-five or more miles, but when we first saw it, it was already huge, and looming up like a mammoth round-topped pyramid above the lower surrounding hills. Its elevation is 4,422 feet, and it rises 1,200 feet above the surrounding plains.

Bear Butte is an inactive volcano, and except for the very top on its westernmost point, the volcanic cone itself is covered with only a few trees and purple rock. On the cone's southeastern side and next higher peak, there are wild mahogany and yellow pine trees at the lower level. This is as high up as the visitor's road goes. A dense growth of evergreens begins there and runs all the way to the top. Off to the east side of the cone is a third peak. This part is almost all sheer and rugged rock, and it looks much like the spiny ridge of a monumental dinosaur's body and tail. It is here that Fools Crow walked into the cliff and talked with *Wakan-Tanka*. Bear Butte is an absolutely spectacular place, and it is easy to see why the Indians would consider it sacred and desirable for a vision-questing place.

A guide was present at the visitor's parking area, and when we introduced Fools Crow to him, he showed instant interest. He had heard of the famous Ceremonial Chief. Before long he disappeared, and shortly thereafter the head ranger drove up to visit with Fools Crow. He knew all about him, and had wanted to meet him for a long time.

When the head ranger left, Fools Crow put on his ceremonial garments, including his beautiful full-tailed headdress, and walked a short way up the trail that leads from the visitor's area to the top of the Butte. Each time he had vision-quested there, he had climbed this very trail. He pointed to where the spirit deer first appeared on the path. Then he described again how the spirit deer had rolled and cavorted in the meadow.

We took some still pictures of Fools Crow and Kate, and also some movie footage. Fools Crow pointed out the arrowhead-shaped opening in the cliff that marked the spot where he walked through the door. It was an incredible climb to get there, and most assuredly he could not have made it without the spirits' help, but I did not doubt that it happened exactly as he said.

Fools Crow gave me Iron Cloud's pipe a second time. After performing a pipe ceremony with it, Fools Crow handed it to me by again using the four gestures, while Dallas recorded it on movie film.

It was late in the day by now, and Dallas and I walked down to the meadow so I could see where the sweatlodges were set up. We examined the framework of one only recently used by someone, and then our group returned to Rapid City for dinner. After dinner, we went to a supermarket and stocked up on groceries for Fools Crow and Kate, and then we headed for Pine Ridge and Fools Crow's house.

Nighttime had fallen and it was pitch dark when we crossed the northern part of the badlands and passed through the town of Scenic. About a half mile beyond Scenic, Fools Crow's car slowed momentarily ahead of us and swung in a wide arc off the right edge of the highway. As his headlights caught two parked cars at the side of the road, we saw perhaps eight young Indian men standing by them and waving frantically at him to stop. I thought we were in serious trouble. But Fools Crow kept going, and Dallas and I were not about to stop either. It was the very kind of situation we anticipated, and both our cars went flying by. As we did so, they seemed suddenly to change their minds, for they ceased waving at us to stop, and, in fact, motioned us on. When we were close enough to see their faces, it could be seen that they were all so drunk they could hardly stand. I shuddered to think of what might happen to anyone else going that way alone that night.

Fools Crow turned off on the side road to his house, and Dallas and I continued on the main road to our motel at Martin. The next morning we returned to get Fools Crow and Kate, and brought them to the town of Martin to continue working on the book. While we were in Martin, Dallas had one further suggestion regarding the pipe. It was to have an attorney draw up a paper testifying to Fools Crow's giving it to me, so that no one could ever question it. So we went to the office of Frederic R. Cozad, and he was kind enough to compose a detailed letter covering the presentation.

Thinking again about that near incident at Scenic, I am forced, as I consider reservation conditions and what Fools Crow has had to say about them, to wonder whether information like this will ever again be available from a traditional Sioux elder statesman. But there is little more to be said now. Fools Crow has obeyed *Wakan-Tanka* and told as much of his story as he feels he can and should tell. He is very old, and has often said that he will soon die. Perhaps he will. Right now he is weatherbound in his tiny, uninsulated home out there on the reservation, and I wonder how he and Kate are making it. South Dakota, along with much of the nation, is enduring one of the worst cold spells in history. Does he have enough wood, and is he well enough to go outside and chop it?

I find some comfort in remembering that the Sioux have been through incredible circumstances for a hundred years, and survived them. Fools Crow has been one of these, and it is my hope that he will be here to see the green grass come up in the spring. Whichever it is to be, he has already left a noble legacy. Fools Crow, grandson of Knife Chief and son of Eagle Bear, has lived up to his name. He has fulfilled his role, and will never be forgotten by the Sioux, by other Indians, or by his white friends.

In July of 1975, the Rapid City *Journal* carried an article, whose byline was Sheridan, Wyoming. It stated, "Frank Fools Crow, a Dakota Sioux holy man, has been named Indian of the Year by the Indian members of the All-America Indian Days board of directors. Fools Crow, 85, a resident of Kyle, South Dakota, was chosen from among nominations submitted by tribal councils from throughout the country." In my view, it was a fitting tribute to a truly remarkable man.

APPENDIX AND NOTES

Several of the articles quoted in this Appendix are so extensive as to be unusual insertions for a book. But they are from magazines long out of print and copyright, and they express most plainly and fully the mood of non-Indians about Indians at the turn of the century. They will help those unacquainted with the situation to understand how it was among the whites, and thus to compare their thoughts with those of Fools Crow. A few short notes are not enough. One must know the whole story. Some time ago, I found in a used-book store two volumes of painstakingly collected and valuable articles about Indians. They were taken from old magazines and newspapers and pasted up by some unknown person—who, I regret to say, often cut from his articles the names of the authors and the publishers. So some articles that I am including in the text and the notes do not cite their sources.

1. Agnes Dean Cameron: "I wouldn't stuff these black-haired heads with the names of the rivers of Africa or the heights of the mountains of Asia; mixed circulating decimals are of less value to them than mixed farming. When an Indian boy or girl leaves school and seeks employment, the question will not be: "How much do you know?" but: "What can you do?" Not what school did you come from, but what has that school done to make you a useful worker in a work-a-day world?

"From white or red, 'I went through college' is a poor plea for preferment with the hard-headed business man who has to be 'shown' every time. If the raw farm apprentice the first week can cure Dobbin of the colic or rescue the old muley cow from the muskeg, it will go further with the farmer than cube root or college athletics.

"Teach the boys to till the ground and to splice ropes and mend wagons and shoe horses. Make a specialty of what lies nearest his own home—prunes, or wheat, or salmon, or sheep, or cattle, or whatever it may be. Let the boy be 'long' on some one thing. He is to be a workman, is it too much to hope to make of him the workman with high ideals?

"Let the girls read and write and sew and learn how to milk cows and cook good dinners and ward off tuberculosis from the next generation. If Indian young men and women can do this and with it acquire also a taste for good reading, they are independent and self-supporting citizens already, and so 'better educated' than 50 per cent of their white cousins, though these wear pins of Greek-letter societies and talk with the tongues of men and angels.

"The Indians of today have in their own persons enough to counteract many generations of standing still and slipping back. There is a necessity for concentration and nervous dynamic force. As one little chap writing back to his old teacher puts it: 'Give my best regards to all the boys, and tell them they *must step lively in the good path.*'

"If the teacher can send away his dusky disciples with a wish to be straight and clean and honorable and kindly, to abominate a lie and to play the game because he himself in comings-in and goings-out among them has tried to do all these things, then the 40,000 embryo citizens are qualifying for enrollment in the Big School of the asphodel meadows, where we all take seats on the primary-benches and individually face the stern demand of Tomlinson: 'By the worth of the body that once ye had, give answer, What have you *done?*' "

2. F. W. Blackmar: "The education which is forced can in no way be as beneficial as that which springs spontaneously within the pupil, but it is the best we have to give the Indian, with the hope that there may spring up within him what may lead him in due time to higher development.

"The recent law passed for the compulsory education of Indians is a step in the right direction. In time it may be made of more permanent value by development and extension. Although we may urge that these people might ultimately be persuaded to adopt voluntarily the means of a higher culture, yet there is no time to wait for such developments in the case of the Indians of today. Their immediate education is their only salvation. They must be forced as far as possible to transform their mode of living in accordance with the customs of modern industrial and civil life.

"It is not to be supposed that parents of Indian children are capable of determining whether education is good for their children or not. Indeed, it is hardly conceivable that those who have reached advanced years would willingly turn away from their savage life, when we consider the past relations of the United States Government to its Indian wards, as they may be called. The Government may stand in *in loco parentis,* and may feel great responsibility for the Indians, but what is to be done must be done at once, and thoroughly, or the good which has already been gained will be lost.

"The compulsory education act passed by Congress and approved March 1891, provides as follows:

" '. . . the Commission of Indian Affairs, subject to the direction of the Secretary of the Interior, is hereby authorized and directed to make and enforce by proper means such rules and regulations as will secure the attendance of Indian children of suitable age and health at schools established and maintained for their benefit.'

"To give a wild Indian, accustomed to the chase or to a roaming life, land and tell him to live upon it without breaking up his preconceived notions of life, will be of little service. He must be taught how to build homes, how to live in homes and to support himself and to provide for the extreme necessities, at least, of modern life. These things can only be taught in schools established and carried on for that purpose, and by teaching the Indian the practice of agriculture and of local government.

"One of the methods by which the Indian youth may make himself useful is service in the Federal army. It was a view of Aristotle and other great writers that the army was the best training school for citizenship. There can be no doubt of this in respect to some barbarous tribes. The discipline, or rather the learning to obey, is indeed, among the first principles of citizenship. It would be the first and best road to self-government. Those who have observed the results of military discipline in our training schools will observe, too, that the Indians take very kindly to army drill and become very proficient as soldiers. There is no reason why that large number of young men who find it difficult to enter modern industrial and commerical life should not find here an opening for distinguished faithful service. Up to this time quite a number of Indians have been enlisted in the service of the army. Yet this work has not been carried far enough to show what can be done. It promises well at least. But it well illustrates a principle in Indian education. The Indian must be drilled, trained, and placed in an occupation which offers protection on the one hand and restraint on the other. Otherwise he will not be able to compete with the white race in the economic struggle for land or the political struggle for power.

"It seems a sad thing to force children to attend school away from home and against the wishes of their parents, but it is the only hope of salvation for the Indian race. The tribal inspiration and the tribal influence must be broken up and the Indians must be taught to take

their stand among the people of their country, to toil for their bread and
to engage in the industries of common life. They must be prepared for
intelligent citizenship; they must know how to gain and hold property;
they must understand their rights and be content with what belongs to
them and ask for no more. With such education the Indian problem
gives fair promise of solution."

3. Sarah Newlin in her article "Indian Treaties and National Honor,"
publisher unknown, told of efforts to help:

"We have long held whole tribes responsible for the ill-doing of a
few, sometimes of one member; have we not taught all Indians that
each one of us should be held responsible for the ill-doings of white
men against them? Bishop Whipple tells us that, after special inquiry,
he has 'Yet to find the United States officer who does not acknowledge
that *in every instance we have been the first to break our treaties with
Indians.*'

"And we talk of 'those treacherous savages.'

"What are the marks of an absolute despotism? Are not some of
them making its subjects dependent on its good-will for their welfare;
making it unlawful for them to move from place to place without permission, or to buy and sell where they wish? Our Indian policy has
these marks. How can it escape the stigma, how can it fail to inflict the
suffering that attends despotism?

"The difficulty in this Indian subject lies not in the Indian but in ourselves. Public opinion alone can effect a change. All who hold their
peace are responsible for the acts of our representative Government.
The few who do 'cry for justice' have already accomplished something,
but to those who are waiting, literally, in the shadow of death, how
slowly and meagrely the help comes! We hear much of a 'strong pressure' on the Government against the Indians for self-interest; let there
be a strong pressure for justice, for right.

"A country that is worth fighting for is worth purifying. We can yet,
perhaps, redeem with good this 'century of dishonor.' We can clear this
dark blot from our national scutcheon. Humanity says to us:

'Prove now thy truth,
I claim of thee the promise of the youth.'

"Two associations exist for the express purpose of rousing the nation
to a recognition of our obligations to the Indians and for securing for
them a long-delayed justice, especially full legal title to their lands, payment of debts, and protection of law.

"The Women's National Indian Association, organized April 1879, is
now at work in twenty-seven States and Territories. It gathers and

spreads information about Indian affairs, sends an officer all over the country to tell facts and extend the organization, petitions Congress for needed legislation for Indians, opens pioneer missions which it turns over to churches willing to take them, and raises the money needful for all this. Bishop Whipple cheered its workers by telling them that they had already done 'immense good' and were 'reaching the heart of the nation.' Bishop Hare compared the effects of its work to that of a 'calcium light thrown down a dark alley; evil-doers could no longer work in the shade there.'

"Indian Rights Association (of gentlemen) was formed in 1883, with the same objects as the Women's Association, but somewhat different methods of work. Both societies need money and workers. Who will help?"

4. Yuwipi means "they wrap, or tie, him up." In doing the Yuwipi ceremony, the medicine man is wrapped in a blanket and then tied securely with ropes. The lights are turned out, and while they remain out he prays, chants, and then is mysteriously released from his bonds and the blanket. It is a very old and a still popular ceremony, whose purposes are to cure the ill, to gain information about medicines to be used for specific healings, to find lost or stolen articles, to gain the permission of the spirit powers to do a certain thing, and to learn from the spirits what will happen in the future.

5. Ruby (1955:95) states, "Red Cloud was eventually converted to Catholicism. One of his last wishes was to be buried in a black robe, like those the priests and lay brothers wore. It was granted." Ruby goes on to say that Red Cloud's two buckskin outfits and war bonnets were sent to museums: one in Washington, D.C., and the other to the Oglala Community High School, in Pine Ridge. "The second chief," Ruby says, "his son Jack Red Cloud, died in the influenza epidemic of 1918. James Red Cloud, his grandson, is chief today. He is nearly eighty. He has never been converted to the Christian religion; he is Yuwipi; but many of Red Cloud's descendants are Catholics."

In 1893, writing in *Harpers New Monthly Magazine,* William H. Wassel wrote "The Religion of the Sioux." It deserves reading in its entirety so that the whole of it, and the white attitudes so plainly exposed therein, may be considered in the light of Fools Crow's own information.

To the Sioux of the past, religion was truly a mystery. From the simple growth of the blade of grass to the complex phe-

nomena of the thunder-storm, all life, power, and strength
were interpreted as the physical acts of unknown gods. The
Great Spirit is a name given us by the interpreter, for the Sioux
had no conception of a single spirit, however great, capable of
ruling the universe. Lightning was the anger of a thunder god,
an awful bird, whose structure varied from wings containing
only six quills to wings with four joints each, according to the
imagination of the medicine-man. The moving god, he whose
aid it was most difficult to invoke, was too subtle to be likened
to any known form, but he controlled the intellect, passions,
and mental faculties, abstractions for which the Sioux has not
even a name. The Hayoka was the contrary god, who sat
naked, and fanned himself in the coldness of a Dakota bliz-
zard, and huddled shivering over a fire in the heat of summer,
who cried for joy and laughed in his sorrow. Rocks and
bowlders were the hardest and strongest things; hence they
belonged to the oldest gods—smaller rocks were fetiches. On
the barren buttes of the Dakotas may be seen many a
crumbling pile of stones erected in by-gone days to propitiate
an unknown god. Many a forgotten chief has gone to the
highest hill when his son was sick, and amidst fastings and incantations reared a mound of little stones in the hope that his
loved one's life might be spared. And still another relic of the
savage belief of the old Sioux is found on the bodies of the
warriors themselves. Take almost any man who is thirty years
old or more, and he can show you long scars on his back or
breast, and dozens of smaller scars on his arms, all inflicted by
himself in fulfilling his vows to the sun. The sun-dance was
one of the great religious and political events of the Sioux life.
Whole villages assembled and feasted, while the worshippers
fasted and exhausted the strength they were to need so badly
in the coming test of endurance. On the appointed day none
but virgins were allowed to cut down and trim the tree that
was to be used, while only chiefs and warriors of exceptional
bravery were allowed to carry it to its place in the centre of
the village. Here, with mysterious pipe-smokings and unin-
telligible incantations, the pole is planted, ropes of buffalo-
hide having been fastened to its top, one rope for each
worshipper. The men, already half dead from exhaustion, are
then brought out and laid on the ground around the pole, always ready knives thrust through the muscles of their chests or
backs, and in the holes thus made wooden skewers thrust, to
which are fastened the loose ends of the ropes. Then round

and round dance the worshippers, their eyes fixed on the blazing sun, while the jerk, jerk, jerk, of the bleeding flesh beats a sickening time to the hi-yas of a Dakota song. Friends and relatives, men, women, and children, gash their arms and breasts to stimulate the dancers and keep up their courage. When the flesh is torn apart the dancer is released, his vow fulfilled, his bravery, his manhood, unquestioned. . . . These and a thousand other monstrous customs were what the early missionary had to combat.

The Sioux hereafter was a particularly happy idea, in the main in keeping with the advanced views of some of their white brothers of the present day. There were happy hunting-grounds, but there were no unhappy ones. When a Methodist minister, attending one of the Indian commissions in the 70s, painted a hell with colors of fire and brimstone, the only necessity for such a future abode was, as an old chief expressed it, for all the whites. Some Indians might lie, steal, or commit murder, but these were tangible offences receiving prompt punishment, and as such were violations of a social rather than a religious code. And, in fact, to kill a Crow Indian, steal his ponies, or lie to him and get him into trouble, were things that made the plenteous game, the clear waters, and the rich grass all the more abundant for the Sioux in the happy hunting-grounds. The medicine-man was not a priest, for their religion had no conception of such. He was self-appointed. Who could displace him or doubt his power? By some shrewdness he predicted a coming event, or by luck he performed an unheard-of act, and then his greatness was assured. Sitting-Bull, medicine-man rather than chief, once predicted rain in a season of drought. With mysterious pipe-smokings and vague incantations he prayed for rain, and sure enough it came. When the crops again needed water he was applied to, but he cautiously answered: "Too much rain will drown you. I can easily make it rain, but no one can make it stop." . . . This utter lack of appreciation of moral right and wrong, combined with an exceptional craftiness, was a towering obstacle for the missionary to surmount.

This much has the missionary done. From the sorcery and jugglery of a weazened medicine-man he has brought the Sioux to confide in the simple teachings of the Bible. From the barbarous self-immolation of the sun-dance he has led him to the few rites of Christianity. From the gross sensuality and selfishness of the awful mystery, the Takoo Wakan, manifested and worshipped under the form of gods innumerable, he has built up a faith in one Supreme Being.

To-day Episcopalians, Roman Catholics, Presbyterians, and Congregationalists are all well represented in the Dakotas, and have rendered great assistance to the government in efforts toward civilization. The younger men wear their Y.M.C.A. badges, and the Roman Catholics their crosses, just as their forefathers wore the dirty medicine charms. The leading men are no longer those who have killed the most Crows or stolen the greatest number of ponies. War-songs are replaced by Christian hymns, and *"Jesus Itancan"* now bursts forth from the dusky throats that formerly knew nothing but the murderous *"kte."*

It would be an error, of course, to suppose that all the Sioux have embraced Christianity. Every one knows that there are still those malcontents who wear the hair long, who withdraw as far as possible from their agencies, and who still yearn for the extermination of the whites and the return of the buffalo. The late Messiah craze is still fresh in the public mind. The standing rock from which the principal Sioux agency takes its name is a large stone. One story makes it a runaway girl turned into stone with her baby on her back when pursued by her father and brothers. Another story makes it originally an Arickaree object of worship that became sacred to the Sioux when a Warrior, defiling the idol, was killed shortly afterward by its worshippers. Whatever its origin, it was held in great reverence. Three years ago last summer an old Sioux suddenly felt himself possessed of divine power, and, as a proof, offered to make the stone remove itself from its masonry to a distant point. His bragging attracted considerable attention, but this hope of gaining followers was cut short when the Indian agent gave him twenty-four hours in which to remove the stone, or else remove himself to the guard-house. At the end of the time it was the Indian who moved.

It is probable that there are still messiahs who at times will give bullet-proof ghost-shirts to their followers and lead them against the law and order of government. The Indian who promised that thirty feet of finely sodded and forest-planted soil should cover all the earth, smothering the greater part of the whites, but allowing a few to escape as fishes, will have successors whose fortune-telling, no matter how absurd, will gain them followers. For, stripped of power, it is but natural that the older chiefs should long for its return, and there is an

19. Fools Crow looking out over the Black Hills from the meadow where the sweatlodges are built.

20. Fools Crow meeting with Theodore C. Marrs, Special Assistant to the President, September 1975. (Official White House Photograph)

21. Fools Crow at the Custer Battlefield National Monument, June 25, 1976, the Centennial of the famous battle on the Little Big Horn.

22. Fools Crow at the September 10, 1976, meeting with the House Subcommittee on Interior and Insular Affairs. Left to right: Fools Crow, Matthew King, Frank Kills Enemy, Red Shirt, Moses Two Bull. (Official White House Photograph)

23. Fools Crow shows Dallas Chief Eagle the commemorative paperweight given to him by President Gerald Ford.

analogy between the excitement produced on the ignorant and uncultivated brain of the Indian by dreams of old-time warfare and that aroused in the immature white lad after a vigorous perusal of the dime novel.

Smarting under wrongs, both real and imaginary, it was not natural for these Indians to receive the first missionaries with friendliness. Always suspicious, always keen to expect bad intentions, they regarded the early missionary in the general class of whites, and therefore unworthy of confidence. The chiefs dreaded a further loss of their following; the medicine-men feared that their enchantments would fall before the white man's god. Even the mass of the people, although afraid to forcibly interfere, nevertheless sought all other means to prevent the establishment of missions. Unlimited in hospitality among themselves, yet in many cases they forbade the missionary to use the water that flowed in the creeks. A missionary's horse had no right to eat a blade of the thousands of tons of grass that annually went to waste on the reservation. Armed with simple remedies, the missionary sought to win favor by healing the sick. If a cure were effected, no thanks were received; but if the patient died, the family of the deceased laid the death at the missionary's door and demanded payment for the loss. When the missionary sought to better their physical condition by giving to one a warm coat, the entire village demanded that they be likewise treated. If an Indian woman were given a dollar for doing a small washing, another woman would be angry unless she, for a like consideration, be allowed to carry the water; while a third woman would insist that she, for another dollar, be allowed to hang the clothes upon the line. When one considers that the good-will of these savages was the first requisite for mission-work, then the tact and untiring perseverance of the missionary will be appreciated. There was no Hiawathan romance about it.

Early converts were principally among the women. "Only a woman—it makes no difference," the warriors said. The woman was only the household drudge, and so long as she chopped the wood, carried the water, and took care of the ponies, her religious beliefs were of small moment. But the man's life was a succession of paganish rites. Wild orgies celebrated all his actions from the time when, as a boy, he killed his first bird to when, as a stealthy old man, he stole his last pony from a Crow. To embrace Christianity was to give up everything that had been his pride. But, as admitted by the most experienced Indian agents, to allow his pagan belief to continue was to so shape his life in the wrong direction as to retard civilization many generations. An instance of the benefits of this change of belief is the report of the Presbyterian Church that of eleven hundred communicants only one was known to have joined in the ghost-dances of 1891.

While government officials could not directly promote Christianity among the Sioux, they have fully recognized its civilizing power. In 1876, with a view to allow the different sects to work harmoniously and to the best good of the Indian, the different Sioux reservations were assigned as fields for missionary work among the Episcopalians, the Roman Catholics, the Presbyterians, and the Congregationalists. This allotment in no way limited the work of the Churches to the fields assigned; it merely gave to each its starting-point, and the control of the contract-schools in that territory.

That the missionary's work has been well done may be judged from the following tables taken from a late report of Mr. Daniel Dorchester, superintendent of Indian schools. I have made such changes in these tables as have come within my personal knowledge, and as the work of christianizing the Sioux has not been stationary, any errors that may still exist will be on the short side.

"The Roman Catholic Church has the following missions in the Dakotas: Devil's Lake agency—3 priests, 2 boarding and 1 day school, 15 employés; Standing Rock agency—3 priests, 2 boarding-schools, 25 employés; Pine Ridge agency—2 priests, 1 boarding-school, 20 employés; Rosebud agency—3 priests, 1 boarding-school, 20 employés; Crow Creek agency —3 priests, 1 boarding-school, 15 employés. Totals—5 missions, 14 priests, 7 schools, 95 employés, 12 churches; Roman Catholic population, 4,740; adult baptisms (for the year), 743; child baptisms, 1,350.

"The Presbyterian Church has the following exhibit, furnished by one of its oldest ministers. Its missions are in the Yankton, Crow Creek, and Lower Brule, Sisseton, and Devil's Lake agencies, and at Flandreau. Native communicants, 1,104; native members or Sunday-school, 736; native churches organized, 15; native pastors installed over churches, 8; stated supplies in charge, 7; admitted on profession of faith last year, 120.

"Congregational (A.M.A.) missions are as follows: Cheyenne River agency—9 stations, 25 laborers, 1 school;

Standing Rock agency—5 stations, 13 laborers; Rosebud agency—3 stations, 6 laborers. Totals—3 missions, 6 ministers (4 at Cheyenne River agency, and 1 at each of the other places), 17 stations, 44 laborers, 1 school. Number of communicants not known.

"The Protestant Episcopal Church has the following: Total —9 missions, 9 churches, 25 chapels, 17 stations, 9 clergy, 8 deacons, 37 catechists; communicants, 1,712; Indian contributions, $2,575; average church attendance, 2,609; church sittings, 4,672; church property, $61,246. Total population Episcopal Indians, 6,200.

"It is not a wild estimate to say that probably there are from 10,500 to 11,000 Indian adherents of the Protestant Episcopal, Presbyterian, and Congregational churches in the Dakotas."

The last two years have witnessed church convocations of the christianized Sioux, events of great importance to the Indians. The different agencies compete with one another for the honor of holding them, the voters good-naturedly swinging from one agency to another, as inducements of watermelons or tales of vicious snakes are held up to them. In 1892 the Episcopalians met at St. Elizabeth, the Roman Catholics at the Cheyenne agency, while the Presbyterians and Congregationalists combined, and held their Paya Owodake (united talk) at the Standing Rock agency.

This latter conference was held in a square booth built of young trees, with the branches strewn over the top for shade. Above the enclosure proudly floated the stars and stripes, borrowed for the occasion from the quartermaster at Fort Yates. One side of the booth was for the men, the other for women. All meetings, whether of a business or a purely religious character, were conducted in the prescribed form. Prayers were offered, hymns sung, and sermons preached—all in the Sioux language—sometimes by missionaries, more often by Indians. There is a terrible force in the prayer of an Indian—a wild, eloquent vehemence in all his petitions. When on Sunday, the last day of the conference, the sacrament was administered, there was an earnestness on every face that said dumbly, "We believe, and we are trying to do the best we can."

Cultivated by their mode of life, all Sioux have remarkable memories for sounds. Their singing is an agreeable surprise, the men, in their deep, rather rough, tones, chanting a thundering bass to the shrill treble of the women. Many of their hymns are merely Sioux words arranged to standard music; others are those that have been composed by educated Indians; while a few, the most popular, are native airs, queer tunes that have a distinctively Indian sound, and that run continually into minors.

Sometimes at one of the conferences an old custom will crop out when, on holding one of their society meetings in the open air, the women, with no apparent thought, arrange themselves in a great circle so nearly perfect that the eye glancing over it can suggest no change to make it more perfect. From this position the delegates rise and make their reports. In case of a contribution, one woman after another goes to the centre of the circle and deposits her offering, whether it be money, a strip of calico, or a fancifully worked bead bag. It is the desire of the missionary, as well as the government, to break up even the semblance of these old-time customs, but when one sees the readiness with which three hundred women will adapt themselves to this kind of a meeting there is some excuse for its preservation.

The christianized Sioux vote and elect officers of their religious societies much after the fashion of their white brothers. Their electioneering arguments, however, are distinctly Indian. In a recent election for secretary of one of their associations, a comely-looking woman nominated Miss Collins, a white missionary, who has been among the Sioux for seventeen years. Before the voting was begun, the same woman arose and declared that Miss Collins should not be elected. "For," said she, "I gave her a quilt, and asked her to hang it up at this meeting, but she wouldn't do it."

"Oh," said Miss Collins, "I was afraid it would rain; then the quilt would have been ruined, and that would have made me cry."

The explanation was satisfactory, and when the voting was begun, "Winona" after "Winona" was recorded for Miss Collins—Winona, signifying the first-born girl, being the name the Indians have given her.

Despite the awakening of Christian enthusiasm among the Sioux, the names frequently given their children show a desire to have them known as great warriors. At one of this year's conferences there was present a poor weakly little chap, with scrofula written all over him, but who bore the great-sounding name of "He-who-shoots-to-kill-past-beyond." In all his sickly existence the poor child has probably never killed anything as large as a field-mouse, yet should he live to be an old man, in some way or other the story will creep out that in his youth he stood in a circle of enemies and killed, killed, until there were none left to battle against him.

Sitting-Bull was a crafty old pagan, but his two widows have stood up in church and said, "We want Christ." A deaf-and-dumb son of this same old fox was told by One-Bull, Sitting-Bull's successor, that he could not be received into the church on account of his infirmities. On hearing this the missionary, who was about to go on a journey, told One-Bull to tell the lad that on her return she would take him as a church member if he were still so inclined. When the little lady had travelled about ten miles on her journey she saw some one coming after her, riding fast over the prairie. It was the deaf-and-dumb boy, bearing a note from One-Bull that said, "We cannot make him understand." The boy dismounted and made signs, touching his eyes, straightening his form, and outlining his figure stretched upon the ground. That was his dead body. Then opening his eyes, he pointed to heaven, and afterward made on the ground the square enclosure of the church. . . . He is now a constant attendant at all church meetings.

In connection with the fatality of revolution which seems to have followed the death of Sitting-Bull is the fact that in the hands of one of the christianized Indian policemen who killed Sitting-Bull was an old carbine which, as a hostile, the same policeman had picked up in the Custer affair.

The Churches and missionary societies were quick to grasp the idea that moral and mental training should go hand in hand. Government officials have stated that religion should be wholly ignored in government schools, but the same officials have never disputed the benefits of the moral teachings of any of the Christian Churches. In 1876, when the assignment of the reservations to the different Churches was made, many of the Churches were given control of the contract-schools in their fields. These are schools built by the government and controlled by a Church, the latter supplying teachers and receiving so much per scholar—about fifty dollars a year—for the average attendance. In addition to this amount the government allows such schools to draw the usual rations and clothing for the attendant pupils. These schools and the mission schools, the latter built and supported, except as to rations and clothing, by the various Churches, are the best schools on the reservation when properly conducted. With the exception of a few day scholars, the children are admitted on the first day of September, and educated morally, mentally, and industrially until the last of June, their training during this period receiving no set-back from contact with Indian village life. The government makes school attendance compulsory for all children between the ages of five and eighteen, and if the ringing of the bell on the first day of September does not bring them in, Indian policemen scattering over the reservation soon round them up. Washed from head to foot, and clothed according to civilized ideas, the scholars are then ready to learn to speak, read, and write English, to get some knowledge of arithmetic and the history and geography of their own country, while a few receive musical instruction. Industrially, the boys work in the school gardens, in the blacksmith, carpenter, and tin shops, and are taught the care of horses, cattle, and poultry. The girls receive instruction in domestic work, cooking, sewing, darning, and laundering. Aprons, blouses, cloaks, pillowcases, towels—in fact, everything in needle-work that is required for the school and scholars is made by the Indian girls. Morally, in addition to the beliefs of the different churches, the children are taught honesty and truthfulness, taught that girls and women are not household drudges, taught that dance rites and medicine charms are relics of the barbarism from which they have emerged.

As auxiliaries to their churches and chapels the Domestic and Foreign Missionary Society of the Episcopal Church has established five boarding-schools for the Sioux—St. Elizabeth's, on the Grand River, South Dakota, near the camps of Gaul and John Grass, two noted leaders of the hostiles who fought against Custer; St. Paul's, the oldest, at the Yankton agency; St. Mary's, at the Rosebud agency; St. John's, at the Cheyenne agency; and Hope School, at Springfield, South Dakota. In all, 228 children are under the control of principals and assistants. Godliness, usefulness, cleanliness, politeness, and learning are the points strived for. When I gave the customary *"How, cola,"* to a little mite at the St. Elizabeth mission, the mite replied, "Good-morning, sir," in a way that made me feel decidedly at a disadvantage.

The churches and religious societies have certainly quenched the fire of barbarism in the Indian children. The Bible, translated into their native language, has been put before them, so that the younger element does not grow up with a belief in that convenient form of prayer—merely pointing the pipe—which expressed so little, but implied all manner of requests for ponies and meat and comfortable old age. Marriage according to Christian rites has succeeded the annual virgin-feast, where a slandered maiden stood face to face with her accuser by the sacred fire and swore a high-sounding oath to her purity. The disappearance of blanket and breech-cloth, long hair and highly painted faces, is a sign that the Sioux has succumbed to a stronger civilization, and with his old customs have fallen his old gods.

6. I was reminded at this point of a very old newspaper article, c. 1900, author and publisher unknown because those data were cut away, which reported, "After a period of investigation and study covering twenty-five years the government is about to issue a monumental work on the subject of the American Indian. It will be a handbook of history and information about the various tribes. 'Where did the Indians come from?' That's a question to which careful and patient study has been devoted and which, by the way, the bureau frankly says it will not try to answer in the forthcoming book. One of its ethnologists has propounded the interesting idea—call it a theory—that 'the Indian didn't come, but just started right here in America.' . . . others of equal eminence have discovered this theory, claiming that the Indian was indigenous to American soil, just as the negro was native to Africa and the Mongol native to Asia."

When Fools Crow said this same thing, and stooped down as he did so to grab a handful of South Dakota dirt, it reminded me of my own remarks in which I stated that the Sioux to all intents and purposes are a people who came into being in the late 1600s, when they first moved as a nation into the Midwest and buffalo country. His statement and action indicated agreement. In the Sioux mind they have always been an integral part of the Plains country, and God created the first Sioux out of that very ground. To understand any of their religious and political views one must hold this fact in mind.

7. Dr. Charles A. Eastman is a Santee Sioux who grew up in Canada with some of his people who fled there after the Minnesota outbreak. In 1887, he graduated from Dartmouth, and in 1890, from the Boston University School of Medicine. He then spent many years among his people at Pine Ridge and Crow Creek. By 1903, he was a well-known author of books and articles. In an article entitled "The Sioux Mythology," written for *Popular Science Monthly* in 1904, he describes in summary form what he has learned of Sioux mythology. In this he states:

"The spirits of the departed Sioux were, it was supposed, admitted at once into the mysteries of God, except those of the very wicked, who were returned to the world in the form of one of the lower animals. This was their punishment. Yet such a spirit might retrieve its misfortune by good behavior, and thus be promoted to its former shape.

"In man there were believed to be three souls. One of these, as I have said, immediately enters heaven by the 'spirits' path—the milky way—escorted by the stars. The second remains where the body is placed, as guardian of the grave; while the third lives and travels with its relatives. On this account the natives believe that everything said of the departed is heard by them. I do not know just how this triune conception originated. No doubt it had a reasonable explanation somewhere in the early life of the race, but the legend connected with it is lost."

8. Ruby (1955:52, 63) makes reference to both Horn Chips and Poor Thunder as outstanding medicine men. Ruby tells about Horn Chips' vision quest, which was made in a pit much like the one Fools Crow was put in as a boy, and Ruby states that Poor Thunder was a Yuwipi medicine man—going on to describe in detail a Yuwipi ceremony he performed. The ceremony was very similar to Fools Crows', even to the sparks flying and the rattles moving around the room during the ritual.

9. There is an age-old skepticism toward the medicine man's power to cure. Many non-Indians are just not willing to believe this, considering him to be superstitious, a charlatan, or a magician at best, and actually a source of death and misery among his people. Naturally, the Indians know this and resent it. What they can show the medicine men have accomplished has, until recently, seemed to be of no consequence.

Henry Craig Fleming, M.D., in his *Medical Observations on the Zuni Indians,* Museum of the American Indian Heye Foundation, Vol. VII, No. 2 (1924), states the common opinion applied to all medicine practitioners of all tribes: "Many lives are sacrificed annually through the ignorant practice of the medicine men and medicine women. And it is unfortunately true that very little medical intelligence and efficiency are evident."

In an old and rare newspaper article in my possession, the name of whose author and publisher, along with the date, are unfortunately removed, there is a lengthy dissertation concerning the medicine practices of the Sioux at the turn of the century. It is most revealing, and it will be valuable to compare the whole of it with what Fools Crow has to say about his profession and practice.

"It is under contemplation by the Indian bureau to institute a vigorous campaign against the practices of the medicine men, or native Indian doctors and magicians. While some efforts have been made in the past to this effect, reports received from various agencies indicate that the medicine men still wield a strong influence over their people. The secrecy with which their operations are conducted and the superstitious awe in which they are held by a large number of Indians, even at the present day, have rendered it very difficult to eliminate them from the reservations, and, though they are proscribed by law from exercising their traditional functions, it has only been the most flagrant cases of their barbarous rites that come to the notice of the authorities.

"It is now believed that no small number of deaths result from the practices of the medicine men and that this is true may readily be gathered from the following account of these individuals by a member of the Indian bureau who has just returned from the field after investigating the subject:

" 'Everything connected with these tawny wizards,' said this gentleman, 'is sought to be involved in the greatest secrecy and this makes investigation difficult. A young Indian who is ambitious to become a doctor and finally a prophet learns from his father or other member of this tribe the name and medicinal properties of some herb. He can also, by presenting a sufficient number of ponies to a medicine man, prevail upon the doctor to impart the secrets of the herbs to him. Frequently Indians allege that the secret is revealed to them in a dream or by a bird or animal. After procuring it the novice is prepared to begin the practice of medicine. Success is, in their opinion, only possible with the aid of the Great Spirit, and in order to invoke the aid of the supernatural they resort to various sacrifices.

" 'Again, while treating a patient they place tobacco in little pouches, which they tie with sinew. These are painted brilliant colors and fastened to willow sticks about the size of the shaft of an arrow but somewhat longer. Occasionally, as a substitute for the bags of tobacco, strips of flannel are fastened to the tops of the sticks and permitted to flutter in the breeze. The sticks are also gayly painted and inserted in the ground or crevices of rock on top of a hill. This is done to gain favor with the Great Spirit and secure his assistance in making their practice successful or curing the patient under their charge. The tobacco or flannel constitutes, in fact, votive offerings.

" 'The Indian doctors also profess to be able to dream out at will any problem which is difficult of solution during their waking hours. After a novice succeeds in effecting a sufficient number of miraculous cures to render him famous he adds prophecy to his curative attainments and makes predictions as to events which will occur in the future.

" 'Generally speaking, the mode of practice of the Indian doctors, after placing the offering to the Great Spirit on a near-by hill, is to give the patients medicine and then chant songs over them to the accompaniment of a tomtom, or crude drum, made by drawing dried skin tightly over a wooden frame, iron kettle, tin can, or other hollow article or utensil that will answer the purpose. Herbs furnish the ingredients for all medicines. In some instances the Indian doctors chew up herbs and blow them on the patient.

" 'The successful doctor first imbues his patient with as much superstition and keeps him or her as ignorant as possible. The so-called music of a tomtom is very weird and dismal and to our way of thinking very much out of place in a sickroom. The Indian doctor when treating a patient paints himself in dazzling colors and arrays his body in fantastic garments and furbelows, which are designed to in a measure increase the awe inspired by his presence at the bedside of stricken brother.

" 'While engaged in his mystic ministrations the medicine man sits over his drum, sometimes directly over the patient. Everything he does is supposed to be wrapped in the deepest mystery. In some cases he applies his mouth to the place of pain after first washing it out with clean water. By doing this he claims he is sucking out the disease with which the patient is afflicted. When a patient is very sick they on rare occasions hold a kind of consultation, which they call a medicine feast, and all who are present are requested to partake of what is placed before them. Dogs enter very largely into these feasts, being considered a rare delicacy. To show how crude their knowledge of medicine and disease is, I came across a case of an Indian doctor who once put brass filings into the eyes of an Indian to cure him of an affliction of the eyes.

" 'One of the most curious and perhaps efficacious remedies the Indian doctors employ is that of the sweat bath, which, properly handled, would, in the opinion of white physicians, prove valuable.

" 'A medicine man having decided to give his afflicted brethren an opportunity to test the efficacy of the sweat bath as administered by him, gives public notice of the time and place for holding the ceremony.

" 'On the day designated he proceeds to the spot selected for the occasion. Stones of various sizes are gathered and placed in a heap on the ground. Sticks of wood are then deposited around the stones and the wood is lighted. While the stones are being thus heated the red-skinned wizard assists in constructing a frame, or wickiup, of saplings, the pliable poles being bent into the form of a semicircle and both ends stuck into the ground. Blankets, quilts, and every imaginable article of wearing apparel are thrown over the frame. The wickiup, or miniature lodge, when completed is usually about 7 feet in diameter at the bottom and 4 or 5 feet high. Into this limited space as many as ten or twelve Indians, who have responded to the invitation of the medicine man, will crowd in the hope of receiving benefit for bodily ills.

" 'When the lodge is completed the afflicted Indians remove their clothing and enter it. As soon as the stones are red hot they are passed into the lodge by the medicine man, who utilizes a forked stick or an ordinary hayfork, if obtainable, for the purpose. These are received by the Indians on the inside and placed in the center of the circle formed by their naked bodies. Pieces of foreign matter, such as dust or charcoal, that may adhere to the stones are carefully removed. In the opinion of the participants any foreign substance if permitted to remain with the stones would detract from the curative power of the medicine, which they believe will cure all ills.

" 'When all is in readiness a bucket of water, into which the medicine has been emptied, is passed into the lodge by the doctor and the entrance is carefully closed. The lodge may appear impervious to the breeze, but occasionally one of the Indians on the inside call to the doctor to throw something over a certain place until they are finally satisfied that it is perfectly airtight and that they are excluded from the evils and temptations of this iniquitious world to allow the steam to penetrate their bodies, thereby healing their afflictions. A small quantity of water containing the medicine is poured on the red-hot stones. Clouds of steam immediately arises and the medicine man begins to walk in a circle around the lodge, chanting as he does so.' "

The article trails off here and is incomplete. For some reason the person who collected it did not bother to save its conclusion. But what he did retain is more than enough to show his disdain for Indian medicine men and medicine.

10. During an important lecture I attended at Sinte Galeska College, Rosebud, South Dakota, in October 1976, the audience was told by Orval Looking Horse that the Sacred Calf Pipe once had a carving of a standing buffalo on its bowl. But the Keeper was careless and the bundle was stolen. When it was recovered and returned to Green Grass, an astonishing thing happened. The Keeper had unwrapped it to examine its condition, and as he looked at the buffalo its head drooped. He looked again and the buffalo sank to its knees. He looked again and it had fallen down. He looked a fourth time, and only a small round spot marked the place where the buffalo had been. In sorrow over the Keeper's carelessness and what had taken place, it had gone away.

11. Views of the contemporary medicine men vary a little as to the meaning of the parts of the pipe, although they agree in essence. During the lecture referred to in note No. 10, Orval Looking Horse described the pipe bowl as the female, and the stem as the male. "When the two pieces are joined, it is the union of all things in renewing life." Notice that the joining *is,* and does not merely symbolize, the union. In Sioux understandings, any religious action or item *is* the thing spoken of rather than simply a representation of it. In a further example, attaching a colored prayer cloth to the Sun Dance Pole is a prayer, and not an indication that separate oral prayers are being made.

Most of the medicine men at Rosebud and Pine Ridge see the pipe head as standing for the union of "God and every created thing, because it brings everything together." The red color of the catlinite stone is "the blood that is common to all things." I was also told that the pipe consists of four parts: the stone bowl, which stands for (is) the earth; the stem, which is everything that grows upon the earth; the animal carvings on the stem, which are the four-legged creatures; and the eagle feathers and pipe smoke, which together are everything that flies and lives above.

12. Fools Crow told me that several versions of the Kettle Dance are still being done here and there. But they use an iron kettle and they do it in different ways. He has heard of some where they didn't even use dog meat. "So," he said, "those dances have no power. They are only social dances, show dances, something to see, but they have no spiritual value for the people who do them or the people who watch."

Dallas Chief Eagle said, "I can tell you about a Kettle Dance I saw performed at a big Indian encampment about four miles east of Mosher, South Dakota, in 1936 or 1937. They had a little boy there, beautifully costumed. They brought the kettle from somewhere else and put it in the center of the dancing area. There was no fire under it. The dog was already cooked when I arrived.

"The singers took their places alongside the kettle, and then the boy danced toward the kettle from the north side with a stick in his hand. It was round, about three feet long, sharpened at one end, and painted red. Then a medicine man in full regalia came out to the center and took the stick. He danced around the kettle and pointed the stick at eight men. They were probably picked out before the dance, but he pointed the stick at them anyway. As each one came forward he touched them with the stick, and they started to dance. They formed two groups, like Frank said, and each time they approached the kettle they crouched and pretended they were sneaking up on the kettle. The fourth time they went forward the leader took the head. I don't know what they did with it. There was a lot of commotion and noise. Then the dancers got some harmless whips and asked the spectators to join in a Round Dance. Whoever refused was whipped, but of course it didn't actually hurt them.

"When they finished a crier went among the people and told them there would be a giveaway. Some people donated food, one contributed a wagon, some gave horses, a quilt, a costume, or something like that. I am inclined to think that if anyone had a Kettle Dance today they wouldn't be able to do it the old way Frank talked about. They would do it the way I saw it."

13. Ruby (1955:20–21) makes reference to the incident with Two Sticks, but gives far different facts than Fools Crow. According to Ruby, the affair took place in the 1890s, when cattle were being distributed to the Indians. It seems that, although he had no order for it from the agent, Two Sticks demanded that he be given a steer. When he was refused, he returned with four other Indians, and they killed five of the cowboys who were guarding the steers. The Indian police rounded up four of the Indians and "shot them on the spot. Two Sticks was captured, tried, condemned to death, and taken to Denver, where he was hanged." Obviously, either Fools Crow or Ruby is wrong. There are several things in Ruby's account that I question: The first is that he does not say where Two Sticks was tried; the second is the idea that the Indian police would shoot their own people "on the spot"; the third is his assertion, as his book continues, that the cattle issues were discontinued in 1905. They were still being made during the ERA period, which was the 1930s.

14. Ruby (1955:87) states that in the summer of 1953, a family of full-bloods who believed in Yuwipi danced the horse dance. "Many Indians and three white people saw the dance." But the dance Ruby refers to was far different, is nothing like Fools Crow's, or for that matter that of Black Elk, who gives a detailed description of a sacred Horse Dance in *Black Elk Speaks,* pp. 166–80. It appears probable that the girl did not do a true horse dance at all. Ruby says that the dance was for an eighteen-year-old girl who dreamed she would be struck by lightning. Her father consulted a medicine man, who advised her to ride the dancing horse. In doing the dance, the girl was hooded, lifted on the horse, and the animal was made to dance by jerking on the reins and kicking it.

15. In the light of a certain interview held with Red Cloud, and reported in the November 28, 1876, Omaha *Herald,* it may well be that the judgments of the chief are overly harsh. As we consider history after him we learn that the Sioux became the perpetual victims of government procedures and programs they could not, because of language and cultural barriers, understand. Red Cloud's sin regarding the Black Hills might have been nothing more than failure to comprehend what exactly the Great White Father in Washington, D.C., wanted him to give up.

A writer named Lyttle sends the following from Red Cloud Agency, Neb., where he interviewed the fallen chieftain, Red Cloud, in a common Sioux tent. He said:

" 'I have done as the commissioners sent out by the President said for me to do. I have tried to do the best I could honestly for the Great Father. I know the Black Hills was my country and there was plenty of gold there before today. I knew it was my reserve and reminded the commissioners about our treaty (making marks upon the ground). I told the commissioners what ground I would let them have.'

"Q. 'What was said about the Black Hills at the time you made the treaty?'

"A. 'I told them that was the ground given us by the Great Spirit and they could not have it. They made imaginary lines which I knew nothing about. I knew what ground I had given away. It was not what the commissioners said. I told the commissioners I would let them have the Hills if they would give me some land to live on and plenty of provisions for my people.'

"Q. 'Have not the whites treated you pretty well?'

"A. 'Some of them have. I was a great friend of Dear and Yeats, the Indian traders. I would have gone to Washington if I had had money or backing. I would like to have given the Great Father my side of the story. The commissioners told many things, promised much in words and did not fulfill what they promised. They lied to me (handing me a lot of papers). I have had these papers for six years.'

"Q. 'Have you counseled the Indians to be unfriendly to the whites?'

"A. 'No. I have been successful with my tribe (meaning the Ogallalas), for which they have not given me anything, not even thanks. I have always thought I was a friend of the peace commissioners and the President. At no time has the government had a right to complain.'

"Q. 'What have you to say about your arrest by Gen. Crook?'

"A. 'I was told to move in near the agency, and I would

have moved had it not been cold and stormy. I told my people they would move the next day and they agreed to it. That night we were captured about daybreak.'

"Q. 'I suppose the government has deprived you of the right to be chief any longer.'

"A. 'Oh, no. I am their chief, the same as I ever was. My people do not know anything about Spotted Tail being their chief, nor do they care. The Indians will recognize me as their chief.'

"Q. 'Did the government take much of your property at the time of your capture?'

"A. 'They took 48 of my horses, and over 100 from me and my children, and all our guns and even the knife from the old woman (pointing to his wife). They took my pipe from me.'

"Red Cloud here shook hands and said he did not want to talk any longer on the subject; that he had suffered shame enough."

The conversation was interpreted by Frank Salius, a half-breed, in the presence of H. C. and Richard Dear. The papers referred to were a commission from the President as acknowledged chief, and numerous letters from silly persons in New England asking for the autograph of the distinguished chieftain, possibly his X mark. What could he do better?

16. Of all the North American Indian religious ceremonies, none has excited the interest and imagination of Indians and non-Indians as much as the Sun Dance of the Sioux. Nor has any other ritual aroused among the non-Indians of the past a comparable indignation. The first white eyewitnesses to the dance were simultaneously enthralled and appalled at what they described as weird pagan rites and savage brutality. Government and church officials were so mortified by it that they moved quickly to outlaw and stamp it out—much as they would a fascinating but poisonous snake.

On the other hand, the Sioux considered the Sun Dance to be a natural and sublime practice of religion. It was and is their greatest expression of worship, and the source of growth and renewal for all things. They were amazed at the failure of the whites to comprehend this, and because the dance was essential to their life-way and well-being, were forced to continue it regardless of the penalties involved . . . moreover, the way they did so is a remarkable revelation in itself.

The dance itself is performed on a flat meadow, in a circle whose diameter varies from 50 to 150 feet, depending upon the number of participants involved. The circle is open to the sky. It is called the mystery circle, and a tall cottonwood tree, called the Sun Pole or tree, is stood upright at its exact center. A pine-covered shade arbor about 10 feet wide surrounds the circle, and bleacher-type benches are set up under the shade for spectator seating. The only other constructions directly related to the Sun Dance are the sweatlodge, a small dome-shaped structure used for purification ceremonies as each day begins, and a preparations tipi in which the dancers dress and ritual paraphernalia are kept.

I have witnessed over the past three years four Sun Dances at the Rosebud Reservation, and am most impressed with the quality of it as a religious ceremony. The dance is held in July or August, is preceded by elaborate preparations, including vision quests, and the dance proper lasts four days. Each day there is purification, dancing, prayer, flesh offerings, and healing. The dancers fast and seek visions. Spectators who are close to the dancers pray and fast too. Each day one or more dancers are pierced. They have one or two wooden skewer sticks stuck through the skin of their chests, to which are attached ropes whose one end is already tied to the Sun Pole. They then pull back on the ropes until the sticks tear loose. The painful act is a thank and sacrificial offering done for all the people. But the piercing is only a small part of the ceremony. Moment by moment over the four days the Sun Dance builds in cadence to a climax, when at the end of the fourth day all of the male dancers are pierced at the same time. The Sioux call the Sun Dance "our religion," because in it, at one time or another, every aspect of Sioux religion as practiced over the course of a year may be seen.

Not many non-Indian people have seen a Sun Dance, let alone read a detailed account of an old-time ritual, done the way it was performed before the ceremony was outlawed by the United States Government. By more than good fortune I came recently across a rare eyewitness account by Frederick Schwatka, written for a no longer published magazine called *The Deserted City*. Since the date is missing, I would guess it was written about 1880, with the Sun Dance itself taking place in the year 1875. He refers to it as being called "the greatest the Sioux had ever held." Its location indicates the main participants to be from the Crow Creek, Lower Brule, and Rosebud reservations, although many Sioux would have traveled long distances to attend such an important ceremony.

As I said, the account is quite rare and possibly the oldest on record. I am acquainted with most of the literature on the subject, and I have not seen it quoted elsewhere. As has been the situation with other articles included here, it provides an excellent comparison to what Fools Crow has to say on the subject. He has been the most active intercessor, or leader of the Sun Dance, at Pine Ridge and elsewhere from 1929 until today.

A few years ago it was the good fortune of the writer to witness, at the Spotted Tail Indian Agency, on Beaver Creek, Nebraska, the ceremony of the great sun-dance of the Sioux. Perhaps eight thousand Brule Sioux were quartered at the agency
at that time, and about forty miles to the west, near the head
of the White River, there was another reservation of Sioux,
numbering probably a thousand or fifteen hundred less. Ordinarily each tribe or reservation has its own celebration of the
sun-dance; but owing to the nearness of these two agencies it
was this year thought best to join forces and celebrate the savage rites with unwonted splendor and barbarity. Nearly half
way between the reservations the two forks of the Chadron
(or Shadron) creek form a wide plain, which was chosen as
the site of the great sun-dance.

In general it is almost impossible for a white man to gain
permission to view this ceremony in all its details; but I had in
Spotted Tail, the chief, and in Standing Elk, the head warrior,
two very warm friends, and their promise that I should behold
the rites in part slowly widened and allowed me to obtain full
view of the entire proceedings.

It was in June that the celebration was to be held, and for
many days before the first ceremonies took place the children
of the prairies began to assemble, not only from the two agencies most interested, but from many distant bands of Sioux to
which rumors of the importance of this meeting had gone. Everywhere upon the plains were picturesque little caravans
moving towards the level stretch between the branches of the
Chadron—ponies dragging the lodge-poles of the tepees, with
roughly constructed willow baskets hanging from the poles
and filled with a confusion of pots and puppies, babies and
drums, scalps and kindling-wood and rolls of jerked buffalo
meat, with old hags urging on the ponies, and gay young warriors riding. Fully twenty thousand Sioux were present, the
half-breeds and the "squaw-men" of the two agencies said,
when the opening day arrived. Probably fifteen thousand
would be more correct. It was easier to believe the statement
of the Indians that it was the grandest sun-dance within the
memory of the oldest warriors; and as I became fully convinced of this assertion, I left no stone unturned that would
keep me fast in the good graces of my friends, Spotted Tail
and Standing Elk.

When all had assembled and the medicine-men had set the
day for the beginning of the great dance dedicated to the sun,

the "sun-pole" was selected. A handsome young pine or fir, forty or fifty feet high, with the straightest and most uniformly tapering trunk that could be found within a reasonable distance, was chosen. The selection is always made by some old woman, generally the oldest one in the camp, if there is any way of determining, who leads a number of maidens gaily dressed in the beautiful beaded buckskin gowns they wear on state occasions; the part of the maidens is to strip the tree of its limbs as high as is possible without felling it. Woe to the girl who claims to be a maiden, and joins the procession the old squaw forms, against whose claims any reputable warrior or squaw may publicly proclaim. Her punishment is swift and sure, and her degradation more cruel than interesting.

The selection of the tree is the only special feature of the first day's celebration. After it has been stripped of its branches nearly to the top, the brushwood and trees for a considerable distance about it are removed, and it is left standing for the ceremony of the second day.

Long before sunrise the eager participants in the next great step were preparing themselves for the ordeal; and a quarter of an hour before the sun rose above the broken hills of white clay a long line of naked young warriors, in gorgeous warpaint and feathers, with rifles, bows and arrows, and warlances in hand, faced the east and the sun-pole, which was from five to six hundred yards away. Ordinarily this group of warriors numbers from fifty to possibly two hundred men. An interpreter near me estimated the line I beheld as from a thousand to twelve hundred strong. Not far away, on a high hill overlooking the barbaric scene, was an old warrior, a medicine-man of the tribe, I think, whose solemn duty it was to announce by a shout that could be heard by every one of the expectant throng the exact moment when the tip of the morning sun appeared above the eastern hills. Perfect quiet rested upon the line of young warriors and upon the great throng of savage spectators that blacked the green hills overlooking the arena. Suddenly the old warrior, who had been kneeling on one knee, with his extended palm shading his scraggy eyebrows, arose to his full height, and in a slow, dignified manner waved his blanketed arm above his head. The few warriors who were still unmounted now jumped hurriedly upon their ponies; the broken, wavering line rapidly took on a more regular appearance; and then the old man, who had gathered himself for the great effort, hurled forth a yell that could be heard to the uttermost

limits of the great throng. The morning sun had sent its com-
mands to its warriors on earth to charge.

  The shout from the hill was re-echoed by the thousand men
in the valley; it was caught up by the spectators on the hills as
the long line of warriors hurled themselves forward towards
the sun-pole, the objective point of every armed and naked
savage in the yelling line. As they converged towards it the
slower ponies dropped out, and the weaker ones were crushed
to the rear. Nearer and nearer they came, the long line becoming massed until it was but a surging crowd of plunging horses
and yelling, gesticulating riders. When the leading warriors
had reached a point within a hundred yards of the sun-pole, a
sharp report of rifles sounded along the line, and a moment
later the rushing mass was a sheet of flame, and the rattle of
rifle-shots was like the rapid beat of a drum resounding
among the hills. Every shot, every arrow, and every lance was
directed at the pole, and bark and chips were flying from its
sides like shavings from the rotary bit of a planer. When every
bullet had been discharged, and every arrow and lance had
been hurled, the riders crowded around the pole and shouted
as only excited savages can shout.

  Had it fallen in this onslaught, another pole would have
been chosen and another morning devoted to this performance. Though this seldom happens, it was thought that the
numerous assailants of this pole might bring it to the ground.
They did not, however, although it looked like a ragged
scarecrow, with chips and bark hanging from its mutilated
sides.

  That such a vast, tumultuous throng could escape accident
in all that wild charging, firing, of shots, hurling of lances and
arrows, and great excitement would be bordering on a miracle,
and no miracle happened. One of the great warriors was tram-
pled upon in the charge and died late that evening, and another Indian was shot. The bruises, sprains, and cuts that
might have been spoken of in lesser affairs were here unno-
ticed, and nothing was heard of them.

  Later in the day the sun-pole was cut down and taken to the
center of the great plain between the two forks of the
Chadron, about a mile away. Here a slight excavation was
made, and into it the butt of the sun-pole was put, and the
tree, the bushy top having now disappeared, was held upright
by a number of ropes made of buffalo thongs diverging from
its top. At their outer ends, probably from seventy to eighty

feet away from the sun-pole, they were fastened to the tops of stakes seven or eight feet in length. These, with a large number of stakes of similar size driven in close together, formed a circular cordon around the sun-pole, and over these stakes were stretched elk-skins and buffalo-robes, canvas and blankets, and a wattling of willows and brush. Sometimes canvas, blankets, and light elk-skins are thrown over the supporting ropes to ward off in a slight way the fierce rays of the noonday sun. To one approaching by the road that led over the winding hills which hem in the broad plain between the two forks of the Chadron the affair looked not unlike a circus tent, the top of which has been ruthlessly torn away by a cyclone.

All day, from the closing of the ceremony of shooting at the sun-pole, the attention of the Indians was occupied in constructing this enclosure, where, within a day or two after its completion, they performed those barbarous rites and ceremonies of cruelty and self-torture that have placed the sun-dance of the Sioux on a level with the barbarisms of any of the far more famed devotees of Juggernaut.

Early on the morning of the third or fourth day the true worship of the sun, if it can be strictly so called, was begun. So far all that that luminary had done was to signal the charge of the young warriors on the sun-pole. It now entered into the calculation of every minute, almost of every second, of the barbarous proceedings. Those who were to torture themselves, probably forty or fifty in a sun-dance of this size, were, as near as I could judge, young warriors from twenty to twenty-five years of age, all of them the very finest specimens of savage manhood in the great tribe.

I was told that these fine fellows fast for a number of days before they go through the self-torture, one informant saying that before the ordeal takes place it is required of them to abstain from food for seven days and from water for two. While their condition did not indicate such abstemiousness as this, I think it true that some fasting precedes the more barbarous ceremonies.

The third day was mostly consumed in dancing and in exercises that did not vary greatly from the dancing and exercises usually seen at any time in large Indian villages. On this day, however, the sun-dance began. Within the arena were from six to twelve young warriors, still in war-costume of paint and feathers, standing in a row, and always facing the sun, however brightly it shone in their eyes; with fists clenched across the breast, like a foot racer in a contest of speed, they jumped up and down in measured leaps to the monotonous beating of the toms-toms and the accompanying yi-yi-yi-yis of the assembled throng. The dancers occasionally vary the proceedings with savage music or with whistles made of bone. Now and then a similar row of young maidens would appear in another part of the arena, and their soprano voices would break in pleasantly on the harsher voices of the men. The dancing continued for intervals of from ten minutes to a quarter of an hour, broken by rests of about equal length, and lasted from sunrise to sunset.

Many trifling ceremonies took place while the important ones were proceeding. Horses and ponies were brought into the arena, and the medicine-men, with incantations, dipped their hands into colored earth and besmeared the sides of the animals with it. As these animals were evidently the best war-ponies, the ceremony was doubtless a blessing or a consecration of war.

On the fourth day of the Chadron sun-dance the self-torture began, and I was told that those who were to submit themselves to the great ordeal were the same young warriors who had been dancing the day before. Those who began the dance on the fourth day took the final ordeal on the fifth, and so for four or five days the dancers of one day became the sufferers of the tortures of the next.

The row of dancers took their places promptly at sunrise, but it was not before nine or ten that the tortures began.

Then each one of the young men presented himself to a medicine-man, who took between his thumb and forefinger a fold of the loose skin of the breast, about half way between the nipple and the collar-bone, and lifted it as high as possible, and then ran a very narrow-bladed but sharp knife through the skin underneath the hand. In the aperture thus made, and before the knife was withdrawn, a stronger skewer of bone, about the size of a carpenter's pencil, was inserted. Then the knife-blade was taken out, and over the projections of this skewer, backwards and forwards, alternately right and left, was thrown a figure-of-eight noose with a strong thong of dressed skin. This was tied to a long skin rope fastened, at its other extremity, to the top of the sun-pole in the center of the arena. Both breasts are similarly punctured, the thongs from each converging and joining the rope which hangs from the pole. The whole object of the devotee is to break loose from these fetters. To liberate himself he must tear the skewers through the skin, a horrible task that even with the most resolute may require many hours of torture. His first attempts are very easy, and seem intended to get him used to the horrible pain he must yet endure before he breaks loose from the thongs. As he increases his efforts his shouts increase, huge drop of perspiration pour down his greasy, painted skin, and every muscle stands out on his body in tortuous ridges, his swaying frame, as he throws his whole weight wildly against the fearful fetters, being convulsed with shudders. All the while the beating of the tom-toms and the wild, weird chanting of the singers near him continue. The wonderful strength and extensibility of the human skin is most forcibly and fearfully displayed in the strong struggles of the quivering victims. I have seen these bloody pieces of bone stretched to such a length from the devotee that his outstretched arms in front of him would barely allow his fingers to touch them.

I know it is not pleasant to dwell upon this cruel spectacle. Generally in two or three hours the victim is free, but there are many cases where double and even triple that time is required. Oftentimes there are half a dozen swinging wildly from the pole, running towards it and then moving backwards with the swiftness of a war-horse and the fierceness of a lion in their attempts to tear the accursed skewers from their wounded flesh. Occasionally some over-ambitious youth will erect four stakes within the arena, and fastening skewers to both breasts and to both shoulders will throw himself backwards and forwards against the four ropes that hold the skewers to the stakes.

Faintings are not uncommon even among these sturdy savages; but no forfeit, opprobrium, censure, or loss of respect in any way seems to follow. The victim is cut loose and placed on the floor of some lodge near by and left in charge of his nurses. The only attempt I saw to break loose from double skewers in front and behind terminated in this manner. Whether the men ever afterwards enter the cruel contest after having thus failed I do not know. It may be possible that some exceedingly ambitious warrior may enter the lists year after year to show his prowess, but I understand it is supposed to be done but once in a lifetime. It is not obligatory, and by far the greater number grow up sensibly abstaining from such savage luxuries. When the day is almost over, and the solar deity is nearly down in the west, the self-tortured warriors file from the enclosed arena, one by one, and just outside the doors, deeply covered with handsomely painted buffalo-robes, they kneel, and with arms crossed over the bloody breasts and with bowed heads face the setting sun and rise only when it has disappeared.

Many other horrible variations have been reported to me; such as tying a saddle or a buffalo's skull to the end of the long rope fastened to the skewer and running over the prairie and through the timber, the saddle or skull bounding after the victim until he liberates himself; or, when fainting, to draw the tortured man clear of the ground by the ropes until his weight overcame the strength of the distended skin. My informants told me that no two of the ceremonies were alike, the self-torture in some form being the one common link in all. The consecration of the sun-pole, much of the dancing and singing, the double efforts of ambitious youths, and other ceremonies might be left out entirely or others substituted. I describe it only as I saw it. I will add that this sun-dance was called the greatest self-sacrifice of the greatest native nation within our boundaries. Within a year they had checked, at the Rosebud Hills in Montana, the largest army we had ever launched against the American Indians in a single fight; had retired successfully to the Little Big Horn, a few miles away, and there, a week later, had wiped Custer's fine command from the face of the earth; had held Reno for two days upon a hill; had never lost a battle worthy of the name in the wars which led to their subjugation; and had proved the utter worthlessness of victory to a savage race contending against civilization.

17. Named for its cattle brand, "101," this ranch was begun by Colonel George W. Miller on his claim at the opening of the Cherokee Strip in Oklahoma, on September 16, 1893. Operated by his sons, George, Joe, and Zach Miller, the ranch covered one hundred thousand acres by 1926. It was world famous for its "White House" headquarters, where many of the world's most noted personalities and high officials were entertained on many occasions. It received wide acclaim for its 101 Wild West show. It was here that the famous black cowboy Bill Pickett developed the rodeo sport of bulldogging.

18. J. L. Smith (July–August 1967:10) relates an incident that was described to him by Joe Thin Elk, in which "some five policemen confiscated the Sacred Pipe bundle at the direction of the agent, Couchman." Couchman opened the bundle and examined its contents. Then he agreed to return it, and ordered the policemen to do so. After it was returned and the policemen were on their way back to the agency, "a cloud of mist, much like the one that appeared with the coming of White Buffalo Calf Maiden, was seen. When it lifted, one of the policemen was dead. This happened twice more during the next few days until all five of the policemen were dead." I do not know whether this is the same incident Agent Roberts in Fools Crow's account refers to. But it probably is, or at the very least it substantiates the story.

19. As we discussed the bringing of the Sacred Pipe by Calf Pipe Woman, several questions arose. One had to do with Fools Crow's dating of the event at between A.D. 1200 and 1500, and placing the encounter in Teton Mountain Country. His rationale for this has been given, but Dallas added it was well established that early people the world over were migratory in nature. Why then should it surprise anyone to find that bands of the huge Sioux nation did the same?

As to how the holy woman was able to wear cloth apparel long before cloth was brought to the Indians by white traders, Fools Crow's terse answer was that such occurrences in holy events need no explaining; "God works his miracles as they are needed."

It is said that many versions exist of the story of Calf Pipe Woman. I shall, however, mention only one other account. Reference has been made to a meeting I attended at Sinte Galeska College, at Rosebud, South Dakota, on October 21, 1976. The importance of this event— billed as a lecture but hardly that—cannot be overestimated, since it was claimed to be the first time in history that the Keeper had visited the Rosebud Reservation. As such, more should be explained about the meeting.

Perhaps fifty Sioux men and a few Sioux women attended the lecture. All were traditionalists, including the college representatives, and several were medicine men. In addition, there were some whites present. The session was filmed and taped by Ben Black Bear, Jr., a brilliant young Sioux who serves on the college staff and is a well-known preserver of the ancient traditions of his people.

The lecture was scheduled to begin at 1:00 P.M., but it did not commence, as is usually the case when things go according to Indian time, until 1:45 P.M., when Orval Looking Horse and his father, Stanley, arrived. Introductions were made, everyone sat down, and the lecture began. The young and handsome Orval, wearing long braids, remained silent with his arms folded while his father, a short-haired, heavy-set, and swarthy man, launched into a mumbling, twenty-minute-long dissertation in Lakota. His eyes were downcast, and he could barely be heard. Yet everyone sat quietly, and, indeed, paid rapt attention.

When he finished, Ben Black Bear made a summary translation. As far as Stanley knew, Orval was the nineteenth Keeper of the Sacred Pipe. The previous keeper was Stanley's mother, Lucy Looking Horse, but she had passed him by and given the responsibility for watching over the pipe to Orval. Furthermore, she had told neither of them the entire story of the bringing of the Sacred Pipe by Calf Pipe Woman—a fact they accepted, but that surely mystified me.

What they did learn compared favorably, insofar as it goes, with the story Fools Crow tells, and some details were added. Their tale began with a warrior who, while out hunting in ancient times, came upon a cave in Devil's Tower, a huge pillarlike formation in Wyoming. In this cave he found some arrows and a pipe bundle. Somehow, he knew he could take only one of the two back to his people, and he chose the arrows. Stanley did not identify the man's tribe, but it was probably Cheyenne, and his discovery would then have something to do with the origin of that tribe's sacred arrows.

Later on, he said, Calf Pipe Woman brought this same pipe to the Sioux village. Mention was made of the cloud filled with wavy lines that descended upon the Sioux hunter who had impure thoughts, and also of the surviving hunter who retreated in fear to the top of a hill, and then came down to find only the bones of his former companion. No details of what Calf Pipe Woman did when she came to the Sioux village were given, except that when she left she changed five times, the last time back into a woman. Stanley explained that he didn't know what else she had changed into, since his mother felt this was too sacred to tell.

When Orval spoke next, it was also in Lakota, and with the same humble demeanor evidenced by his father. Orval first acknowledged his gratitude at finding people at Rosebud who still had respect and concern for the Sacred Pipe and its Keeper. There was less respect for it on his own reservation, and none at all among the BIA people or the Tribal Council. He said he could not find employment because local residents thought he was a devil worshiper, and in consequence he had to make a living by breaking horses. Then he answered a few questions put to him by the medicine men.

Most of the discussion that followed for the next ninety minutes had to do with why the Sacred Pipe and its Keeper are not better supported by the Sioux. The conclusions were without exception the same: In their view the white man is always at fault; he, in one way or another, caused the people to lose their understanding. Sitting there in the midst of the Indians, I felt more than a little uneasy, and along with the other whites under attack. I did not appreciate it. I was an invited guest. And, as much as I understood the century-old resentment involved, I represented whites who were not a part of that fault. Some Indians there knew it. And further, I realized that all of the complaining would not change or alter the fact that the Sioux must themselves make things right. Only they, by proper ceremony and firm resolve, can restore the Sacred Pipe to its rightful place among their people.

A few further comments regarding the Sacred Pipe are in order. J. L. Smith, in an article entitled "A Short History of the Sacred Calf Pipe of the Teton Dakota," *Museum News,* Vol. 28, Nos. 7–8, University of South Dakota, Vermillion, South Dakota (July–August 1967), makes several statements that at first appear to contradict Fools Crow. Smith visited Green Grass in 1966, and while he did not see the pipe he did see the bundle. Its two outer wrappings were a man's gray overcoat covered by a yellow overcoat winter liner. The building in which the pipe was housed was approximately nine feet by twelve feet, made of wood, and covered on its four sides by corrugated metal. It had a wooden door on the south, and a small window on the west. The interior was littered with tools and debris, and the pipe bundle itself lay upon an empty milk rack, which itself rested on a ten-gallon drum. The bundle was oriented on a north-south axis, and was "no longer taken outside mainly because all are afraid to go near it."

Smith does describe the contents of the Sacred Pipe bundle, yet his description is based for the most part upon an article by Sidney J. Thomas in *American Anthropologist,* Vol. 43 (1941). Thomas claimed that the bundle was opened for him by the Keeper in 1934, and gives the very detailed description of its contents, which is quoted by Smith.

Smith records a version of the Calf Pipe Woman story that varies considerably from Fools Crow's. She was dressed in a white buckskin dress, leggings, and moccasins. She carried a sage fan in her right hand, and the bundle in the crook of her left arm. On her back was a quiver, herbs were in her left hand, and her face was painted with red stripes.

The lodge in which the pipe was presented faced east. She opened the bundle, and the pipe was removed and placed on a pipe rack. When she finished giving her instructions, she took six bows and six arrows from her quiver, gave them to six young warriors, and sent them to a specified place to kill six men, whose ears were to be cut off and attached to the pipe.

While Smith cites probable dates for the receipt of the Sacred Pipe as 1785–1800, he also gives credence to Fools Crow's view by mentioning that Garrick Mallery, *Picture Writing of the American Indians,* Tenth Annual Report, BAE, Washington, D.C. (1889), shows two different pictographs with the dates A.D. 901–930 and 931–1000; that High Hawk, an Oglala, gives a date of 1540, and says, "from 1610 to 1617 fifty-four offerings were made to the Sacred Calf Pipe."

An insert chart in Smith's account gives four different lists showing the Keepers of the Sacred Calf Pipe bundle: one by Curtis, in 1916, lists seven Keepers; another by Mekeel, in 1931, lists nine; a third by Left Heron, in 1931, lists eight; and a fourth by Thomas, in 1934, lists ten Keepers, to which Smith adds three more to make a total of 13 by 1966.

In all of these lists, Standing Walking Buffalo is shown as the first Keeper, and his name is not listed again. Therefore, if they are correct, no one named Walking Standing Buffalo could have brought the pipe bundle to Pine Ridge in 1929. Moreover, Smith names Martha Bad Warrior as the probable Keeper in 1934, the general period during which the Sun Dance in question was held.

Nevertheless, Smith also calls himself into question by admitting that "since the death of Red Hair in 1916, the custodianship of the pipe bundle has been somewhat contested." Add to this the fact that none of the four lists previously mentioned agree as to the names of Keepers cited or sequences, and Stanley Looking Horse's statement that Orval is the nineteenth, and not as Smith has him the thirteenth, Keeper, and it becomes probably that several names are missing from all of the lists— including a Walking Standing Buffalo, who had the pipe in 1929.

The difference between the Smith and the Fools Crow descriptions of the pipe bundle wrappings and the condition of the building interior are easily explained. Accounts by those who have seen these over a period of many years show that the wrappings have changed, and that at times the building was clean, with a sage-covered floor. When Fools Crow saw it, its condition was as he stated. Moreover, he saw the bundle opened, and he saw it brought outside, his is no secondhand account, and all the more valuable because of it.

20. Those who read books and articles about Indians know that some of the writers of olden times were spellbound as they watched medicine men of the Plains tribes do wondrous things. Tipis were made to shake, large and small items were caused to disappear and reappear, men walked on hot coals, sword blades and fire were swallowed, and it is claimed that on occasion the medicine men would even have dramatic contests to determine which had the greater power. Usually these were put down by the authors as feats of magic, even though many of the "tricks" defied explanation. The question is, of course, whether all of these accomplishments were indeed feats of legerdemain, or whether some of them at least were something more.

A certain Professor H. Kellar, who claims to have made "an exhaustive study of this fascinating subject," wrote entertainingly and skillfully about 1890 of his observations in an article entitled "Magic Among the Red Men," *North American Review,* pp. 591–600. As is the case with other articles previously included, it presents an interesting comparison to what Fools Crow has to say on the subject.

There was a thrilling scene on the prairie at the Indian station of Rosebud, in South Dakota, a few years ago, which first awakened my attention to the fact that what we heedlessly term magic exists with deeply interesting complications and weird suggestions among the Indians of North America. There was to be a beef allotment by the agent, and the braves had assembled for hundreds of miles to share in the distribution of their staple of food and the festivities which attended it. Near by were the agency buildings and the cattle stockade. A magnificent expanse of flower-spangled verdure stretched to the north, dotted with the tepees of the newly-arrived warriors, while the log cabins of the progressive Indians, as those are called who adapt themselves to white men's civilization, were gathered near by. The great chief Red Cloud, to whom the Ogallalla Sioux looked up with a veneration genuinely characterized by affection, stood surveying the scene. On his serene but stern brow there was an expression of melancholy, but the interest which all that concerned his people awakened in his manly heart shone from his eyes. He was a man of tremendous physical force, and a warrior and counsellor who could hold his own with any mighty men of ancient or modern times. The sun had set and a cold moon in the first flush of its full splendor whitened the prairie with a ghostly frost. From hundreds of camp fires there came the sounds of rejoicing. A medicine man, that is, a morose, rather flabby-looking Indian who had been pointed out as the high priest of the Ogallallas, strolled by where we were standing, on his way to his tepee, which was at some distance from the others. It was larger, and the skins of which it was composed were beautifully painted in colors with battle scenes and those emblematic outline sketches which the Indians have for centuries loved to make of their favorite "medicine." A rather massive looking centre pole, curiously enough, supported this tepee, instead of the slanting poles which met diagonally over head and rested upon each other in the skin tents of the braves. "What is the red man's medicine?" was the question which his white visitor put to Red Cloud. The old man said nothing; but after repeated solicitations consented that his Caucasian friend should go to the medicine man's wigwam and say that it was the wish of Red

Cloud that the mysterious priest should give this paleface whatever enlightment he chose upon the question.

No one familiar with the strong religious nature of the North American Indian, his marvellous confidence in and reliance upon the Great Spirit, whose worship is almost the same in all the great Indian families and tribes in North America, would have been likely to ask any such question of a chief. To the Indian medicine means mystery; it is the essential element of his religion and has a sacred and solemn significance which has for generations guarded its secrets from the curious and unworthy. To go through the medicine lodge was the greatest ordeal that awaited a brave prepared to take his place among the warriors of his tribe. On the rare occasions when this privilege was demanded by and accorded to a squaw, the event was of such moment as for a time to eclipse all the other matters of interest. The secrets for which an Indian would give his life would naturally not flow out in answer to a white man's idle curiosity.

The medicine man heard in silence what the intruder had to say. He took down a beautifully fashioned bow which hung from his tent-pole and carefully selected seven finely-finished arrows, the shafts of which were of the color of the wood, the feathers from a gray hawk and the points, not of the steel at that time so freely used for the purpose, and, indeed, manufactured by white men, but of a pale flint as hard as cornelian. The seeker after knowledge watched the seer as he examined his weapons, and, when he strode out on the prairie a distance of thirty or forty feet from his tepee, followed him. There was an extraordinary brilliancy in the atmosphere that evening, which left no doubt that, whatever the medicine man chose to do, a practised eye could readily follow. Drawing an arrow to the head on his bowstring, and looking up one moment into the zenith as if to locate the exact spot he proposed to pierce with his shaft, he released his powerful bow, and the dart that left its cord flew straight and swift and glittering for a moment, in the moonlight, in a course which it seemed would inevitably bring it down upon the very head of this beautiful messenger from earth to heaven; there was, one fancied, a smile upon the face of the medicine man as, with growing attention, we waited to hear the whistle of the returning arrow. After an interval which seemed doubly long to me, he dispatched the second shaft after the first and, it seemed, in exactly the same airy channel. There was still no indication of what had become of these arrows and the medicine man was still silent. The third, fourth, fifth, and sixth shafts were drawn from the quiver and dispatched in succession at the zenith. As the last sang its farewell to his bowstring the medicine man dropped the tip of his bow to the prairie and leaned upon it thoughtfully. A glance at my watch showed that just fifteen minutes had elapsed since he dispatched the first of his airy missiles, no one of which had fallen to earth so far as I could tell. Five minutes more and returned to his tepee, closed the skin flap, and strode away toward Red Cloud's house. I was determined to see the thing through, and after waiting a decent time for him to return, opened the tent flap and entered the tepee. The bow and the now empty quiver, save for one shaft, hung where I had first seen it. I waited for hours intending to give the fellow all the money I had to tell me his secret. He did not return any more than did his mysterious arrows.

A subsequent discovery that the Indian medicine men have known for centuries of the existence of magnetic iron ore, and have utilized this great secret knowledge in their own way, has given some plausibility to the suggestion a friend has made that the hollow centre-pole of this tepee was of magnetic iron, and that the medicine man was an archer of sufficient skill to be able so as to direct his shafts one after another that upon their return to earth, unseen in the pale moonlight, they buried themselves in the ground at the bottom of the centre-pole, swerved, it might be, a few inches by its magnetic attraction. Whether or not this was the case, I do know it to be a fact that among the Minnesota Sioux, who were responsible for the awful massacres of the early sixties, it was the custom for a medicine man upon the eve of the declaration of war to conduct the warriors of the tribe to a plain on the upper Mississippi which terminated abruptly at the base of a bluff some forty feet high. Upon this bluff in rude aboriginal painting there were a number of allegorical figures and several large war shields drawn in what was apparently the solid rock. The medicine man would marshal his braves within easy bowshot and fire an arrow at the cliff. If the arrow stuck to the stone and did not fall to the ground he gave it out that the Great Spirit intended his red children should fight and win. If the arrow fell to the ground, however, the red men were warned that they would be defeated in the coming strife. Of course, knowing which part of the cliff's surface was of the magnetic iron ore, and which of the baser material, that would not attract and hold a shaft head, the medicine man, were he so disposed, could influence the coming event.

An exhaustive study of this fascinating subject has convinced me that few races at any time in the history of the world have been more powerfully moulded by their religious beliefs than the American Indian. As Charles Godfrey Leland says in a note to the marvellous adventures of that frontier half Indian, half whiteman, Jim Beckwourth, whose fame, among the knowing, is not less than that of Kit Carson himself, the word medicine as used by the Indians means magic, supernatural knowledge, inspiration, and the use of amulets and charms. The origin of this curious interpretation lies in the belief that all diseases are caused by evil spirits and so require magical powers to exorcise them. A sick Indian could only be cured by a sorcerer, and the more hideous the sorcerer made himself by paint, horns, skins, and skulls, the more potency there was in his spells, and the better chance the patient had. In no time or country of which I have ever heard was it true that the doctors of a people ranked even higher than their warriors, and were high chiefs, high priests, and high medicine men all in one. But this comes very near to being the case among the North American aborigines, among all of whome it must be remembered the form of government is a theocracy of which the medicine man is the high priest.

The veneration with which the Parsees regard fire, which is the sacred symbol of the benevolence and power and beauty of their unseen god, is akin to the feeling of mysterious awe with which the Indians have always surrounded the secrets of their medicine. This their religion, their fleshly and spiritual consolation in one, is almost the only possession they now have left to them from their forefathers. Secrecy is its keynote. The medicine men of the Sioux and Cheyennes and Arapahoes and Pawnees have known for a much longer period than the white men can estimate of the existence of the famous pipe-clay ledges in the upper Mississippi valley from which the red pipes so wonderfully fashioned by the Indians have been made for generations. It was not until a long and fruitless search had been made that the whites discovered one of these pipe-clay ledges back of Mankato, Minn. Sitting Bull, perhaps the best known red man to the white people of this decade and at whose door the more recent disturbances among the Sioux have been laid, was no war chief at all. He was simply the high priest or medicine man of his tribe developed among influences which brought out the peculiar ruthlessness of his nature. In the great medicine lodge or council chamber of the Sioux, Sitting Bull was feared as much, almost, as among the lonely cabins of the frontiersmen. When a chief differed with him, Bull would stride over to where he sat and brain him with a blow. Nobody dared to punish him for this.

The medicine lodge of old was built in the first moon of each May, and before the lodge poles were raised the medicine men of the tribe selected a medicine chief who was to lead the fighting men to battle during the ensuing year. This chief was bound with thongs to the top of a lodge pole forty feet tall and upon his shoulders were fastened in like manner a pair of wings from a freshly killed eagle. The medicine men then took hold of the butt end of the lodge pole as if to raise it to its position and the brave with it, but if the medicine of the latter was to be good and powerful, his eagle wings did most of the lifting and he and the pole floated gracefully up into the air until the great spar was in a perpendicular position. The other poles were then set up and the great medicine lodge or council chamber was complete. Rather than violate one of its secrets, any real Indian would cheerfully hack off every one of his ten fingers.

There has been a tradition that the medicine men of the once famous Pawnee tribe were peculiarly gifted. That this is anything more than a tradition I do not believe, for at a time when the Sioux and Cheyennes, Crows and Blackfeet in the north, and the Comanches, Apaches and Navahoes in the south, were the most famous of the aborigines, and showed, as they still show, the most powerfully developed types, the horse-stealing Pawnees who lived along the valleys of the Platte and the Arkansas, whose hand was against every man and whose treaties were only made to be broken, had already begun to dwindle into that insignificance in which we find them to-day in their transplanted home in the Indian Territory. James Beckwourth, the famous scout, who became a war chief under the name of Medicine Calf among the Crows, has related to a friend an extraordinary feat of levitation which a great war chief of the Crow Indians performed in his presence on the eve of leading his warriors to battle. The chief was an aged man and professed to have a premonition of death. For many moons he had led the Crows successfully against their hereditary foes, the Blackfeet. It was not his heart that failed him now, but his medicine had lost its potency. In the dusk of the gray morning he led his braves out on an open prairie, and, setting his shield on edge some fifteen or twenty feet in front of them, pointed to it with his lance. As the eyes of the fighting men rested upon the embossed surface of the buckler it appeared to rise slowly from the ground until it reached a height corresponding to the head of the chief; it then, by the same invisible means, passed through the air until it obscured his face and hid it from his warriors. A thrill of horror pervaded the assemblage, but no word was spoken. It was taken as an emblem of his approaching eclipse, his banishment from this world, his journey to the land of the Great Spirit, to which all Indians, good and bad alike, went with unhesitating faith. The great chief was killed that morning. On the robe of a famous Pawnee medicine man I have seen drawn in outline his warlike exploits with the allegorical figures of the animal or bird which was medicine to him, such as the bear, for example, and those phases of the sun and moon to which the medicine man attached such importance.

Prior to the inception of any great enterprise, such as an expedition of war, a great hunt, or the like, the medicine men of a band of Indians invariably "made medicine" for several days. They sang a monotonous chant during this time, beating their medicine dums and dancing as with muscles of iron. On one occasion, to avert the wrath of the Great Spirit, a great Crow chief had the brass medicine kettle of his tribe brought out and placed in full view of the assembled village. It held ten gallons and was as bright as the sun. Into it each brave threw his most cherished possession, and three Indian maidens then carried it to the river and threw it in. This was a sacrifice like that of the Roman Curtius, to save the commonwealth.

One of the most general of all the customs of the aborigines was that of the medicine bag which each brave carried on his person from the time he became a fighting man until his death. Without it he could succeed in nothing he undertook. To lose it in battle unless he lost his life as well, or captured the medicine bag of another brave, was a disgrace fully equal to that of the Roman who lost his shield. On approaching the age of puberty the Indian boy retired to a solitary spot, where for several days he lay on the ground without nourishment, praying to the Great Spirit. When at last he slept the sleep of exhaustion, his mind was still intent upon that image of his dreams which was to indicate to him his medicine. Whatever bird or animal first appeared to him in his slumber he at once set out to hunt down on his awakening. He took its skin, whether bird, reptile, or beast, stuffed it with moss, ornamented it elaborately, and thenceforth it was dearer to him than life. As a rule, the medicine bag was, of course, the skin of some bird or smaller animal, but a great chief has been known to use an entire wolf's skin.

There is, however, a curious absence of the supernatural in Indian life. A brave never saw the spirit of his deceased brother. There were no ghosts in the Indian country. There was one Great Spirit who ruled the world and was worshipped by all red men of all tribes. The medicine men were the priests or only mediums of communication with the Great Spirit. There were no images or idols to which the warrior paid his devotions either specific or symbolic. When he died he went straight to the Happy Hunting Grounds, not his spirit, but he himself, and his warhorse was killed to accompany him, just as his most beautiful buckskin clothes, his finest bow and arrows and lance, and his most cherished possessions were either buried with him or broken upon his tomb. The red man's magic after all is pervaded by a spirit of deep devotion which admits of no trifling, depends upon no charlatanism, and is born in him whether he be Sioux, Cheyenne, Apache, or Navahoe, along with that spirit of indomitable bravery and of stoical fortitude which none may know but to admire.

21. The Wounded Knee battle of 1890 has weighed heavily upon the hearts of the Oglala people since it happened. They can hardly escape it, since the mass grave of its Indian victims is the most prominent monument on the Pine Ridge Reservation. Each time they pass it they are reminded again of the terrible thing that happened there, and that the reservation experience really began with it. When one looks at the long list of names engraved on the monument, it is seen that many are relatives of families who still live on the reservation. Thus it is a constant and painful reminder, and a symbol of all the unfortunate things the Sioux have endured for the past century.

It was a natural site for the restless, frustrated, and embittered young people to choose when they decided, in February of 1973, to do something desperate to draw attention to the plight of the Indians. At that time several hundred members and supporters of the American Indian Movement, led by Russell Means and Dennis Banks, seized the historic hamlet of Wounded Knee. The hamlet and the Indians were immediately surrounded by a large force of federal marshals, FBI agents, and policemen from the Bureau of Indian Affairs—and the Indians received some extensive publicity from the media at last. The Indians demanded that the Senate Foreign Relations Committee re-examine the nation's Indian treaties—particularly that of 1868—and asked for the investigation of government treatment of Indians.

Seventy-one days of varying degrees of tension followed, during which time considerable gunfire was exchanged, and a large number of concerned but not directly involved Indians assembled near the perimeter where the government people were dug in. Two Indians were killed and a U.S. marshal was seriously injured. Finally, after considerable arbitration, the Indians received a peace document through Fools Crow, laid down their weapons, and submitted to arrest. This document, known as the Agreement of May 5, 1973, promised to prevent civil rights violations against Indians by government authorities, to take action against the tribal courts of BIA police, and to take action against unlawful behavior of tribal councils.

Little has been done to fulfill these promises, but 600 Indians were arrested; 114 were indicted, including a Lutheran minister, Dr. Paul Boe; and 127 cases were soon pending. Finally, in a last effort to get around what they felt would be an unfair trial, 65 defendants persuaded a federal court to hold hearings as to whether the Sioux treaty of 1868 did not provide them the rights of sovereignty to avoid trial in U.S. courts. After an 11-day hearing, U. S. District Judge Warren K. Urbom decided that although the Sioux had "a residue of sovereignty . . . the conclusion that Indian tribes do not have complete sovereignty is irresistible, if I am to follow an unbroken line of decisions of the U. S. Supreme Court."

Nevertheless, by the time the hearing was over, Judge Urbom had become clearly sympathetic to the Indian cause. He let witnesses take the oath on a Sioux pipe rather than the Bible, and he specifically criticized one U. S. Supreme Court precedent that had been used to reduce the sovereignty of Indian tribes. In 1823, Chief Justice John Marshall had called the Indians "fierce savages, whose occupation was war. . . ." The hearing record "should go far to dispel that assertion," Urbom said. "The Sioux, and undoubtedly many other tribes as well, had a highly developed governmental system, a religion proclaiming the sacredness of all nature and life, and a disposition toward peacefulness at least as effective as that of the white intruders."

In an interview after he released his opinion, Judge Urbom said that the Wounded Knee cases had a strong effect upon him personally. "Before I was involved, I was as naïve about Indian history as most Americans. . . . I had the subterranean feeling that we had abused the Indian badly, but I hadn't realized the extent of that abuse." Urbom condemned as "an ugly history" U.S. treatment of Indians. "White Americans may retch at the recollection of it," he said, asserting that the government has been unfaithful to its promises to the American Indian. In concluding, he hoped the hearing would "make the citizenry of the United States more aware and more willing to grapple with the hard decisions that need to be made [concerning Indians]."

Those who would like to understand the Sioux Indian's questions about justice must know something about the United States Government-Teton Sioux, Arapaho Treaty of 1868. It has never been revoked, but it has been shamefully violated. The more important sections of the treaty are as follows:

• Peace between the United States and the Indians; the United States will punish anyone, Indian or white, who violates the treaty, and reimburse the injured person for the loss.
• The Sioux and Arapaho will have a reservation of everything west of the Missouri River in present South Dakota; the area north of the Northern Platte River and east of the Big Horn Mountains (in Wyoming) will be unceded Indian Territory, where no whites will settle or pass through. The Indians give up claims to other land.
• If the reservation yields less than 160 acres of farming land per person, the United States will provide nearby land. Anyone living on the reservation may take land for his own or his family and own it privately; otherwise, land is held in common by the tribe. The United States may pass laws about passing down land to descendants.
• The United States will provide: educational and economic buildings; an agent who lives on the reservation and who can forward complaints of treaty violations for prosecution; assistance for farming; clothing and necessities for thirty years; food for four years; oxen and a cow for every family that farms.
• The treaty can only be changed by a vote of three fourths of the adult members of the tribe.

22. After 101 years of religious suppression, the American Indian Religious Freedom Act, Public Law 95-341, was passed as a joint resolution of Congress in the summer of 1978. Henceforth it will be U.S. policy within federal agencies to "protect and preserve" the rights of Indians, Eskimos, Aleuts, and Hawaiians to exercise their traditional religions. Native Americans are to be granted, among other things, access to sacred sites on federal land, use and possession of sacred objects from nature, and other freedoms to perform ceremonial rites.

BIBLIOGRAPHY

Hassrick, Royal B. *The Sioux—Life and Customs of a Warrior Society*. Norman: University of Oklahoma Press, 1964.

Kellar, H. "Magic Among the Red Men." *North American Review*.

Marshall, S. L. A. *Crimsoned Prairie*. New York: Charles Scribner's Sons, 1972.

Neihardt, John G. *Black Elk Speaks*. New York: William Morrow & Company, 1932.

Robinson, Doane. *A History of the Dakota or Sioux Indians*. Minneapolis, Minn.: Ross and Haines, 1956.

Ruby, Robert H. *The Oglala Sioux*. New York: Vantage Press, 1955.

Smith, J. L. "A Short History of the Sacred Calf Pipe of the Teton Sioux," *Museum News,* The W. H. Over Dakota Museum, University of South Dakota, Vol. 28, Nos. 7–8, July–Aug. 1967.

INDEX